D1430954

# Advance Praise for
## *Supermoms Activated*

"Jacqueline beautifully illustrates the difficult yet inspiring challenges that modern day moms fighting for liberty face. She stresses the importance of agency and our power to choose to fight for what we believe in and for the people most important to us. And just like Jacqueline says, it only takes one person to start a tidal wave, be the person, join the wave."

–Tina Descovich, Co-founder
of Moms for Liberty

"Moms fight like our children's lives depend on it, because our children's lives do in fact depend on it. Toboroff's profile on ordinary moms shines a much needed spotlight on today's revolutionary heroes fighting to save America against the global Marxism of the Fourth Industrial Revolution."

–Undercover Mother

"The most dangerous place in nature is between a Mama Bear and her baby cubs. Supermoms Activated is an indispensable book that outlines ways for American Moms to usher in the next wave of Conservatism in America!"

–Kari Lake, Newscaster, Broadcast Journalist, and Leader of the Largest Grassroots Movement in Arizona

BOMBARDIER

Published by Bombardier Books
An Imprint of Post Hill Press
ISBN: 979-8-88845-243-1
ISBN (eBook): 978-1-63758-720-1

Supermoms Activated:
12 Profiles of Hero Moms Leading the American Revival
© 2023 by Jacqueline Toboroff
All Rights Reserved

Cover Design by Jim Villaflores

This is a work of nonfiction. All people, locations, events, and situation are portrayed to the best of the author's memory.

Post Hill Press
New York • Nashville
posthillpress.com

Published in the United States of America
1  2  3  4  5  6  7  8  9  10

# DEDICATION

To my rock, my father, Leonard Toboroff, who spent countless hours editing my book only highlighting moms. Dads, you're critical. To my mom, Joy Toboroff, you're my role model. To my brother, Matthew Toboroff, thank you for always having my back. And to my babes, Gem and Axel, I fight for you, all day, every day, with pleasure. Lastly, to the moms out there who have been silenced for three years, I love you, I see you, and I hear you.

# TABLE OF CONTENTS

# INTRODUCTION

**A**merican moms have had it.

They've watched their country fall apart and public servants turn against them. They've been stripped of rights and subjected to McCarthyism by their own children, who've been programmed inside the educational complex. They'll take a lot; they negotiate with "terrorists" all day long—from kids to partners to work associates. But they will not coparent with the government. That is the red line they won't cross.

I interviewed twelve supermoms who have recently risen up and become "activated" to fight the government on various levels. And it wasn't just one cataclysmic event that caused this activation. Between March 2020 and the November 2022 midterm elections, there was a tectonic shift in how political candidates and elected public servants at the local, state, and federal levels operate. Decades-old stump speeches stopped working. Too many life-changing events transpired in too short a period of time for those public servants to carry on like it was business as usual. Real issues related to the survival of our country—the COVID pandemic, Black Lives Matter, mandates including lockdowns, masks, and COVID vaccines, the broken education system, the indoctrination of kids, crime, the economy—became the focal point, replacing paper dragons. And all these fractious issues were politically inspired by Democrats to gain electoral points. The Democrats sold these issues to misinformed citizens at the local level.

Moms now find themselves in a fight they didn't start but are going to finish. The twelve torchbearers of the revolution I interviewed weren't drafted to the war; they volunteered. They ran to the front lines without armor, practice drills, diagrams of the battlefield, or marching orders. That's how moms roll—when they anticipate danger and their antennae go up, they don't sit around waiting for instructions. These moms are fighting to ensure that the American dream still exists for the next generation—not only their kids, but yours.

I never thought I'd run for office. I have enough to do as a divorced mom of two living in downtown Manhattan; I deal with landmines 24/7. Just leaving home to bring my two kids, ages ten and fourteen, to school feels like a matter of life and death. First, we navigate homeless encampments and junkies. When we get to the subway, we see people bracing themselves against the walls so that criminals don't hurl them onto the tracks. Once on the train, we're trapped inside a metal box with more junkies and mentally unhinged vagrants threatening, defecating, screaming, smoking weed, and stumbling about.

We often see posters supporting drug use on the subway car's walls. One says, "Don't be ashamed if you are using, be empowered that you are using safely." Another says, "Fentanyl test strips can help save your life." These posters making drug use aspirational are brought to us by the New York City Department of Health (a mirthless joke) and Mayor Eric Adams, who are tagged at the bottom of each poster. I internalize my fury every time I see them. All the conversations I have with my children about not doing drugs are challenged by these ads created by unelected bureaucrats and a supposedly health-conscious elected official, publicly promoting drug use.

And all of this—the encampments, the junkies, the subway cars filled with the terrorized, the posters—we deal with every weekday before eight a.m.

This is just part of the scenario that drove me to run for city council in 2021, in District 1—which covers downtown Manhattan's neighborhoods (Chinatown, Soho, Tribeca, the Lower East Side, the Financial District, and other areas). I was at my wit's end and could take it no more; I feared for my safety and my children's safety. Things already had been dire in the Big Apple, and COVID made everything even worse. When I was campaigning, the city felt like something from the film *Death Wish*. And although I lost my race on November 2 that year, I was part of a movement that was the forebear of what was to come: moms impacting policy and effectuating change.

Democrats outnumber Republicans in New York City seven to one (68 percent). In District 1, Democrats outnumber Republicans by eight to one, so the city council election was a numbers game that I knew I had little hope of winning. However, even though I was a first-time candidate, I helped flip the only area in Manhattan that went from deep blue to pink: Chinatown. I was in the top 1 percent of fundraisers and the first female Republican candidate to ever get matching funds for District 1. And I had the highest percentage of Republican voter turnout ever for that seat.

My message clearly resonated with voters, and I embodied the change that was to come.

But before we get to that change, a little backstory on NYC politics. First, the city council is a big deal. The fifty-one-member body controls the Department of Education and the police department. And education in NYC sucks. New York City taxpayers spend $38,000 per public school student annually.[1] The prize is being in the bottom half of the nation for reading and writing. It's a deplorable return on investment.

When I ran for city council, only three of the fifty-one members were Republican. The legislature in Albany is majority Democrat. The governor and mayor are Democrats. The district attorney and attorney general are Democrats. The citywide judiciary is about 90 percent Democrat. This is what is meant by one-party rule.

And one-party rule by the Democrats has led to failure.

In the November 2021 election, the Republicans picked up two more seats in the city council, bringing the total to five. Still less than 10 percent. And the Democrats have been implementing changes for the worse for decades; we just didn't see it until now. It was like they were slowly boiling a frog, until 2020 came along and the dead frog was floating at the top of the pot.

In all cities and states, moms who have never been politically engaged are becoming activated. These aren't the vagina hat–wearing, Gucci shirt–burning activists who slap up a black square or a Ukrainian flag on Instagram and think they've made a difference. These are moms getting shit done. And they're not hiding behind masks; they're demanding to be seen.

Supermoms from all political parties, ethnicities, socioeconomic backgrounds, and religious faiths are devoting time they don't have to fight battles they must win. They're taking on school boards, running for office, starting advocacy groups, lobbying politicians, filing lawsuits, crafting policy, starting schools, and organizing networks to save the day.

Here's what I've learned, and why *Supermoms Activated* is necessary to read right now: the people composing the biggest voting bloc in the November 2022 midterm elections, moms—of which there are eighty-five million in the United States—are leaving the Democratic Party in droves. Also, mothers are no longer offering blind devotion and a free pass to higher office to their party's candidates. The days of political party loyalty are receding, with many moms prioritizing loyalty to their children. The government *isn't* coming to save America or Americans, and the Mom Army is stepping into the breach.

These activated moms know that there *was* a red wave in the 2022 midterms—that Republicans got more than four million votes than Democrats did and captured the House. Don't forget that to do something like this, the Republicans must swim against the tide of a prejudiced media and active branches of the government. Look at what Twitter did as an example: based on what new Twitter boss Elon Musk has thus far turned over to independent journalists, the American government was paying Twitter (and likely other media and tech platforms) to censor conservatives.

The FBI, under Jack Dorsey's reign, used taxpayers' money to pay Twitter $3,415,323 since October 2019. Conservative accounts were banned and targeted under the guise of protecting the country from "foreign influence." This didn't happen just to big names like Donald Trump, the sitting president at the time. It happened to everyday people who questioned the Biden administration, the COVID vaccines' efficacy and origins, the Chinese Communist Party, the purpose of open borders, and more. Going against the Left's narrative on Twitter merited getting flagged, put on a list, or having an account deactivated. Any dissent led to being branded as an election denier (unless you were a Democrat, like Stacey Abrams). "Right after the 2020 election, during the Stop the Steal movement, Twitter deplatformed Moms for America," notes Kimberly Fletcher, founder of Moms for America and mother of eight.

What do we know about COVID, George Floyd, BLM, the vaccines, the economy, the border, illegals, education, and the Democrats? Only what the government has told us through its "affiliates": the *New York Times*, the *Washington Post*, Facebook, Twitter, CNN, MSNBC, TikTok, and many other media outlets.

The purple wave of moms is now fighting back, and throughout this book you'll hear their stories. Some of the moms I interviewed are people you've been hearing about on the news and through word of mouth. They have stormed school boards, created new types of schools, been first-time candidates for office, founded advocacy groups, fought medical tyranny, and battled at the United States Supreme Court to legally ban critical race theory (CRT). Other moms are lesser known, but their impact has radiated out and been felt by the public.

America already had the Founding Fathers. Now it has the Founding Mothers. Moms that risked it all before the term "Year of the Mom" was coined by pundits in 2020. Some were doxed and canceled, like former California public school teacher Kali Fontanilla. For exposing CRT being taught at her school, she was harassed online. "The abuse involved rhetoric like, 'your right wing husband is shooting blanks,' 'white supremacist,' 'house n**ger,' 'bed wench,' and 'OnlyFans for white men,'" she says. Others relocated from tyrannical cities and states to ones that were more hospitable. Some of the moms were fired or pushed out of careers. Some made the difficult decision to pull kids out of school. Some were labeled public enemy number one and called "a danger to democracy" on a CNN Anderson Cooper segment.

All twelve moms profiled here chose a path that was uncharted and uncomfortable, to say the least. As mom of four, radio host, and former political candidate Sandra Whitten says, "I love making people uncomfortable; we're all uncomfortable together."

Collectively, the moms cite being guided by a force larger than themselves. They talk about spirituality and faith—even the moms who aren't necessarily religious.

The moms are intrepid, whether speaking before a hostile school board or Supreme Court justices, on live television, or in front of politicians and aggressive drag queens sexually exploiting children. "We've got to save the kids," maintains Sara Gonzales, mother of two and host on Blaze TV.

These warriors don't view themselves as victims but rather as being chosen. Every mom I interviewed used all the incoming missiles as a springboard rather than a sentence. They didn't have a road map but are grateful to be in this fight and thankful for the clarity of purpose. And now they have provided a blueprint for the rest of us.

Many of them had never been in politics before, getting involved when it appeared they were down for the count with nothing left to give. "I was a student mom when my youngest was a newborn and my husband was working as a border patrol agent for DHS and not getting paid. Sitting there at the kitchen table, helpless, like all these other families, I felt G-d say, 'This is why I called you,'" Whitten recalls.

Whether going through a divorce, raising kids single-handedly, fighting against a justice system that offered zero justice, or being financially strapped or at an emotional breaking point, they ignored the million reasons to stay quiet and follow the herd. Their reason for stepping up outweighed all else: protecting their kids.

"I started referring to ourselves as mama bears and papa bears, and insisted that the school system is treating us like pariahs," says single mom Asra Nomani. "We can't let the Left hijack children."

Republican governor of Virginia Glenn Youngkin, in office since January 15, 2022, is one of the moms' first triumphs. He was running a sleepy campaign when the then governor of Virginia, Democrat Terry McAuliffe, said, "I don't think parents should be telling schools what they should teach. I'm not going to let parents come into schools and actually take books out and make their own decision." Youngkin sided with the parents and adopted their issues, and was rewarded with a groundswell pushing him over the victory line. As a result, he became a national hero and an example that current Republican candidates across the United States refer to when plotting a win.

Youngkin isn't the only candidate to win on a pro-parents'-rights agenda. Florida's Republican governor, Ron DeSantis, has been unequivocal in his commitment. He signed into law House Bill 7, also called the Individual Freedom bill, which bans educators from teaching certain topics pertaining to race and prevents educators from guilting and shaming students about their immutable characteristics because of past events.

DeSantis aligned with Moms for Liberty, cofounded by Tina Descovich. During his appearance at the group's first ever summit in July 2022, there were "Mamas for DeSantis." DeSantis told the group's attendees, "Now is not the time to be a shrinking violet. Now is not the time to let them grind you down. You've got to stand up, and you've got to fight. We have drawn a very clear line in the sand that says our school system is for educating kids, not indoctrinating them. We have drawn a clear line in the sand that says parents have a fundamental role in the education of their kids."

DeSantis' presence at the Moms for Liberty summit immediately followed his endorsements of local school board candidates. He said, "I think what's happened over the last couple years is, parents now realize that these are really significant elections. Certain elections—the midterm, who's running for governor or senator—those are important; don't get me wrong. But [school boards] probably have a significant impact on families' lives in a way that some of these other offices may not be able to do." That a governor would do this speaks to Moms for Liberty's relevance. One of the most powerful politicians weighing in on a previously unknown role, school board member, was historic.

Back in the Democratic enclave of New York, where I live, Republican gubernatorial candidate Lee Zeldin lost on November 8, 2022, but also made history. He ran on a platform that was pro-parental rights, pro-meritocracy, anti-discriminatory mask and COVID vaccine mandates, and anti-CRT. He got over 30 percent of New York City's votes, a figure we haven't seen since Republican governor George Pataki won with 28 percent of the vote in 1995.

I helped organize Moms for Lee, a group composed largely of registered Democratic moms who could no longer tolerate the betrayal of the Democratic Party. Because of the Democrats' policies, they felt unsafe amid soaring crime. They were terrified for their children's educational future, due to American Federation of Teachers president Randi Weingarten's taking a wrecking ball to the educational system.

Moms for Lee did something historic. They rallied, created social media groups, harnessed networks of mom friends, dialed for dollars, wrote op-eds in the top national and local publications, went on national and local news, and created a grassroots groundswell that led to more voters coming out to support a Republican.

While Zeldin was defeated, New York won. The nation owes these Democratic moms a thank-you; they helped ensure that New York picked up four House seats and that Republicans won the majority in the U.S. House of Representatives.

There are other wins to celebrate, including that Moms for Liberty has helped flip school boards to pro-parental rights candidates. Why are school boards important? Because *everything* insidious is deposited and sprouted in the educational complex, as malleable minds are the easiest to brainwash, indoctrinate, and activate.

More than five hundred school board candidates were endorsed by Moms for Liberty chapters in 2022, and 275 won seats. And once pro-parental rights moms win seats on school boards, they understand their power, become familiar with the importance of the immense budget and operations, and feel emboldened to run for other local, state, and federal positions.

According to Pew Research Center, as of November 3, 2022, the top three issues for voters *are* mom issues. They are the economy, the future of democracy in the country, and education. Crime is number six. Immigration is prioritized ahead of climate. Race, climate, and abortion don't even make the top seven issues, and race is in the bottom four on the list of eighteen topics of importance. [2]

The Left, however, is anti-America and anti-Americans. Therefore, *it's anti-mom.* It has come out and said it and, via policies, has implemented an anti-United States agenda. The entire premise of "reimagining" America is to transform it fundamentally, which began in earnest with the Obama administration and has continued with the Biden administration.

For one thing among many, Barack Obama helped destroy education. Common Core—that is, government-imposed academic standards—which cost the taxpayers $80 billion, has been an unmitigated failure. So has the "free education" that he championed. Julie Gunlock, director of the Independent Women's Forum Center for Progress and Innovation, says, "Schools have become social welfare centers. You drop your kid off at seven a.m., which is called 'before care.' They get food because feeding kids is fundamental. Then there's actual school, lunch, and wellness centers so that teenagers who need condoms or STD assistance can be taken care of minus parental notification. This system really begs an answer to the question, 'Why do we need parents?'"

Joe Biden has grifted off of Obama's failures, which are too numerous to count. Knowing he couldn't get support, Biden rammed through twenty-two executive orders within his first week in office and 105 to date as I write this. Since assuming office on January 20, 2021, President Biden has hobbled America by every metric. Crime is through the roof, specifically in urban cores governed by Democrats. The economy is on the verge of collapse due to obvious mistakes. Overspending on woke initiatives, taking the country from being energy independent to being an energy slave, dereliction in managing the supply chain, and on top of this, funding a proxy war between Ukraine and Russia have made chicken, eggs, gas, rent, and travel prohibitively costly. It is lost on no one that the Biden administration is using American taxpayers' money to secure borders, national traditions, and safety in a foreign country while opposing these very necessities here at home.

Also, while mothers fight to keep their children off drugs, the Biden administration has become a de facto drug dealer and pusher. The invasion at the southern border—even when Title 42 was in place—exceeded, by conservative estimates, three million illegals. Many feel the number is closer to ten million. It should come as no surprise that there's no official number, because the government suppresses it, as does the media, in a strenuous effort to obscure the horrors. On May 9, 2023, days away from the end of the Title 42 border policy, Biden told Americans that the southern border will be "chaotic for a while." With this porous border comes child trafficking and drugs, sent in by the Mexican cartels.

While refusing to label the Mexican cartels terrorists, Biden's administration, United States attorney general Merrick Garland, Randi Weingarten of the AFT, unelected bureaucrats, and the mainstream media have gone to war against concerned parents, who have been labeled domestic terrorists.

It is proving to be the biggest misdirection play of all time. According to registration data, over one million voters across forty-three states have switched to the Republican Party since 2021. Voter registration has increased among suburban, white, Hispanic, Asian, and black moms. Fifty-six percent of married women voted Republican in the November 2022 elections.

To be clear, by and large, politicians—even Republicans— aren't doing squat; moms are. While it's true that the Republican candidates and politicians are far superior to the Democrats when it comes to bringing moms into the fold, it is only because the moms have come to the front lines of the battlegrounds.

Two classes of people are emerging in the Biden-era educational complex: losers and winners. And of course many other government efforts are continuing to nosedive as well. In Democratic bastions, some of which include sanctuary cities, the mayors have admitted they are useless. Despite beckoning illegals, greeting them with concierge services, smothering them in "free" taxpayer-funded luxuries, they're now begging for help.

Media darling Mayor Eric Adams of New York City welcomed illegals with concierge service, putting them up in $400-a-night hotels in midtown Manhattan during a financial crisis. This, when moms couldn't even find, let alone buy, tampons and baby formula due to the supply chain breakdowns. Suddenly, on May 15, he threw in the towel and said, "The city is being destroyed by the migrant crisis,"[3]

New York Democratic governor Kathy Hochul's $230 billion "budget" includes $220 million of Medicaid to go toward illegals in the state. *Only* New York taxpayers are on the hook for this because federal law prohibits using federal money to foot the bill. On December 14, 2022, Mayor Adams insisted that the federal government fork over $1 billion so he can deal with the unforetold flood of illegals overwhelming New York City. Then, threatening taxpayers, he said on December 18 that "basic services will be cut" *if* federal money doesn't come. Federal money didn't come, but more illegals did and the burden on the tax-base grew. In January, it was projected illegals would cost taxpayers $2 billion, then in February, they would cost $4.2 billion, and in March, it was estimated illegals would cost $10 billion.[4] The Mayor's Office of Immigrant Affairs predicts that with the expiration of Title 42, the Big Apple is on track to receive between *nine thousand and fourteen thousand illegals a day*!

On July 28, 2022, police defunding–advocate Mayor Muriel Bowser of Washington., D.C., a Democrat, requested mobilization of the D.C. National Guard to address the "humanitarian crisis" of bused-in illegals. Democratic mayor of Chicago Lori Lightfoot has displaced illegals, immediately moving them from Chicago to its suburbs. Democratic mayor of El Paso, Texas, Oscar Leeser declared a state of emergency over the continued influx of illegals. Democratic mayor of Del Rio, Texas, Bruno Lozano is also in a panic, referring to the horror show as the "Biden Border Crisis."

Moms' brains are working overtime, calculating all the ways their children will be adversely impacted and how the tax dollars they pay are funding the ruination. A *New York Post* article published on January 1, 2023, takes away some of the guesswork, saying that the cost is "a huge penalty to the lifetime earnings of students forced to suffer through remote schooling, totaling possibly as much as $28 trillion (more than the nation's entire GDP) over the remainder of the 21st century."[5] It's the first stab at putting a price tag on the abomination.[6]

However, this number is incomplete, as it fails to account for the illegals. Moms are paying taxes to fund criminals (which illegals are by definition), who will be in direct competition with their children. And how will already broken schools with students at below-grade level proficiency in various subjects absorb illegal children, who might have zero proficiency and not even be able to even read and write in English? How will American taxpayers meet the financial demands of expanding schools, hiring additional teachers and general staff, and funding more resources? Then there's the issue that illegals will be competing for limited spots in higher education and jobs.

There's so much work to be done, and the twelve supermoms profiled here have begun it. They've exposed corruption at all levels and forced a reluctant media, politicians, and unelected bureaucrats to acknowledge the rot. They've forced journalists to do their job and report on the decline. But the moms have done something else: they've offered solutions. "Being *just* angry isn't effective. We need to focus on education and local issues if we want to win. We don't need cheerleaders for the broken system," says Fletcher.

When they can't find a politician to support, moms are offering themselves up as candidates. And you know why moms make for good candidates? "Because we're CEOs of our homes. I was juggling two kids and their respective sports, dealing with school and lack thereof, taking care of the home, preparing meals, mowing the lawn in the evening, working full time during the day, divorcing, running a campaign, paying bills, budgeting, and socializing. I know how to do so much—all moms do. And we're born fighters," says Lindsay Cole. Kimberly Fletcher sums it up: "I am a lioness. A Sherman tank is how I identify if you mess with my kids."

As Winston Churchill said, "If you're going through hell, keep going." These twelve supermoms will keep going to change the hell created by the Democrats. I hope that these profiles of them will both educate and inspire you—because these activated moms and others like them, maybe even you, are the ones who will help parents get their voices back as they work to save the future for all of our children.

# CHAPTER 1:
# KALI FONTANILLA

**WORKED FOR FIFTEEN YEARS AS A PUBLIC SCHOOL TEACHER IN COMPTON, CALIFORNIA. FOUNDER OF EXODUS INSTITUTE, WHICH SUPPORTS HOMESCHOOLING FAMILIES. FORTY YEARS OLD AND MARRIED. THE ONLY NONMOTHER I INTERVIEWED, BUT AS KALI SAYS, SHE'S "MOM TO AMERICA'S KIDS." A FORMER DEMOCRAT, NOW AN INDEPENDENT CONSERVATIVE WHO VOTES REPUBLICAN WHEN SHE LIKES THE CANDIDATE.**

K ali Fontanilla has firsthand experience with the educational complex, having been a public school teacher for fifteen years. She knows what good educators can accomplish with solid core curriculum and high expectations. She also sees the results of detaching from a traditional core curriculum and attaching to CRT: dramatic learning loss and feelings of inadequacy, resentment, and laziness.

Kali taught in one of the most dangerous areas in America—Compton, California. The city is notorious for gang violence, specifically by the Bloods and Crips. On a scale of one (low crime) to one hundred (high crime), Compton is rated 56.8.[7] This might deter most people, but not Kali.

Among many parents who are frustrated with a quantifiably significant learning loss, blaming teachers has become de facto. It's a lazy tactic. Yes, plenty of teachers have been derelict in their duty of teaching kids how to think. They've shifted focus away from ensuring that students are proficient in various subjects and toward CRT, which anyone with a grievance can teach—in classes that anyone with a grievance can pass.

But it's important to recognize that there are good teachers, even great teachers, who have been victimized by the teachers' unions and held hostage to an ideology that is diametrically at odds with the purpose of school. Teachers have seen the landscape of their profession change, along with the respect they used to garner. For the good ones committed to educating, the death of their profession has been a bitter pill to swallow. They're faced with the difficult choice of staying in their career with the children they love or walking away.

Kali understands what it means to have a difficult home life. "I never met my father; he left while I was still in my mother's womb," she says. She grew up in poverty, struggled with a drug addiction at age nineteen, and is a survivor of sexual assault. Not exactly a recipe for success.

She knows that everything from stability to success starts at home—not at school. Sure, school plays a role; it is equipped to educate those with support and structure at home, whereby good habits are reinforced. But teaching a kid from an unstable home life is extremely difficult—a concept that opposes the narrative that federal school funding is a cure-all.

As of 2020, almost nineteen million children, 25 percent of the children in the United States, live in single-parent households. Children in this situation have a higher risk of dropping out of school, becoming pregnant in their teens, and divorcing in adulthood. Kali also faced two other uphill battles. Relapse rates after drug rehab are high (approximately 50 percent of addicts relapse within the first year of sobriety), and approximately 50 percent of sexual assault victims have post-traumatic stress disorder, according to a study from Harvard.[8]

Starting in 2007, Kali taught in an elementary school composed of marginalized and predominantly brown and black kids. Many of the kids' parents were addicted to crack cocaine. "The atmosphere was so intense; I took over for a teacher who had burned out after two months on the job," says Kali.

According to a Gallup poll, K–12 workers are the most burned-out employees in America—36 percent of them reported being burned out prior to 2020, but since the pandemic, the percentage has gone up to 52.[9] Only Kali didn't burn out; she was on fire. She loved her job, even the location. Teaching kids that had a rough start to life hit close to home. She felt a genuine connection to her class and looked to be a source of inspiration to a body of students that could stand to be inspired.

Kali was at the school in Compton for only a year (her grandmother passed away and she moved back home to Capitola, California). Nonetheless, her time there was fruitful and instructive. "I raised the standards, expected academically rigorous work from the students, watched them keep up with my demands, the curriculum, and ultimately excel," she says. It confirmed what she already knew: black and brown kids aren't victims and don't need special treatment. They need, like all kids, discipline, encouragement, and challenging curricula to maintain engagement and self-esteem.

During this time, Kali considered herself politically Left-leaning. However, when it came to education, her beliefs skewed Right. Even back in 2007, she was against the Left's push to get rid of homework. Anyone with brain activity above that of plant life, and certainly an educator, understands that homework gives students extra time to review class material and parents the opportunity to see what the students are learning in school. Finally, homework necessitates responsibility, on behalf of both the student and the parent monitoring the educational process.

Kali rejected the blanket no-failing policies that had already started to take root, seeing these policies as opposing academic excellence and setting kids up for failure in the real world. Finally, she was firmly against affirmative action. Black and brown kids didn't need to be treated like losers who needed an artificial boost; they were capable—and she saw this firsthand.

After grieving the loss of her grandmother, Kali returned to teaching in Santa Cruz, California. Like Compton, it was an educational quagmire. Students in this community rank in the bottom 50 percent of all schools in California for overall test scores. For math proficiency, they're in the bottom 50 percent—and only 6 to 9 percent are grade-level proficient in math.[10] The student body at the school Kali taught at was approximately 65 percent minority—mainly black and brown kids.

During her seven years at the school, Kali was committed to instilling accountability via a holistic approach focused on the global picture—owning one's future and understanding the alternatives to forgoing self-agency. She insisted that her students work hard, complete assignments on time and well, and contribute to classroom life. Just like in Compton, Kali saw positive results with her students in Santa Cruz. They were able to meet high standards, and they flourished.

Though she loved teaching in Santa Cruz, after seven years there Kali was ready to try something new. In 2015, she started her third and final position in a public school, teaching English language learners in middle and high school in Salinas, California. Three-fourths of the residents there were Hispanic.

Salinas is famous for all the wrong things. It's the gang capital of California. It's part of Monterey County, which has California's highest homicide rate among ten-year-olds to twenty-four-year-olds. The majority of these murders occur in Salinas, Monterey County's largest city and its county seat. With a population of one hundred fifty-seven thousand, Salinas is ranked 37.7 out of one hundred for violent crime. (The national average rank is 22.7.)[11] This is the environment that Kali chose to teach in. Just making it to school alive was, and still is, a real problem. And students had, and still have, an added pitfall to avoid: getting rolled up into gang life.

"There's no question that Salinas' gang problem is on the high end compared to most other cities in California," says Salinas police chief Kelly McMillin. His department attributes this to the "unlimited supply of firearms." The Salinas gun homicide rate is more than seven times higher than the national rate. "These kids are growing up in a battleground area," McMillin says.[12]

Crime rate notwithstanding, Kali's time teaching in Salinas was going well. Future planning remained one of her educational platforms along, with financial literacy, and it was well received. "Many kids told me my class changed their lives," Kali says. Kids living in dire circumstances appreciated instruction on ways to pull themselves out of poverty and being shown a vision of a different life. "The more teachers we have telling kids to take accountability of their future, the better," Kali says. "High school kids are cynical." She wonders, if the school's modus operandi is to lower the bar and treat students as if they are "less than," why would they even go to school?

The depressed educational outlook the Left offers has proven to be a disaster—and a lie. According to the National Center for Education Statistics, for the school year 2018–2019, Asian/Pacific Islander students had the highest adjusted cohort graduation rate for public high schools, 93 percent, followed by white students at 89 percent, then Hispanic at 82 percent, black at 80 percent, and last, American Indian/Alaska Native at 74 percent.[13] However, these numbers don't tell the real story. Not only public high school graduation rates must be taken into account, but also the lowered standards the educational complex have adopted. According to the website EdSource, some of California's largest school districts are dropping D and F grades, and other districts are mulling over phasing out grades below a C for high school students.[14] To remove accountability, the goalpost is being moved.

Teacher and student results must be worrisome, because "the California Department of Education is withholding the release of the results of the Smarter Balanced tests that students took last spring until an undetermined date later this year," according to a separate EdSource article published in the fall of 2022.[15] "The result will be a monthslong delay before the public can view results in English language arts, math and science for the state, districts, schools and charter schools." It's an admission of failure on the part of both the federal government and the bureaucrats running our public schools.

Throughout Kali's fifteen-year career as a public school teacher, she took kids that weren't grade-level proficient and got them up to speed. "We have a literacy issue in this country," she says. But "at first-grade level and by the end of the year, I was able to get my students literate."

One would think that the educational complex would use Kali's efficacious methods, but one would be wrong. Kali's methods would be appreciated and supported only if the goal were to raise the bar, protect the children, and respect taxpayers funding the school system. And this is *not* the goal of the educational complex.

Even before the pandemic, there were too many failing schools with children performing below grade level. Now, post-pandemic, rather than get serious, schools are doubling down on failed policies, making the education gaps even wider. First, the students missed a precious two years of education and socialization due to the teachers' unions' insistence on school buildings remaining closed. The results were so damning, an investigation by the House Oversight Committee's Subcommittee on the Coronavirus Pandemic have been ongoing, focused on out-of-nowhere changes made to CDC guidance to reopen schools, released in February

2021, approximately one year after the first cases of COVID were reported in the United States. Randi Weingarten, leader of one of the country's largest teachers' unions, told Republican lawmakers that claims that the union conspired with the Centers for Disease Control and Prevention to keep schools closed longer than necessary at the height of the pandemic are "patently false."[16] However, Republicans maintain the teachers union and the CDC worked in unison to keep schools closed. Rep. Brad Wenstrup, R-Ohio, who chairs the pandemic subcommittee, sent a letter to Weingarten in March, alleging the CDC "deviated from standard practice" by allowing her and AFT leaders to "revise and edit an internal draft," and that the exchange "coincidentally shifted CDC's guidance to align with AFT's agenda—keeping schools closed."[17]

When children returned to school, they were confronted by a new landscape. Due to so-called COVID mitigation, "spacing" in school became a national conversation. Desks were spaced six feet apart, class size halved, lunchtime no longer a beehive of socialization but a seating plan challenge because to date, we've yet to figure out how to eat or drink with a mask on. The schools should have been hyperfocused on teaching a core curriculum. The exact opposite happened.

"Three issues—closures, mandates, and CRT—weighed heavily on me," says Kali. The pandemic served as an excuse for so many teachers to *not* teach but still collect a salary. Others went into overdrive and, like superheroes, were hell-bent on helping to save kids starved for consistency, human interaction, mental stimulation, and contact with the community they spend the most time with outside of home. Kali was one of the superheroes. "I mastered online teaching," she says. "As the school day was cut in half, I cut out all the fluff."

Every caring parent took issue with the "fluff"—that is, anything unrelated to traditional core curriculum—once school went online, and they continued to do so once the schools reopened. Yet schools couldn't even keep track of their pupils, let alone focus on a curriculum. Compounded gross negligence ensured that the schools closed, then moved online. Teachers failed to keep track of attendance, didn't hold students accountable for not showing up or turning in assignments, had a relaxed grading policy and, finally, gaslit the parent body into believing that this came from a place of worry about students' safety and health. Rather, these changes were well thought out and intentional. Many teachers were in dereliction of duty and following orders to purposefully change the landscape of school in order to change the ideology of American children.

Kali remembered her duty. Her students showed up, and they did great—despite all of the above and despite a mask mandate. When the school building reopened to students, masks were required. However, "as a two-time survivor of sexual assault, wearing a mask was out of the question," Kali says. During one of the attacks, her breathing had been restricted. So at school, she refused to cover her face. The school's reaction was illuminating. Zero accommodations for someone who had survived an assault or struggled with asthma were granted. "The educational complex claimed to champion mental health and safety, yet created openly hostile breeding grounds toward those who didn't feel healthy or safe in a mask," Kali says. It wasn't just the flashbacks of her sexual assault that prohibited Kali from wearing a mask; it was the fact that the policy created a forced traumatizing environment. It placed a barrier between student and teacher, between trusted confidants. Children were even told they could kill others if they were not masked, so masks became a symbol of death.

But the straw that broke the camel's back for Kali, resulting in her soon-to-be departure from teaching at public school, was CRT. In 2020, spurred by George Floyd's death and the Left's encouraging of and using BLM for its own purposes, all manners of institutions were "reimagined"—that is, reworked for the worst. Kali witnessed the absolute demise of education based on sweeping curriculum changes implemented without any data or proven track record. "I watched my district choose to focus less on academics and more on activists and activism," she laments. And there was no workaround. Unlike avoiding mask mandates by having classes online, teachers and students could not opt out of CRT whether online or in-person; it metastasized and was everywhere.

Parents who speak up about the negative repercussion of CRT for their children are swiftly rebuked by the unelected bureaucrats running the educational complex. Whether it is inquiring about the removal of honors classes and gifted-students programs, questioning why classic literature is no longer part of English, or why black families are invited to certain school events excluding other races, CRT is baked into the decision.[18]

Then the media gets to work, downplaying the events and telling parents that their concerns are overblown. Critics of CRT are diminished and labeled crazy conspiracy theorists by "trusted" mainstream media personalities as well as leaders of the teachers' unions.

MSNBC's Joy-Ann Reid, with the ironic Twitter handle Joy-Ann (Pro-Democracy) Reid, tweeted on June 18, 2021:

> Maybe y'all should choose a different fake analogy for this apparently terrifying graduate level / law school theoretical school of thought that's not being taught in a single K–12 school? Or maybe just have the balls to come at the #1619Project and antiracist education by name…[19]

On July 8, 2021, CBS News reported: "Randi Weingarten, the head of the American Federation of Teachers (AFT), said critical race theory (CRT) is not even taught in elementary schools—and she vowed to fight 'culture warriors' who are 'bullying teachers.'"[20] *This* is the power that parents are up against: mainstream media outlets and their star talent, and the head of the second-largest teachers' labor union in America.

The account of a teacher with longstanding experience in the field at the elementary, middle, and high school levels detailing the transformation in schools merits close attention—especially in a time of pervasive lying, silencing, and threats. And for Kali to not only hold tight to her teaching principles but go to bat against the profession demonstrates not only her commitment to students but her concern around what is to come: a lost generation.

"My district inserted explicit CRT theory," Kali says. Administrators began to analyze all aspects of school life, from academia to educators to staff, through the lens of race; the guiding principle was to look at America's institutions as racist. This meant that the core curriculum *couldn't* be taught, because it had been put into place by racists, and because each of the components of the traditional core curriculum—English, math, science, and history—not only had been developed by racists but fostered racism. Grading, homework, and proficiency standards are considered racist for the same reasons, and are pitched as constraints put forth by the white man to oppress blacks.

In addition to being fixated on race, CRT demands that sexual mores are pushed onto babies at their very inception, promoting the farce that the existence of two sexes is one of the white man's constraints. In other words, to follow science is racist. And it isn't enough to not be racist in schools; one must be actively "anti-racist." Schools are obsessed with brainwashing children about gender and racism as early as they can get their mitts on them, making them reject both facts and common sense.

"During the entirety of my fifteen-year-long career as a teacher, I had one transgender student," says Kali. "Nonbinary didn't exist three years ago; it wasn't a thing. Kids didn't know about it." However, within the past couple of years, students' identifying as both transgender and nonbinary has become mainstream: one in twenty Americans under age thirty now identifies as either transgender or nonbinary.[21] Pew Research Center data shows while about 1.6 percent of the overall American population identifies as transgender or nonbinary, for those under thirty, the figure rises to 5 percent.

If these gender concepts barely existed before, why are they so prevalent now, and especially in the educational complex? The answer is: woke teachers have systematically replaced traditional teachers. According to the National Education Association (NEA) in a February 1, 2022, article about a survey it had conducted among its members: "A staggering 55 percent of educators are thinking about leaving the profession earlier than they had planned. However, the poll found that a disproportionate percentage of Black (62 percent) and Hispanic/Latino (59 percent) educators, already underrepresented in the teaching profession, were looking toward the exits."[22]

The NEA is one the largest labor unions in the country. It represents public school teachers and other support personnel, faculty and staffers at colleges and universities, retired educators, and college students preparing to become teachers. So those percentages cited truly *are* staggering. And as traditional teachers leave or are pushed out, new radical ones come in and run the show, implementing all things woke. And that includes indoctrinating the kids they teach, insisting there are multiple genders.

"We are supposed to address nonbinaries as 'they/them.' Teachers get in trouble if they don't," says Kali. Furthermore, "We are supposed to hide it from the parent—use the old pronouns in front of the parents, and in school use new ones." Kali describes a staff meeting she and her husband, also a teacher, attended. They witnessed a fellow teacher mistakenly use the student's new pronoun while on phone with the student's parent. The parent was upset, confused, and caught off guard, and asked if his son had changed his name. The administration then hatched a sinister plan. A file was created with two sets of pronouns: the new ones the teachers would use to address the student worked over with identity confusion, and the real one to be used when discussing the student with the parents. Directives stated that this deceit was necessary to protect the child.

Through policies such as this, an immediate power hierarchy is set in place, with the teachers as the boss and with the parents as enemies that the children need protecting from. And who is the protector? The educator.

Under Governor Gavin Newsom in October 2021, California became the first state to require that all high school students pass a one-semester ethnic studies course to graduate. Kali's district, wasting no time, had the ninth-grade students take the course. During the pandemic, as the teachers were sharing their lesson plans, Kali gained access to some details of her peers' instruction components. "The education consisted of intersectionality and counting one's oppression," she says. For example, black lesbian women experience three forms of oppression: from being black, being lesbian, and being women. The students were shown pie charts, with cis white Christian males placed in the middle—the best position.

In addition to that, the students were given a quiz to rank their privilege. "This was meant to teach the concept of hegemony, a key concept of CRT," says Kali. The educational complex wants its students to know that society was built to benefit the white man and oppress people of color. Colonization and decolonization are hammered hard.

Kali noticed that her male students were the most averse to this new lesson plan; 50 percent of them failed the course. "They thought it was a waste of time, because the class was stupid," she says. Strange that learning about what a loser one is isn't the attention-grabber that schools have insisted it is. Who would have anticipated that teaching kids to focus on hate and teaching that nice white boys must be considered the enemy would backfire?

Kali was so appalled by the components of the ethnic studies course that she took screen shots of the teachers' lesson plans.

These included Sylvia Duckworth's "wheel of power/privilege" pie chart with color coded tranches. Beginning with "sex" and going clockwise, "heterosexism," "ageism," "ableism," "ethnocentrism," "transphobia," "gender," "xenophobia," "classism," "colonialism," "racism," "sexism," and "homophobia," each individual tranche had additional labels to segregate people. In the center of the pie chart were two words, "marginalized" and "power."

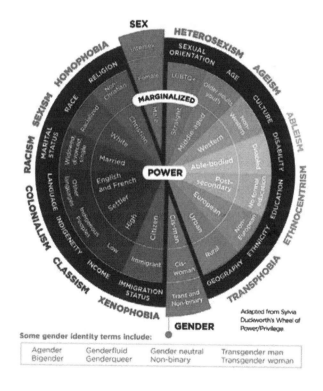

Some gender identity terms include:

| Agender | Genderfluid | Gender neutral | Transgender man |
| Bigender | Genderqueer | Non-binary | Transgender woman |

Adapted from Sylvia Duckworth's Wheel of Power/Privilege.

There were also quizzes with "yes" or "no" questions like: "You have been stopped or questions [sic] by the police because they [sic] felt you were suspicious," "Your religious holidays are celebrated in this country," "You are a citizen of the United States," "You studied the culture and the history of your ancestors in elementary school," "You have felt uncomfortable about a joke or statement you overheard related to your race, ethnicity, gender, appearance, or sexual orientation but felt unsafe to confront the situation," and "You were encouraged to attend college by your parents and family."

**English is your first language**
Yes
No
**Either one of your parents graduated from college**
Yes
No
You have visible or invisible disabilities
Yes
No
**You were encouraged to attend college by your parents and family**
Yes
No
**Your family has health insurance**
Yes
No
Your religious holidays are celebrated in this country
Yes
No
**You studied the culture or the history of your ancestors in elementary school**
Yes
No
**You have been bullied or made fun of based on something you cannot change (gender, ethnicity, age, sexual orientation, etc.)**
Yes
No
You have been stopped or questions by the police because they felt you were suspicious
Yes
No
**You are a citizen of the United States**
Yes
No

| There are more than 50 books in your house |
| --- |
| Yes |
| No |
| You have felt unsafe walking alone at night |
| Yes |
| No |
| You have felt uncomfortable about a joke or statement you overheard related to your race, ethnicity, gender, appearance, or sexual orientation but felt unsafe to confront the situation |
| Yes |
| No |
| Your teachers look like you |
| Yes |
| No |
| Reflection |
| How did it feel to be one of the students at the bottom? How did it feel to be one of the students on the top? |

Kali wanted to expose what the schools were busy doing and denying, using taxpayers' money—and furthermore leaving students to further regress in essential academic subjects, like math and writing. What happened next was astounding. The school board president said that Kali was anti–people of color.

This is astounding first because Kali *is* a person of color—she is Jamaican as well as white. And second, because she has dedicated her entire professional career to helping students of color: building their self-esteem and arming them with skills such as reading, writing, math, and financial literacy so that they'll be able to get good jobs and more.

Sadly, Kali was the only teacher who spoke out against CRT. It could be because her district in Salinas heavily leans Left: 69.5 percent of the people voted Democrat in the 2020 presidential election. The kicker? She was inundated with racist treatment by those claiming to not be racist and insisting that racism comes from the "others." In addition to being the victim of a racist smear campaign from her own colleagues, she was harassed online by a district leader. "The abuse involved rhetoric like, 'Your right-wing husband is shooting blanks,' 'white supremacist,' 'house n**ger,' 'bed wench,' and 'OnlyFans for white men,'" says Kali.

A school board meeting was held that included an indigenous drum circle. The board members largely blocked public comments around CRT; parents, teachers, and community members at large were vocally suppressed. Kali spoke out on online, even though she feared for her safety. She was right to be concerned. After a white parent spoke out against CRT, pieces of bloody meat were left in front of his home, and his door was vandalized with racist messages.

Kali left her position in the educational complex at the end of the 2021 school year, due to mask mandates and the toxic woke culture that has at a minimum damaged many lives and at a maximum destroyed them. Witness those who have committed suicide, practiced self-harm, couldn't withstand the school closures and other mandates due to learning disabilities, became indoctrinated with hate, and had their self-esteem lowered.

The finale to Kali's fifteen years of hard work in the educational complex was tragic. "I worked so hard, achieved so much, was head of my department every year for five years, but to my peers, it meant nothing," she says. Because she was still teaching online in 2021, the principal used it as an excuse to not even say goodbye. "The reaction was, 'Peace out,'" she says.

Although she quit teaching, Kali didn't quit fighting for students. All successful fighters figure out how to adjust to win the battle. They don't waste time trying to fix a broken system mismanaged by broken people. So what did Kali do?

She created a new system.

On May 2, 2022, Kali and her husband launched Exodus Institute, designed to provide a quality alternative to public schools. It supports homeschooling families with supplemental educational programs that include video instruction and assignments. It places the power back into the hands of the parents.

Pre-pandemic, only 3 percent of American families engaged in homeschooling, according to the U.S. Census Bureau.[23] Between the 2020 and 2021 academic years, the number increased to 67 percent. There are now 3.7 million homeschooled students, up by more than one million compared with the year before, according to the National Home Education Research Institute.[24] While there's been a dip of 17 percent between the 2021 and 2022 academic years, homeschooling still has gained serious momentum. Translation: parents are rejecting what is and is not being taught in school, and how schools are being managed.

The outmigration in public schools, especially those in sanctuary cities and states and close to the southern border, isn't only due to curriculum problems. Public schools—and their students— are increasingly taking the hit from the entry of illegals into the educational system. Let's look at California, for example, the state where Kali taught. According to the website The Center Square, California's taxpayers spent a total of $119.8 billion on K–12 education for 6.7 million students in 2020.[25] That's $20,642 per pupil. This was up from $12,143 in 2019. Can you guess why the per-student cost shot up so quickly? Hint: California is a sanctuary state. Taxpayers not only cover the cost of illegals absorbed into the educational complex, but also shell out additional money to schools with kids labeled English learners. And the financial hit has no end in sight because under the Biden administration, open borders are righteous.[26]

California schools have dedicated migrant programs providing all sorts of expensive special services, such as mobile medical care and dental work. Kali saw illegal English learners favored over struggling American students, and preferential treatment doled out to migrant kids. "They were allowed to go back to their country of origin, and schools would pause their grades," she says. This is another way "equity" is meted out—giving more to those the Left deems most oppressed. Of course, the problem with this way of thinking is that everyone has their own beliefs as to who is most oppressed.

The Exodus Institute is aimed at truly supporting American students, including by attempting to undo the effects of CRT. It goes beyond the core curriculum and teaches accurate American history, the good and the bad, without revisionism—unlike in public schools. Kali notes that schools fail to teach that Cherokee Indians owned slaves, as did free blacks; or that Africans owned slaves and then sent them to the Western Hemisphere; or that slavery was worldwide and legal. Revisionist history intentionally keeps people angry and stuck in the past, based on false or incomplete pretenses, to demonize America and the Constitution. Revisionist history and every other form of woke indoctrination have no place at the Exodus Institute.

While the Exodus Institute is a start, it's only a part of the solution. Kali is a torchbearer but understands that no single person can be tasked with the revolution; it requires a groundswell. She believes the path forward is clear and that the task falls to the parents, America's bedrock. Parents need to get much more involved—to demand school transparency, to learn not only about the curriculum being taught but also *how* it is being taught and who is teaching it. Kali also believes that cameras should be present in classrooms to hold both the faculty and students accountable.

"Our schools are supposed to be politically and religiously neutral," she says. Instead, they're unequivocally politicized and G-dless. Parents must put in the work to hold school districts legally accountable. And yes, there's risk involved. It's a financially daunting and time-consuming process, and critics of the educational complex likely will be met with hostility from some very loud and aggressive Lefties. But the time to fight is now. As the legendary film director Cecil B. DeMille once ordered his cast on set, "Don't be extras. Be a nation."

# CHAPTER 2:
# TINA DESCOVICH

**COFOUNDER OF MOMS FOR LIBERTY.
FORTY-EIGHT YEARS OLD AND MARRIED
WITH TWO BIOLOGICAL KIDS (A TWENTY-
ONE-YEAR-OLD IN COLLEGE IN VIRGINIA
AND A FOURTEEN-YEAR-OLD AT HOME) PLUS
THREE STEPKIDS. REGISTERED REPUBLICAN
LIVING IN MELBOURNE, FLORIDA.**

Warning: you are about to meet a woman whose group, Moms for Liberty, has been called "a danger to democracy" by CNN.

Tina Descovich was a pissed-off mom who turned her anger over the loss of parental rights and the breakdown of education into action. First, she served on the school board for Brevard County, Florida, and learned how this type of body functions. The COVID pandemic coincided with the end of her term, so with the lessons she learned during her tenure, Tina cofounded Moms for Liberty on January 1, 2021, with fellow mother Tiffany

Justice. This organization—which is "dedicated to fighting for the survival of America by unifying, educating and empowering parents to defend their parental rights at all levels of government," according to the mission statement on its website—has quickly changed the landscape of schools.

For example, Brevard County alone has a population of 606,612. These residents pay taxes that go toward the school boards' monetary allocation and is factored into the budgeting. All the school boards that have flipped to pro–parental rights bodies, thanks to Moms for Liberty, have a direct impact on the residents within the jurisdiction of the school boards.

Democrats, teachers' unions, unelected bureaucrats, and the mainstream media have repeatedly and vociferously gone to war against the nuclear family and moms. Under the Biden regime, a wrecking ball has been swung at the glue holding this nation together for 246 years. Moms are no longer revered but labeled "domestic terrorists." So the current regime has laid the foundation for spreading fear and silencing the voices of the American bedrock.

What happens to terrorists? Here's what Code of the District of Columbia § 22–3153 says regarding penalties for certain kinds of terrorism: "As per (n) 'A person who solicits material support or resources to commit an act of terrorism may, upon conviction, be punished by imprisonment for not more than 20 years.'" Biden's proxies, United States attorney general Merrick Garland and American Federation of Teachers president Randi Weingarten have lobbed dangerous and defamatory remarks toward eighty-five million people in America who happen to be moms. President Biden "'was excited…to go after parents'" with the FBI after receiving the National School Boards Association letter asking his administration to treat concerned parents as "domestic terrorists" and use the Patriot Act, said House Judiciary Committee ranking member Representative Jim Jordan.[27] Weingarten, for her part, also agreed with the content in the NSBA's letter.[28] Both the Biden administration and the teachers union have made it clear how they view concerned parents and the lengths to which they will go to silence them. It's a monumental misdirection play.

Moms for Liberty has brought together moms from myriad political, religious, ethnic, and socioeconomic backgrounds. The Left is so terrified by this rapidly expanding mom army that CNN was called to the ramparts—hence the "danger to democracy" label. Why? Moms for Liberty was founded less than one year ago as I write this, and already it has flipped school boards to a parental-rights majority in some of the largest school districts in America. This directly challenges the Left's attempt to capture our nation's kids.

CNN's Anderson Cooper says that "school boards have become flashpoints in the culture war gripping the country. Angry parents [are] facing off over everything from critical race theory to mask mandates. What was once a scattered operation is becoming much more organized."[29] This is in no small part thanks to Moms for Liberty and is precisely why the group is a threat. During the segment, a chyron flashed reading, "Parent activist group has turned 'parental rights' into a rallying cry for conservative parents."

Putting "parental rights" in quotes made it seem suspicious or even spurious. The Left believes these rights don't exist. Its embrace of Marxism translates to a belief that parental rights belong to the state and are then handed over to the schools, with which it works in tandem. On April 24, 2023, Biden claimed that the children of America don't belong to their parents, but to the nation at large. He said, "Rebecca put a teacher's creed into words when she said, 'There's no such thing as someone else's' child. Our nation's children are all our children."[30] On Mother's Day, May 14, 2023, MSNBC ran an opinion piece. The title, "Happy Mother's Day to everyone except for Moms for Liberty." A few days later, Democrat kook Rep Ilhan Omar said that Moms for Liberty is "Moms for Dictatorship."[31] The irony is rich—Omar frequently sides with radical Muslims.

A small group of leaders in key power positions—such as teachers union higher-ups, unelected bureaucrats acting on behalf of the Biden administration, and Democratic politicians—has hopscotched over devaluing mothers and flat out designated them enemies of the state. The goal is to strip moms of authority over their children and create a transfer of power. Our nation's greatest resource, our kids, belongs not to individual parents but to the Left, according to leftists.

Tina Descovich was elected to the Brevard County, Florida, school board in 2016 and served until 2020. The county population is half a million people, and the school district is the forty-seventh largest in the United States, with eighty-eight schools, seventy thousand students, nine thousand employees, and a $1.1 billion budget.[32] The main purpose of the five Brevard County school board members is to oversee and approve the budget and set policy. Federal, state, and local monies are involved, so there are many layers with which to contend. For instance, federal money has to be spent a certain way, and the rules vary from state to state. After the school board members decide on a plan, the superintendent is charged with implementing it.

"Being on the school board was a four-year term. It was a time-consuming and complex full-time paid position," Tina says. "School board meetings were twice a month, workshops were twice a month, and I would take on jobs within the district—dishwasher, anything—to really understand the breadth of the community and job. I would also visit the schools."

Tina ran for school board "due to concerns with laws the state of Florida had passed and the Department of Education had pushed related to high-stakes testing," she says, referring to standardized tests used to rank and measure the knowledge of students and effectiveness of teachers. They take place at the end of each academic year in every state, and have been used for years. Critics argue that these types of tests fail to diagnose individual learning needs and shape instruction.

When Florida decided to administer these standardized tests from kindergarten through twelfth grade in March 2024, Tina and other moms were unhappy—and Tina decided to do something about it. "I met with key people and felt empowered to have impact and influence," she says.

Empowerment like what Tina experienced is exactly what is terrifying the Left. Once moms get a taste of how they can effectuate change and impact policy at the school board level, a ripple effect occurs. Running for city council, state legislature, and Congress becomes an achievable goal. Thus the Left must prevent pro–parental rights mothers from getting any seats on the school boards.

During Tina's tenure on the school board, cracks in the system were apparent. School board meetings already could get heated, according to Tina, and the Parkland, Florida, school shooting in 2018 added fuel to the fire. It was a volatile time, and school boards were emotionally charged. Discussions around having armed guardians were intense.

Then came COVID. In mid-March 2020, schools nationwide were shuttered. The members of the wrecking ball crew—the teachers' unions, local government, unelected bureaucrats, the Centers for Disease Control, and the World Health Organization—blamed each other. Perhaps this was part of the plan; making it difficult to isolate one person or organization in control created confusion, which bought time for those implementing unconstitutional rules, mandates, closures, and sweeping curriculum changes. Incontinent orders were given, rules were nebulous and nonsensical, and there was no unified message. From block to block, zip code to zip code, school to school, state to state, "science" was different. Scrambling parents were left in the dark—furious, frustrated, and bereft of any concrete answers or the ability to get information. Instantaneously, problems occurred.

After three months (mid-March to mid-June) of unrelenting chaos—no school, no after-school programs, little to no scholastic instruction or homework—summer recess came. This two-month period (July and August) did nothing to quell the angst. The landscape was total uncertainty leading up to September 2021. Parents were struggling to figure out whether their kids would be in school or have remote schooling, have core curriculum or CRT, be and forced to wear masks and get "vaccines." Not only were they kept in the dark, but they were dismissed like boobs.

"I saw a mom show up to a meeting [during this time], and the union heckled her. She was crying as she left the meeting," Tina says.

September 2020 saw the implementation of the calamitous educational experiment known as online, virtual, or remote learning. The "experts" couldn't even agree on a name. It was an epic failure on all levels save one—exposure.

Moms couldn't unsee what they saw, both while school was virtual or, in many cases, not virtual; myriad public school teachers couldn't get it together or flat out refused to participate. Regarding educators' refusing to provide their students with virtual learning, the repeatedly offered refrain was, "It's unfair to those kids lacking personal devices." This meant that the kids who had them were screwed. This philosophy made perfect sense; the educational complex divorced itself from capitalism and meritocracy and married itself to Marxism, meaning that everyone was entitled to the same crap.

Whether their kids experienced virtual learning or not, moms received a crash course in just what the hell was going on, and it was alarming.

"When my son was in middle school, he scored a five [on the standardized civics test]—the best score. I thought he was an expert in civics. Then, the teacher calls and says my son really got fifty percent," Tina says. "Nonetheless, he was in the group of the best in the state. The way standardized tests are reported tend to make the children and educators look better than they are in reality. Parents were busy and blindly trusted the school. They assumed everything was fine. Everything wasn't fine."

Then the house of cards buckled. We have the COVID response to thank for shining a light on just how broken the educational system is. Parents have been asleep for decades, and now, the sleeping giants have awoken. R.I.P., parental silence. The decades of moms sitting in the passenger seat and outsourcing their children's education died in March 2020.

It wasn't just the response to COVID that galvanized moms. In fact, had schools only stuck with the tyrannical mask mandates and building closures, things might have been fine. Many moms were okay with masks. Many moms were in favor of the experimental "vaccine," even though the Food and Drug Administration hadn't approved it. Had education been solid while it was remote, the fury might have been contained. The death knell to education, and what unleashed the critical mass of moms' ire, was CRT, which was ushered in on the heels of BLM in June 2020—three months after COVID shutdowns began in the U.S.

Tina offers one example of the effects of teaching CRT. "My eldest son brought home an assignment, scored a one hundred," Tina says. But there was a problem. "Within the assignment was an attack on Christopher Columbus, and I was concerned."

Now, parents were faced with severely reduced school hours *and* severely degraded education for their children.

The federal government provides 8 percent of funding for public K–12 education in the United States.[33] Taxpayers spend $9,482 per Brevard County public school student annually. Among those students, 62 percent are proficient in math and 61 percent are proficient in reading.[34] Another way to look at this is that almost 40 percent of the public school kids in Brevard County are *not* at grade-level proficiency despite the nearly

$10,000 taxpayers spend annually on each one of them, along with all the federal money injections and the $1.1 billion school budget. If this business model were being graded, it would barely receive a D (which begins at 60 percent).

With precious learning time lost due to the response to COVID, robust efforts should have been made to ramp up teaching the core curriculum. The textbook definition of "core curriculum" is a body of knowledge, skills, and attitudes expected to be learned by all students, related to a set of subjects and learning areas that are common to all students: languages, mathematics, history, and science. These provide the foundational knowledge and skills needed in college, careers, and adulthood.

The opposite occurred. Time and financial resources were allocated to implementing CRT and its offshoots, DEI (diversity, equity, inclusion) and SEL (social-emotional learning), into all aspects of school life. It's important to understand SEL before addressing CRT. According to Undercover Mother, SEL is the gateway drug to CRT. It is used to embed tremendous insecurities, guilt, and emotional instability in children. It programs them with doubt about gender, the nuclear family, and open to "mindfulness" in order to prime them for CRT.[35] It has recently come to light that Yale medical school has developed curriculum that deploys "emotional persuasion tactics to trigger children attending thousands of public schools to become angry about social justice causes and aid them in developing an 'intersectional identity.'"[36] This is SEL in a nutshell. It primes the children for the onslaught of CRT and DEI initiatives.

The main tenet of CRT is a pathological obsession with race. Everything is viewed through the lens of pigmentation. White people, from inception, are subjugators. Black people are victims and losers. Asians are basically ignored. The educational complex's adoption of CRT makes teaching the core curriculum impossible, because following CRT means rejecting the America that was created in 1776 and the Constitution—because it holds that our Founding Fathers, white Christian men, were racists. Therefore, the rule of law, Judeo-Christian traditions, capitalism, meritocracy, and education, addressed in America's principle documents which formed its creation in 1776 on must be undone.

A way to further disrupt America's Judeo-Christian ethos is to reject American traditions such as Thanksgiving, Christmas, July Fourth, and the nuclear family, under the premise that they're the constraints of the racist white man. Therefore, CRT is hyperfocused not only on race but also on gender. The sexualizing of children is paramount to disrupting the nuclear family, biology, science, gender roles, mating, and procreating.

CRT, DEI, and SEL are like shell companies whose owners can't be tracked down. The point is to intentionally confuse, fatigue, and disperse parental anger. Just as with the COVID response, there's no one person or organization to blame for these concepts.

In fact, concerned parents initially were told they were crazy, that CRT, DEI, and SEL didn't exist. The government, famous media personalities, and educators said ad nauseam that CRT *wasn't* being taught in schools and that it was a figment of racist conspiracy theorists' imaginations. CNN reporter Eva McKend said critical race theory wasn't being taught in Virginia's public schools despite the phrase's appearing multiple times on the Virginia Department of Education's website, and that officials in the state had promoted it.[37] The AFT's Randi Weingarten parroted the lie. She said, "Let's be clear: critical race theory is not taught in elementary schools or high schools," she said. "It's a method of examination taught in law school and college that helps analyze whether systemic racism exists—and, in particular, whether it has an effect on law and public policy. But culture warriors are labeling any discussion of race, racism or discrimination as CRT to try to make it toxic. They are bullying teachers and trying to stop us from teaching students accurate history."[38]

Overwhelming evidence proves that CRT is already prevalent in schools and is continuing to spread to every corner. And when the government, the media, and educators could no longer deny it, they adopted a new stance: "Fine, CRT exists. But if you don't like it, you're a racist." When a Missouri parent said, "Just because I do not want critical race theory taught to my children in school does not mean I'm a racist, dammit!" MSNBC's Joy Reid laughed and said, "Actually, it does."

Parents have been faced with the reality of medical tyranny, school closures, remote learning, limited rights, and the force-feeding of CRT, which has no proven success rate. That is, if success is viewed as becoming proficient in reading, writing, math, and history—skills that translate into getting into higher education or securing a job.

"While serving on the school board, I learned about the imbalance of power. Children and parents' voices were being eroded. Unions negotiate contracts for teachers' salaries. Now they negotiate schools opening and closing. This directly impacts families and children," says Tina. "Unions elect school board members, and we saw school not reopening because board members were beholden to the union."

In late summer 2020, Tina's biggest challenge was her teenage son. He was experiencing severe contamination obsessive-compulsive disorder. It was devastating for her family; he could do very little because he was paralyzed with fear. He had picked up on the panic from the media, was prevented from going into school, and felt the pervasive fear in society. The family found three therapists that would meet on Zoom, but he wouldn't even get on Zoom. "Therapists tried to give therapy through a screen, unable to read his facial expressions," Tina says.

She notes how the COVID response manufactured a real mental health crisis. Her son had limited care when she was away from home, and that affected Tina's ability to concentrate in school board meetings. "All I could think of was my son—the spacing, lunch, six feet separation with kids facing one direction," Tina says. And when it came to a mask mandate, she lost the vote four to one.

She ended up removing her son from the school. "I needed a normal environment for my son, so I found a private school that had no mandates," she says.

The end of Tina's school board tenure coincided with the end of Tiffany Justice's. They connected toward the end of their terms and realized that serving on a school board was just the beginning of their education, commitment, and goals. "We wanted to help parents organize and find their voices," says Tina.

So many moms felt that one of the most challenging parts of COVID was the isolation. But broaching concerns and fears, even asking questions, was a nerve-wracking endeavor, thanks to educational rulers and unelected bureaucrats' pitting maskers, vaxxers, and Progressives against skeptics or resisters and likening them to serial killers. Such a successful campaign of fear porn was unleashed and whipped people into a frenzy. Even actor Sean Penn weighed in, saying being unvaccinated is equivalent to "pointing a gun in somebody's face."[39] Once parents were able to overcome the fear of speaking out, next came the revelation that while some parents might agree on a few issues, like masks, school closures, and CRT, a chasm occurred because views on vaccines and sparked a divide, by way of example. There was a trepidation to speak out and be totally candid for fear of not knowing how far to take the conversation.

The task of bringing together nearly a hundred thousand moms is like herding cats—next to impossible. Tina and Tiffany were prescient; they knew what was at stake and what could be accomplished. They also understood that the winning approach wouldn't be based on being dogmatic. As long as the chapters of the organization they were planning would be helmed by pro-parental rights advocates, the moms could determine what they wanted those rights to be.

So, why is the group's focus on moms and not dads or parents in general? "Tiffany and I are both moms. Also, the majority of parents at school boards were moms. This is the group we want to help organize," says Tina. However, dads and grandparents are indeed members of the Moms for Liberty chapters.

"Our goal is a chapter in every district, showing up to every school board meeting across the country. Our mission is to fight for the survival of America. We want to empower parents to stand up for parental rights", says Tina. The most local level of involvement is at the school boards. "School districts feed kids, administer health care, but they're not doing their job, which is to educate students in core curriculum. The concern is about what kids are being taught and not being taught," says Tina.

In a short amount of time, Moms for Liberty has grown to be in forty-three states with 260 chapters, mobilizing over one hundred ten thousand members. Growth has been organic, mainly through word of mouth and the mainstream media. Ironically, the mainstream media's attempts to torpedo Moms for Liberty has done the opposite. This is likely due to many factors. Moms for Liberty is inclusive; it's not about the two founders. The message is one any mother can rally behind—parental rights. By targeting Moms for Liberty, the mainstream media is attacking the genetically wired feeling that the majority of mothers innately tap into: that we are in charge of our individual kids.

Then there's the timing of the ill-fated attacks. The mainstream media, acting as an arm of the Left, is complicit in suppressing and in many cases denying just how bad the federal government's involvement and the teachers' unions have been for education. Again, the grade-level-proficiency numbers speak for themselves. In 2021, 99.9 percent of teachers union donations went to Democratic candidates and causes.[40] Going after mothers for demanding that their kids get a solid education is alienating to mothers across party lines.

Moms for Liberty continues to grow at warp speed. As Tina rightly states, "People are talking. Two weeks after launching, a mom from Long Island, New York, wanted to start a chapter. We knew nothing about New York; we were based in Florida." The initiative moms are taking in starting their own chapters speaks to the desire that Moms for Liberty has tapped. "Within a few weeks of launching, we started to explode," says Tina.

I interviewed many moms across the nation—of different races and religions, and with different socioeconomic backgrounds. When I asked, "What's the first step mothers can take to reclaim their power and get involved?" many cited joining Moms for Liberty. Why? First, the moms mention how alone they felt during the pandemic and that they were unaware that others felt equally outraged by being silenced and then ridiculed. Second, there's strength in numbers; knowing there's a community of moms out there that can not only commiserate but effectuate change is intensely gratifying. Third, and this goes to the quick and right thinking of Moms for Liberty, the group harnessed the sentiments of so many that had no outlet, no place to go, and no organization.

"The mission has not changed. The goal is to have three thousand chapters, one in each of the three thousand plus counties in America, with thirteen thousand district leaders so that each school district has representation and to have a Moms for Liberty member at every school board meeting from now until the end of time," says Tina.

"There are a variety of reasons people join. Tiffany and I don't push our agenda. Each chapter has a monthly meeting to review the respective school board agenda and to examine what's happening in the district," Tina continues. That being said, there are lots of similarities among the chapters. The chief concern that moms have is "children being indoctrinated and not educated," notes Tina.

Thanks to mass maternal outcry, twenty-three states have banned or proposed bans on teaching CRT. Florida is one of these states. Governor DeSantis has said, "The woke class wants to teach kids to hate each other…but we will not let them bring nonsense ideology into Florida's schools. I find it unthinkable that there are people in positions of leadership in the federal government who believe that we should teach kids to hate our country."[41]

Despite the tremendous strides that Moms for Liberty is making, the government, media, and unelected bureaucrats have ramped up efforts to scare moms into silence, which is challenging. Tina notes that "a big problem is cancel culture. Our way forward is conversations and citizen engagement. Everyone has to be heard. People that questioned anything were banned from social media. Even doctors. Silencing people makes bad feelings escalate. The most beautiful part of our government is citizen engagement." And there's virtually no issue closer to a mom's heart than her kids; this is why engagement with Moms for Liberty and in the school boards is the zeitgeist. "Education in foreign countries is top-down. In America, local school districts get to decide. This only works if parents are involved. Parents have neglected that duty. We need a reengagement of parents," says Tina.

"We want to see everyone at the table. What is a good curriculum? Parents have been cut out of discussion. A call to action is to join a Moms for Liberty chapter. Teach about school board agendas, budgeting, engagement, and help build a network. The best thing to come out of COVID is, we made COVID lemonade," she continues. "An improved education system is one with no indoctrination and [one heavily focused on] reading and math."

It's apropos that CNN featured Moms for Liberty on December 20, 2021, in what appeared to be a bitter assignment for Anderson Cooper. On October 24 of that year, the same network reported what almost all mothers, including Tina, had been screaming from the top of their lungs for two years: closing schools and taking a wrecking ball to education by focusing on CRT are catastrophic. Here is CNN figuring it out:

> Fourth and eighth graders fell behind in reading and had the largest ever decline in math, according to a national educational assessment showing the devastating effect of the COVID-19 pandemic on America's children. The alarming findings are based on the National Assessment of Educational Progress reading and math exams, often called the "Nation's Report Card" and conducted by the National Center for Education Statistics, a branch of the Education Department.[42]

The decline in education is so great and wedded to the Left's principles that the failure can no longer be hidden or ignored, even by the outlets doing its bidding. All that the Left can do is now gaslight. U.S. secretary of education Miguel Cardona said on CNN, "If this is not a wakeup call for us to double down our efforts and improve education, even before it was—before the pandemic, then I don't know what will." Cardona, who is a Democrat, went on to say that "since Day One, the Biden-Harris administration has worked aggressively to safely reopen schools, help students recover academically, and support their mental

health, because President Biden knew that a once-in-a generation pandemic would have a once-in-a-generation impact on our
nation's students."[43]

The reason for the success of Moms for Liberty is that the
administration hasn't, as Cardona claims, worked aggressively to
reopen schools, help students recover academically, or even support mental health. These are statistically proven to be outright
lies, which Cardona even admits by saying, "The results released
today from the National Assessment of Educational Progress
are appalling, unacceptable, and a reminder of the impact that
this pandemic has had on our learners."[44] The problem with
this statement goes back to the root of the issue; children didn't
suffer learning loss because of the COVID pandemic, they suffered because of the Democrats and teachers' unions' response to
the pandemic.

Moms for Liberty doesn't sound like the "danger to democracy" that CNN purports it to be. In fact, just the opposite is
true: Moms for Liberty is democracy is motion. The people fear-
ing democracy the most are the government officials on the Left
and the unelected bureaucrats given unprecedented power. The
media isn't even hiding its bias.

The Middle Eastern new site Al Jazeera had this to say about
Moms for Liberty:

> In a political climate marked by violent insur-
> rection, unhinged conspiracy theories, voting
> restrictions, anti-Black and anti-LGBTQ cen-
> sorship and denials of basic history and science,
> a group of mothers attending local school board

meetings seems like the least threatening thing coming out of the current conservative movement. Yet the veneer of respectability and benevolence that comes with the image of "concerned mothers" is in fact a thin veil for a broader and more sinister movement. Moms for Liberty is an offshoot of the far-right movement that has come to dominate modern American conservatism, with its tactics representing a dangerous shift in strategy for this movement.

Why would a publication headquartered in the Middle East—where women, gays, and Jews are subjugated—make such divisive claims about and cast aspersions on a group based in America? Because upending America's Judeo-Christian core values weakens America. A surefire way to weaken these values is to go after the next generation, and that is easiest done in school. Slandering Moms for Liberty shows just how terrifying democracy is for tyrants, and this terror comes in the form of moms.

At the onset of COVID, "parents politely appealed to school boards," says Tina. They were overwhelmingly ignored. Then the silence turned into rejection, castigation, and segregation. What we're witnessing is parents reclaiming education.

Here's the proof: 74 percent of the candidates that Moms for Liberty has endorsed are first-timers, and they're pulling in the wins.[45] As of the November 8, 2022, elections, the group endorsed 282 school board candidates, and 142 won. In 2022 alone, over five hundred school board candidates were endorsed by Moms for Liberty chapters, and 275 won seats. Across the nation, the endorsed candidates have a win ratio of 50 percent, and in Florida, they have a win ratio of 80 percent. Their impact can be felt in Charleston County, South Carolina (took five seats); Berkeley County, South Carolina (took six seats); York County, South Carolina (took four seats); Rock Hill, South Dakota (took four seats); Colleton County, South Carolina (took three seats); New Hanover County, North Carolina (took four seats), Pinellas County, Florida (took two seats), as well as in Miami Dade County, Florida (took two seats); Sarasota County, Florida (took two seats); Brevard County, Florida (took three seats); Duval County, Florida (took two seats); Clay County, Florida (took three seats); Hamilton County, Indiana (took four seats); Dakota County, Minnesota (took three seats); Cape May County, New Jersey (took three seats); Dry Creek Elementary School District, California (took one seat), and Auburn Union Elementary School District, California (took one seats).

Thanks to Moms for Liberty, many boards now have a majority of members who stand for parental rights.

This is a message to every elected official in America: parents are concerned about their children. It's folly to ignore the in-your-face referendum and the members of the massively powerful voting bloc with the most to lose—their kids. Pro–parental rights moms are going to be on boards (and already are), helping to direct policies, control budgets, and ensure children are being given the skills that they need to succeed.

Tina sums it up like this: "The biggest worry parents have is being ignored when they have concerns about their children. The most important thing in my life are my children, and this administration, the school board, and unelected bureaucrats ignoring me, telling me I don't have a say, only drives me to prove otherwise. We're just getting started. Florida is just the beginning. We're setting the track for the nation. Florida has led, and this is the road map. Moms for Liberty pro–parental rights school board members are future public office holders."

Tina's perseverance hasn't only strengthened moms' positions across the nation; it has helped her win a personal battle that led to her running for the school board back in 2016. Governor DeSantis is looking to overhaul Florida's policies around standardized testing. The plan is to end the Florida State Assessment (FSA) system, and one of the items on the docket is high-stakes testing. DeSantis envisions the new way of measuring progress to be more individualized as well as cost- and time-efficient. As per the *Washington Post*, DeSantis has said, "We will continue to set high standards, but we also have to recognize…the FSA is quite frankly, outdated. There will be 75 percent less time for testing, which will mean more time for learning."[46] If the effort is successful, other states might follow suit.

Tina, a mom of five who was never in politics before, is now having a huge impact. Because of her and other parents, analysts have said that "parent power" shaped the 2022 midterm elections, spanning from school board and county races to elections for federal offices. Tina would be the first to recognize that this isn't about her. Moms for Liberty is not about one person (or the two mom founders); it's about the moms nationwide. A sleeping giant has awakened, and it's fighting to save democracy.

# CHAPTER 3:
# SAMAIRE ARMSTRONG

**ACTRESS WHO RAN FOR MAYOR
OF SEDONA, ARIZONA, IN 2022.
FORTY-TWO-YEAR-OLD DIVORCED SINGLE
MOTHER WITH ONE SON, NINE YEARS
OLD. A "REGISTERED REPUBLICAN,
NOT THRILLED TO BE," SHE SAYS. "THE
ESTABLISHMENT SUCKS OUT HERE."**

Samaire Armstrong is a public figure: she's an actress reliant on public support, given that generating a vast fanbase is helpful to securing starring roles in a highly competitive field. Alienating various groups might seem like a counterintuitive strategy for an industry that needs an audience, but Hollywood as a whole has risked its livelihood by choosing to align with one side politically rather than staying neutral. And Samaire has bravely deviated from her industry's sociopolitical script. She's done so fully aware of the risk to her income, employment opportunities, ability to network, and ability to support her family.

Born in Japan to American parents, she spent the first five years of her life in Tokyo before returning home with her family to Arizona. Her parents were yin and yang: Dad studied combative behavior, and Mom studied healing—two practices that prime a young actress for Hollywood and then its escape.

In 1999, Samaire moved to Los Angeles—ironically, in search of balance. Attracted to storytelling, individual accounts of integrity, varying moral codes, and motivations behind adopting behavioral extremes, she found that acting and developing characters were a natural fit. For decades, Samaire fit in as part of an exclusive and elite community, working and creating.

In 2020, she experienced a break from that copacetic existence. "I woke up," says Samaire.

It wasn't that Samaire had no experience with the political side of Hollywood. She'd already lived through the Me Too movement and the Obama administration. Here's a bit of backstory for those of you who aren't familiar.

Me Too was a movement that started in 2006 in order to draw attention to the sexual assault and harassment of women and girls. Hollywood powerhouse Harvey Weinstein was the catalyst. He indiscriminately sexually harassed and assaulted women, some very famous, who stayed silent for years after appearing in his films, receiving awards, and sitting at his table. Some of these women jumped on the Me Too bandwagon only when it was expedient, almost as a career pivot and an opportunity for more fame; they failed to speak up earlier when it would have actually been helpful in preventing a predator from harming others.

Not letting a tragedy go to waste, those involved in the filmmaking industry sprang into action. "They concluded all men are bad," Samaire says. The created more smoke and mirrors in an industry that is an expert at smoke and mirrors. The idea that all men are bad became the new mantra. At awards ceremonies, celebrities would wear custom-made designer clothes embroidered with the names of victims. "Say her name" was the rallying cry. Samaire understood that there was no middle ground, only an extreme viewpoint.

Then there was Obama. Samaire recalls how he lit up the community in Los Angeles. She explains, "Topically, he appealed to the producers', actors', screenwriters', and studio owners' sensibilities." Tackling climate change, affordable and accessible health care for all, and significant changes to the criminal justice landscape were just some of his core platforms that they rallied behind.

Samaire internally struggled with the phoniness. "My neighbors championing Obama's plans were full of shit," she says. The entire premise was a pretense. They weren't committed to climate in any way other than verbally. They loved their private planes, gas-guzzling SUVs, and palatial homes with extensive grounds that needed oodles of water to be maintained. They didn't care about the financial toll that health care for all was taking on everyday Americans, because they could afford the monetary hit. And radical changes to the criminal justice system? Please. These were the most overly protected and coddled eggs. They enjoyed private armed security and lived in hermetically sealed homes. Conversations about what Obama's policies would mean at large, outside the Hollywood bubble, couldn't be had.

Perhaps critical thinking and pushback toward complex policies impacting many Americans which Hollywood celebrities seem to be obtuse to is a byproduct of a profession wholly dependent on public adoration and uncomfortable facing critique. "It was as if they'd crumble. They were so entitled to a firm belief that everyone had to share the same belief, and couldn't even handle the possibility of entertaining otherwise," Samaire says. Conversations within the tight-knit upper echelons of Hollywood about how they lived—with their homogeny, wealth, and safety—versus the experience of blue-collar workers who were truly financially impacted by exorbitant initiatives was daunting.

And Samaire eschewed getting political. She remained an observer, understanding that Hollywood demanded obedience.

Fissures began appearing, then lengthened and deepened, around being able to go along to get along. The cult-like mentality was suffocating to Samaire. She felt it blunted the creative process, not just hers, but the industry's. It restrained and restricted content, concepts, and the characters that felt politically skewed in one direction, the Left. Movies, TV, and theater went woke in the wake of BLM and Floyd. For example, the remake of *Cinderella* in 2021 has a man, Billy Porter, cast as the Godmother, Coincidentally, the original character of the Godmother (an Old English word) was also remade—into "Fab G"—erasing both G-d and mother in one fell swoop. Historical period pieces have also been reworked to make them move "inclusive." As a result, they're no longer historically relevant and they are intentionally misleading. Netflix's 2022 series, *Vikings: Valhalla*, has a black female jarl, which is historically inaccurate. Netflix's 2020 series, *Bridgerton*, set in early 1800s Regency period, about elite families presenting their children to society, has a cast that isn't representative of the plot during that moment in time. The series is centered around

Queen Charlotte, who was white in real life, and played in the series by a black women. Samaire felt that a lot of the work being put out was less funny, thought-provoking, and original.

Samaire grew up in a family that accepted and encouraged different viewpoints, under the umbrella of freedom and as a hallmark of American values. The ability to have and voice varying points of view is what made her feel safe, because provided these utterances are tethered to a moral compass, there's an implicit understanding that it's one's right to feel and think differently. In an effort to make people feel artificially safe by curating what's permissible, Samaire notes, no one is safe.

As for so many, COVID was a turning point for Samaire. She was in Hawaii on March 16, 2020, when lockdowns began. She saw the movie *Outbreak*, and thought, "I know how things work." She was acutely aware of strange behavioral modifications she'd seen from work associates. That fascination with extremes that originally beckoned her to Hollywood was now in full effect. "People's primal instincts came out," Samaire says.

Then that video came out. Ten minutes depicting the death of George Floyd while he was in the custody of Minneapolis police officers. Samaire was outraged, glued to her phone, watching in a state of fear. It was a snapshot of the smallest sliver of Floyd's life, but it now meant everything, overshadowing Floyd's history of criminality, ranging from guns to drugs and even holding a pistol to a woman's stomach. Hollywood's Me Too proponents overlooked these historical details as they resolutely moved on to the next political stance. Women were no longer in favor; Black Lives Matter became all-consuming.

"I went outside one day and remember thinking, 'Nothing has changed from yesterday, but I need to fear everything,'" Samaire says. Social justice became more important than dying. At least nineteen people—a majority of whom were black—died during the initial weeks of the "Summer of Love" Floyd protests.[47] The truth was suppressed—there was scant coverage, as if to keep the focus off of the victims in order to not detract from BLM. It not only didn't matter but became an impediment to the goal of transforming America. The way in which Hollywood demanded toeing the line during all the other lead-ups—Me Too, Obama, and COVID—had sufficiently cowed the bubble people. To prove their allegiance, civilized members of society—the producers and contributors—sat back while rioters routinely disrupted and degraded wealthy, thriving areas. Capitulating, Councilman Mitch O'Farrell of Los Angeles found a way to combine two movements in one, announcing on August 24, 2020, "Today, after years and years of violence against our Black and queer communities, we are creating the first memorialized space in Los Angeles dedicated to transgender people of color."[48] A rainbow BLM mural was painted on a swath of Hollywood Boulevard.

Cynthia Renaud, the police chief of Santa Monica, California, said at the time that 95 percent of those arrested during the looting didn't live in Santa Monica.[49] Samaire saw excuse after excuse proffered as to why it was okay for society to self-destruct. Logic was gone. Now, the "defund the police movement" was born and swiftly implemented—astoundingly, amid national civil unrest.

Starting in March 2020, Samaire noticed inconsistent messaging. BLM wasn't pitched just as being about supporting people caught up in the system and protecting victims, no matter how imperfect. "The message became conflated with something else far more sinister: a robust effort to victimize everyone that *wasn't* in the system," she says. Innocent, law-abiding citizens had to be punished, had to feel the pain, the financial devastation of being looted, the fear of being assaulted, the discomfort of living in permanent unrest. Los Angeles self-destructed during the initial wave of BLM, and Los Angelenos sat back and took it seemingly as a source of pride, in solidarity or fear of being labeled racists.

Samaire was curious. Like so many others, she was frustrated and concluded that little made sense. Not the series of events, the reporting, the reaction, or the apparatuses in place meant to protect that were in dereliction of duty and adding to the fear and panic. She started researching, going on a quest to arm herself with information, piece together events, and draw her own conclusions. She didn't like what she was being fed.

According to Bureau of Justice Statistics, Americans and the rest of the world have been fed a false narrative of "systemic racism" toward blacks in order to activate foot soldiers to dismantle the nation. On the heels of George Floyd, those in power, as if reading from the same talking points, parroted a tale that white people are born racist and black people are overwhelmingly dying by their hands. This is a lie. The interracial violent crime incidents numbers portray a different picture that government, mainstream media, and educators justifying the implementation of CRT don't mention. As of 2018, there were 547,948 cases of black on white crime; 112,365 cases of black on Hispanic crime; 59,778 of white on black crime; 207,104 cases of white on Hispanic crime; and 365,299 cases of Hispanic on white crime. And Hispanic on black crime was 44,551.[50] What's important to note in order to configure the percentages of interracial crime is the population percentage. Whites represent 75.8 percent, blacks represent 13.6 percent, Hispanics represent 18.9 percent, and Asians represent 6.1 percent.[51]

Samaire learned what other critical thinkers discovered: George Floyd's death was not the result of racism; it was never proven in court, and moreover, the police officers involved came from multiethnic backgrounds. She wondered why all lives didn't matter and why one race was being singled out as the one that did.

In May, 2023 Biden gave the commencement speech at Howard University, a historically black private school in Washington D.C. He said, "White supremacy … is the single most dangerous terrorist threat in our homeland."[52] This is a boldfaced lie, purposefully told to a predominantly black crowd of young adults, to make them believe false information, feel like victims, and seek vengeance. Now, compromised federal agencies and mainstream media hosts are indiscriminately labeling people white supremacists. While discussing the Dallas mall shooting perpetrated by thirty-three-year-old Mauricio Garcia, that left eight people dead, Ana Navarro told her *The View* co-hosts that being Hispanic or black doesn't make a person "immune" from supporting White supremacy.[53] Under the Biden administration, it seems like anyone that commits a crime can be labeled a "white supremacist."

This dip into the well of an alternative viewpoint led Samaire to question other false narratives and rely more heavily upon personal agency.

Prior to June 2020, Samaire wasn't political. "I voted for Trump, but that was the extent of it; I wasn't proselytizing or looking to recruit others," she notes. But as it so often happens, once a thread comes loose, the rest of the cloth unravels. Samaire became a citizen investigative journalist.

Perhaps the biggest revelation occurred while she looking into various Marxist groups—that they're transparent. They tell you their plan and aren't shy about admitting their agenda to destroy the nuclear family. Samaire started finding parallels between Marxist ideology and BLM. She learned that the organization terrorizing the nation, expanding its real estate portfolio, and bilking donors supports Venezuelan president Nicolás Maduro. Opal Tometi, cofounder of BLM, posed with Maduro and went to Venezuela to observe the electoral process, writing that it was a "[g]reat day observing 6 polling sites in Venezuela. calm & seamless process."[54] This discovery set off alarms for Samaire. Venezuela is globally recognized as a place where the Maduro regime deprives voters of their rights to participate in a free and fair electoral process. Samaire saw the hypocrisy for what it was—Hollywood elites claiming to be pro-democracy by way of empowering BLM, which was committed to antidemocratic processes and practices here in America.

The more Samaire explored, the freer she felt; there's power in being self-reliant. She was no longer allowing external sources to dictate her beliefs and shape the causes she'd rally behind. She saw her community on fire and also saw that the people getting hurt weren't the monied and protected public servants, unelected bureaucrats, and movie stars; they were the small business owners, employees, and average citizens just looking to get to and from work or their children's school safely.

This was her "aha" moment. Samaire was pissed off. "I felt like a manipulated tool, first by the COVID spin—which created emotional, physical, and financial vulnerability—and then by the way BLM was weaponized," she says. Because the rules were amorphous and the dictates disparate, intuition called for the general public to slow down, analyze, and regroup. Instead, those in charge whipped the public up into a frenzy. It seemed intentional—there was no time to think. The obvious goal was to dismantle our system via lawlessness, division, and subterfuge in urban cores—to disrupt economies, education, and quality of life.

Samaire saw so much hate in Tinseltown, despite the fact that the median age of its 60,812 residents was thirty-six—they were in the prime of their lives—that they were blessed with heavenly weather and endless possibilities, and that they resided in one of the world's most iconic locations.[55] The film industry, where make-believe comes true, apparently has it so good that it needs to invent problems. Prior to BLM, there were more officers thanks to regular police patrol and prevailing law and order.[56]

Two police officers were shot in their car in the name of BLM and racial and a protest erupted in order to prevent them from being transported to the hospital.[57] Samaire felt the community was silent in response. "The same people who had convinced themselves they were standing up for victims were ignoring real victims," says Samaire. She saw self-proclaimed morally superior elites use COVID and BLM as a license to support nefarious characters and reprehensible behavior via money and messaging.

There was a total breakdown in leadership from governor down to city council member; constituents were left imperiled because of a Democratic ruler's dereliction. Los Angeles mayor

Eric Garcetti declared a mandatory curfew from eight thirty p.m. to five thirty a.m., bolstered by the Los Angeles Metro's suspending all services. The insanity was that people were being prevented from going to work, and thereby supporting the economy, because BLM rioters posed too high of a threat to the community and those in charge let them terrorize unabated. The curfew was used as a Band-Aid to stop a hemorrhage.

Garcetti asked Governor Gavin Newsom to mobilize the National Guard but Councilman Marqueece Harris-Dawson, representing a portion of South Los Angeles, criticized that move, saying, "It's clear that our fear is real that additional law enforcement will only further violence against people of color."[58] Law-abiding panicked people were punished, locked inside their homes again—first because of the government's response to COVID and now because of the government's encouragement of and refusal to swiftly condemn BLM. The rioters ruled.

Within the first week of the riots, 533 people were arrested on suspicion of burglary, looting, violation of probation, battery on a police officer, attempted murder, and failure to disperse, among other charges, according to police.[59] All but eighteen of those arrested were released on their own recognizance. Melina Abdullah, cofounder of the Los Angeles chapter of Black Lives Matter, was unfazed by the approximately $2 billion worth of riot damage (the most expensive in insurance history), saying, "I don't consider property damage anywhere in the ballpark of the theft of life, or even the brutality experienced by protesters who were protesting police brutality."[60] Abdullah continued, "I think we have a right to rage. We have a right to yell. We have a right to be in the streets. We have a sacred duty to shut down business as usual. And that doesn't make us violent, that makes us freedom fighters."[61]

Life in this alternate reality, where criminals are seen as "freedom fighters" and the law-abiding citizens have curfews but the looters are maybe arrested and likely released, became too ridiculous. In 2021, Samaire had had enough. "I got vocal and received pushback—but surprisingly, more praise than hate," she notes. People she had been friendly with for twenty years, whom she'd assumed weren't conservative (that's how clandestine those in the Republican Party in this industry in this town are), called her up to say thank you. Her bravery gave oxygen to others looking to breathe.

Samaire credits her friend and fellow actress, Gina Carano, with being an inspiration. In the midst of a very active career, Carano lost a lucrative job in the Disney's *Star Wars* spinoff *The Mandalorian* when she compared being a Republican in society to being a Jew during the Holocaust. To Samaire, Carano's being canceled was monumental. Carano wasn't actively against anything; she just wasn't going along with the Hollywood dogma. Firing Carano, a woman, also highlighted Hollywood's pecking order and the tenuous nature of its loyalty to trendy causes.

"I knew it was the end of her career in Hollywood," Samaire says. Glossed over were the people getting murdered, streets on fire, businesses destroyed, and employees fired. She couldn't continue pretending with the rest of her industry. Too much was at stake. And she wasn't going to sugarcoat it—it wasn't a disruption; it was destruction.

"We're all playing pretend. It's like an abusive relationship. Once you leave, there's more on the other side. You open up to so much more," says Samaire. She was done playing make-believe and conforming in order to coexist. This was a journey she was ready to take, living her truth and not being silenced.

It wasn't the first time Samaire had taken a stand; when she was twenty-seven, she chose sobriety. The core tenets of Alcoholics Anonymous are being honest and accountable. She harnessed that honesty and accountability again in 2021. "Hollywood won't have me, and I won't have it," she says. Fear wasn't going to control her; she saw any unemployment as temporary. And "no childhood dream to be an actress is worth it," she adds. She was being guided by something bigger.

Samaire has kept circling back to balance, maintaining a level of truth not centric to an ideology. She believes the Constitution shouldn't be partisan, that it's not necessary to agree on everything, but we should all agree on the importance of personal freedom. This commitment to freedom, along with the understanding that everyone deserves respect, is what Samaire instills in her own child now.

At the time of her "Hollywood refugee" status, Samaire's son was seven years old. He was the impetus behind her subsequent move back to Arizona as well as her mindset shift. Samaire chose freedom, and it looked like Sedona. There was a time when she never thought she'd return to where she had been raised and where her family was still living, but those red mountains and the earthy persona of the residents were a tonic. The people were grounded, organically eccentric without the pressure of needing to stand out in order to be recognized, unlike in Hollywood. "They didn't dive into the bullshit of California," Samaire says. Sedona is home to independent thinkers. People selling crystals are able to coexist with people selling guns. Devout vegan hippies share space with hunters in search of javelinas, minus a conniption.

It's not necessarily that Samaire's priorities changed; she had always been in search of truth and gravitated toward creativity and storytelling, but the arena where she thought she was free to pursue those passions changed.

Samaire's reality is now her community; this is what matters most to her. She has intentionally distanced herself from artifice, planting roots in Sedona—one of the most beautiful places in the world, with its stunning vistas of red rock buttes, pine forests, and canyons. And while planting those roots, she saw discord along with the vistas that attract three million visitors annually.[62]

Sedona is a rural community, home to fewer than ten thousand full-time residents.[63] And, supposedly in an effort to preserve its natural beauty, the concept of sustainability and other "green" initiatives had begun appearing in local political measures. This concerned Samaire, recalling the havoc it wreaked on Californians.

Samaire had seen firsthand how the green agenda had financially and physically taken a toll on Los Angeles. Adopting and inserting a green agenda into so many aspects of life in the nation's most populous state, California, steering its forty million residents away from fossil fuels, has resulted in regular rolling blackouts and a financial boondoggle. California has the highest poverty rate—and some of the highest electricity prices—in the country.[64] And despite attempts to tap into renewable energy, there's talk of needing to outsource power from other states. As per *The Daily Signal*, in an August 2020 heat wave, nearly one hundred thousand homes and businesses in California lost power. And

California is poised to spend $54 billion fighting climate change over the next five years.[65] It isn't just the taxpayers' money being spent and the preventable fiascos that are problematic, it's the phony cultish climate-warrior stance of California's celebrities leading the state off the cliff.

Samaire looked into some of Sedona's green policies and cringed; she'd seen this movie before. Sustainability was on the politicians' docket, but she felt there was nothing in place to make Sedona sustainable. It was more pretending. "All this feel-good bullshit on 'green' stuff means giving up liberty and money. Sedona's political plan read like San Francisco's," Samaire says. She concluded that the local politicians' goal was to have all the power go electric. But "we have no infrastructure to make this a reality," she says. "Sedona is in the middle of the desert."

Sedona is blazing hot in summer and cold in winter. The trendy climate-warrior positions of Sedona's governing class are reminiscent of the harebrained ideas of a college dropout. Yet, there's a Sedona City Council and City Management signing on to just about every "green" deal that makes it onto the desk of the Sustainability Department. Charging stations are scant— not to mention, they need fossil fuel and natural gas to function. Sedona's climate action plan is to eliminate half of the city's carbon emissions by 2023, but Samaire posits that officials don't even know how much carbon is currently being emitted. But her biggest gripe is the pretense and posturing of the politicians, which almost always ends up meaning spending more money and constituents receiving less. Samaire recalls hearing the city council say, in effect, "We will spend as much money as necessary to get to zero fossil fuel."

Worried by the parallels between California's failed policies and Arizona's likely-to-fail ones, Samaire grew more political. She had identified as a Republican at sixteen years old but as an adult was an independent; she thought both political sides were repulsive. However, in 2021, living in Sedona, she decided to become part of the solution and took a side.

Samaire's first order of business was standing up for parental rights. She had enrolled her son in a Montessori charter school in Sedona, and masks were mandated, but she had uprooted her family to escape California's craziness. "I'm not coparenting with the state, the school board, and CDC," she says. Furthermore, she was over the fact that the state and the school board were using what the Centers for Disease Control and Prevention was spouting to wield control.

Arizona Governor Doug Ducey had charged the individual districts with enforcing the mask mandates, and Samaire's district was still praying at the altar of mask worship. But her son refused to muzzle. That's when this mama bear sprang into action. She attended school board meetings and listened to the same drivel that other bureaucrats had been repeating ad nauseum for over a year: they were following the experts. She spoke up and told them the school would lose half of its families due to the masking mandate, but her warning fell on deaf ears. She then threw down the gauntlet and said, "If you don't decide to make masks optional, I will be pulling my child from the school."

There were four weeks of school left, and Samaire decided to use them to make a difference. She protested loudly and civilly outside of the school every day for the rest of the school year, fighting for and in her community for the freedom of children.

Other parents caught on and honked in solidarity. Moms joined her to protest outside of school, bringing signs and their children. It was unifying, creating a connection that had been lost since the start of COVID. And as more and more parents joined Samaire in protesting the mask mandates, she realized the power of the community and local politics. She also recognized what many have missed: that parents have *all* the leverage. She intended to use that leverage.

Samaire's second order of business was looking for candidates to run on platforms that truly would benefit her community and solve the day-to-day issues with which they were grappling. She was over believing in the paper-dragon problems that politicians were embracing; she knew that they couldn't be solved and would just suck up money. Sedona's day-to-day issues included the struggle of local businesses following the reaction to COVID; Left-leaning policies that previously had been moving slowly but now were being fast-tracked and were clear threats; a housing crisis spurred by going "green"; and updated building codes that required closed garages, electric vehicle outlets, and solar panel wiring—requiring a Herculean effort to follow.

Not wanting to be a silent participant in her family's demise, Samaire joined the Republican precinct committee in her area. The purpose of this committee is to develop and promote the Republican brand and political platform, educate the public, fundraise, and define an election strategy. Ultimately, her experience was disappointing. She was dejected by the leadership, as Sedona Residents Unite chose radical leftists instead of supporting conservatives. She was suspicious of leadership's motives and questioned why they decided to support a relationship with people vehemently opposing views rather than strengthening the demographic they allege to represent. However, it was educational. "I discovered [that] focusing on county- and state-level candidates is important, but it's the local elections that have the closest impact on one's home and community," says Samaire. Also, some of the people Samaire met while in the precinct committee meetings helped her during her Mayoral campaign.

She took the temperature of the room, of the precinct committee, of her block, of her neighborhood, and of her town. She saw dissatisfaction as a bipartisan problem, particularly since 2020, although Sedona is moderately conservative. The common-denominator goals among its residents are preserving quality of life, maintaining small-town charm, and protecting personal freedom.

While being a precinct committee person didn't work out, a seed was planted. Samaire's interest in storytelling and figuring out the motives behind a character's behavioral patterns, along with her creative spark, persists. Here's the thing about entering politics: there might be a checklist for a successful campaign—filing documents on time, fundraising, building a network, marketing and branding, recruiting voters—but there are myriad ways to complete that checklist. Standout campaigns require authenticity, out-of-the-box thinking, and a connection between the candidate and constituents.

In March 2022, Samaire decided to run for mayor of Sedona. Her platform was balance. While it was perhaps not edgy or provocative, she thought it might feel soothing to fatigued, frustrated, and financially strapped voters. She's not an attack dog, not a polarizing figure. Her campaign ads were subtle, nostalgic, whimsical Sedona vignettes of a magical community that one wanted to be a part of and preserve. Samaire is not wishy-washy, though. She has command of the issues, and through storytelling painted a picture of the problems and solutions.

Her website tackled zeitgeist issues plaguing Sedona, in articles such as "The Woke Agenda Is Here in Sedona Arizona," "The Great Reset Climate Agenda Is Real and in Sedona," and "Creative and Conscious Housing Presentation."

Samaire says she isn't anti-anything except being out of balance, which is a byproduct of being inauthentic. "To choose the right path for Sedona's future, we must come together as a community and listen to residents and local business and protect our sacred land," she told me right before the election. "We need new leadership who can create a vision of our life in Sedona—*together*."

On November 8, 2022, Samaire lost the mayoral election to Sandy Moriarty, but she has found the journey to be rewarding. She left Hollywood, a place not known for truth, on her own terms and with true friendships. She acted as a responsible mom, making the tough decision to move her family for a strong purpose. And Sedona has been full of abundance because Samaire was open to receiving the bounty. Rather than let political tyranny control her, she found freedom. Her time as a precinct committee woman might not have lived up to her expectations, but she built a network and made connections with like-minded people. She's inspired by the smorgasbord of personalities devoted to their land of vortexes known for radiating energy and an aura of mystique.

Coming up on fifteen years of sobriety, Samaire uses many of the lessons learned in Alcoholics Anonymous to move through life in general. She sees success as being not about the end result but about following a path of integrity and getting the ball rolling so that others can carry on with the mission.

And even though the election results didn't fall in her favor, Samaire was one of the initial torchbearers fighting to end the mask mandates in her district, and she succeeded.

Samaire went to Hollywood so she could work in an industry that encouraged creativity. "What I learned is that creativity is dead without freedom of expression," she says. In order for there to be any dynamism, there must be yin and yang; there must be discussions and counterarguments. Some tension must be present on both ends of discourse to stabilize the center and achieve balance. And along the way from Hollywood back to Sedona, she discovered that she's an expert in her own life; she's not farming her life out or ceding authority to any external entity.

Creativity is about taking risks. An astounding thing about COVID and BLM is that these two life-changing events should have unleashed a new art movement. Just the opposite happened. Rather than creativity, there was mass destruction across the board: in the economy, quality of life, government, and arts and entertainment. Culture is now broken. Books have been banned. Art shows are being curated based on immutable characteristics and ideologies.

What is interesting to note is that a few creatives getting a lot of airtime are pushing against the Left's narrative. Kanye West, Ricky Gervais, and Dave Chappelle are some of the talents generating viral moments and commanding hefty sums. It's a referendum on how the majority of people feel. The stripping away of freedom is what made a politically quiet Hollywood actress run for mayor of Sedona on a platform that rejected everything the Left promotes. Samaire is quiet no more, and neither are the moms she's brought into the fold.

# CHAPTER 4:
# SANDRA WHITTEN

**FORMER CANDIDATE FOR U.S. REPRESENTATIVE, CONGRESSIONAL DISTRICT 28, AND CURRENT HOST OF THE AWARD-WINNING RADIO SHOW AND PODCAST *TEXAS FULLY LOADED*. LIVES IN LAREDO, TEXAS. THIRTY-EIGHT YEARS OLD AND MARRIED TO A BORDER PATROL AGENT, WITH FOUR KIDS, AGES EIGHTEEN, FOURTEEN, FIVE, AND THREE. HAS ALWAYS BEEN A REGISTERED REPUBLICAN.**

Sandra Whitten doesn't rely on the mainstream media for facts about the invasion at the border; she's living through it. She isn't snowed by fictitious stories from the Biden administration's press secretary or secretary of Homeland Security, casting aspersions on border agents on horseback, falsely accusing them of whipping illegals streaming in through the southern border. And she certainly rejects the Left's narrative that those who demand that people entry the country legally are racists. Sandra is the wife of a Hispanic border patrol agent and mom to four Hispanic kids: three boys and a girl.

Outraged by the threat to safety of both Americans and foreign children being smuggled in on a harrowing journey, Sandra took action. In March 2019, she threw her hat in the ring and ran for Congress. Her two platform items came naturally and hit close to home: border security and human trafficking. While she didn't make it through the runoffs in May 2022, this mama bear put precious time and financial resources on the line to take a position on an issue that is ranked in the top three of American voters' concerns and growing more relevant by the day: illegals. Absorption of illegals directly impacts the other two top issues: crime and the economy.[66]

Sandra has been paying attention for a while. She was fearful during the 2016 elections, worried the Mexican drug cartels would "freak out," as she terms it, and issue reprisals if Trump won the election. Sandra anticipated two different scenarios: "fight or flight if Trump proved victorious, or chaos, violence, and civil unrest if Clinton was in command, she says."

During the frenetic 2020 election, Sandra tuned in to Fox News. Congresswoman Alexandria Ocasio-Cortez was on the screen yammering on about what young women should aspire to be and from where they should draw their inspiration. Sandra, holding her newborn baby girl, was triggered. "Over my dead body," she said.

Ocasio-Cortez drew Sandra's ire because of comments like these: "People [migrants, are] drinking out of toilets[;] officers [are] laughing in front of members [of] Congress," she tweeted.[67]

"I go back and forth on whether to go on Fox News. The main reason I haven't is squaring the fact that the ad revenue from it bankrolls a white supremacist sympathizer to broadcast an hour-long production of unmitigated racism, without any accountability whatsoever."[68] Also: "In the last facility, I was not safe from the officers," Ocasio-Cortez told CNN's Natasha Chen on her way into the Clint border patrol facility.[69] Ocasio-Cortez claims, "The entire PREMISE of a wall is not based in fact. It's based in a racist + non-evidence based trope that immigrants are dangerous. Yet some Dems are willing to "compromise" & spend BILLIONS on a trope because we've accepted some kinds of racism as realpolitik in America."[70]

There are multiple problems with the propaganda Ocasio-Cortez spreads. With a vast social media network—8.6 million Instagram followers and 13.4 million Twitter followers—she has a significantly more substantial reach than many other politicians. She expertly relies on emotions rather than facts to gin up support and push through radical, harmful notions.

The majority of border patrol agents are minorities. According to 2016 data, Latinos constitute slightly more than 50 percent of the border patrol.[71] This is the sort of statistic the Left intentionally ignores, because it dismantles the narrative that America is racist and that a bunch of white supremacists are guarding it from well-intentioned people who are entitled to living off American taxpayers' fat. By definition, *all* illegals are criminals; they have illegally come into America and then benefit from the American taxpayers' largesse. Democrats, like Ocasio-Cortez, denigrate the border patrol by calling them racist despite the fact that over half the border patrol agents are minority. Simultaneously, Democrats like Ocasio-Cortez accuse Americans of racism all the while they're footing the bill for illegals.

Sandra had a visceral reaction to Ocasio-Cortez because she knows what financial albatrosses are in store for American taxpayers and law-abiding citizens on account of Ocasio-Cortez. Ocasio-Cortez lauds boondoggles like the Green New Deal (which isn't green, isn't new, and certainly isn't a deal), "violence interrupters" (random people trying to talk criminals out of criminalizing in lieu of police), and allowing countless illegals to enter the country with the express intention of "reimaging America."

What Ocasio-Cortez and Democrats mean by "reimaging" is banishing whites, now interchangeably referred to as "white supremacists." This is done by defunding police and changing the demographics of traditionally safe communities. She says, "It's funny because when people ask me, what does a world where we defund the police—where, you know, defunding police looks like? I tell them, it looks like a suburb." In response to Ocasio-Cortez, Fox News' Tucker Carlson wrote an article on July 14, 2020, "Unfortunately, not everyone lives in a suburb as placid and protected as the one Sandy Cortez grew up in, with all the bake sales and pool parties. Cities like St. Louis and Baltimore are more violent than El Salvador, and they're getting more dangerous by the day. In Milwaukee, homicides have risen nearly 40 percent just this year. Killings there could soon break the city's all-time record. That's likely to happen soon in Chicago and Kansas City. Just this weekend in the City of Chicago, 64 people were shot and 11 murdered—11 corpses in one weekend. None of those people died because there were too many cops on the street, they died because, thanks in part to sloganeering from pampered dilettantes like Sandy Cortez, there were too few cops. Less law enforcement in dangerous places means more killings. There's not much debate about that, at least not among adults."[72]

Sandra understands the Left's intention: to allow the unfettered illegals to vote. A case regarding this has recently been tried in New York City. Mayor Adams championed giving approximately eight hundred thousand noncitizens the most basic and cherished right of Americans. The Left *knows* this is illegal; it just doesn't care because it doesn't recognize American rule of law. A state supreme court judge from Staten Island did; he struck the measure down, saying it violated the state constitution.

We're midway through Biden's presidency. The Center for Immigration Studies says that "in January 2022 there were 11.35 million illegal immigrants in the country—a 1.13 million increase over the 10.22 million in January 2021."[73] Experts say this number is grossly low, as it doesn't include "got-aways"—illegals that haven't been apprehended and thus haven't been counted.

Flooding America with illegals is critical to the agenda of the Left and globalists (present in both the Democrat and Republican parties) because it transforms America under the pretense of America being inherently racist. Those citing the racism rarely speak about China, Russia, Iran, or Pakistan. These countries' regimes believe they benefit from the takedown of America because they reject American principles, though their economies are greatly reliant on American money and commerce. To advance the takedown, there's been a strong push to foment racial discord. The Chinese government supports BLM.[74] So do radical Islamic regimes "coordinating with and getting support from the Council on American-Islamic Relations (CAIR).

When the woke army became involved with Black Lives Matter, it enshrined 'from Ferguson to Palestine; occupation is a crime' as the organizing principle of the movement. It plays a pivotal role through CAIR, Students for Justice in Palestine, and activists such as Linda Sarsour in moving the BDS movement into a mainstream component of social justice. It quickly exploited anti-Trump fears to turn the Women's March into a mouthpiece and platform for anti-Israel and antisemitic activities."[75] As of December 2022, China's population stood at 1.4118 billion. According to the 2020 census, 91.11 percent of the population was Han Chinese, and 8.89 percent were minorities, with five hundred thousand Africans—in other words, it doesn't have a leg to stand on.[76] Whether it is through open borders, which means no country, TikTok, BLM and CRT spurring racial division, broken education, weakened military, and financial decline, the Biden administration has been infiltrated and held hostage by globalists that benefit from America's demise. The problem is, at present time, we don't yet know the full extent to which Biden has been compromised and thus, owned by China and other advocates of globalism.[77] The Constitution, Judeo-Christian principles, and capitalism is anathema to the Democrats, many of which that have embraced Marxism.

Flooding America with illegals puts people in imminent danger, including Sandra's border patrol agent husband and, by extension, her entire family. Worse, the Left's claims are predicated on a lie. Americans by and large aren't racist. The deadliest military conflict in American history was the Civil War, whereby approximately six hundred twenty thousand men lost their lives.[78] Forty-three percent of white Americans helped elect President

Obama.[79] If America is so racist, why would illegals want to come here? As per Pew Research Center, Mexico is the top origin country of the U.S. immigrant population.[80] The next largest origin groups were those from China (6 percent), India (6 percent), the Philippines (4 percent) and El Salvador (3 percent).[81]

Due to American's industrious nature and free market, and the ability to get ahead here through hard work irrespective of race, religion, or sex, it's paradise to virtually everyone from other countries, clearly. This is why refugees aren't going to failed Socialist countries or third-world countries with dictatorships. What the Democrats say about America is a lie on its face, proven by the sheer number of illegals flooding America *and* passing by countless other countries on their way.

Illegals are creating undue economic stress for Americans, who are already breaking under the Left's monetary inflation. They are responsible for the drug crisis that is killing Americans. The Cato Institute says, "U.S. consumer payments for illicit opioids ultimately fund fentanyl smuggling. Consumers pay retail dealers who pay wholesalers, and the cash is then transferred back in bulk cash form to Mexico. These funds are then used to pay smugglers to bring drugs back into the United States again."[82] Fentanyl overdose deaths among teens accounted for 77 percent of adolescent overdose deaths in 2021.[83] According to the U.S. Department of Justice's own website, "The southwestern States that share a border with Mexico—Texas, New Mexico, Arizona, and California—are put under strain when they must process illegal immigrants caught with illegal drugs. Illegal immigrants arrested for drug smuggling are not deported, rather they are processed through the local criminal justice system."

Sandra is over the Left's mischaracterizations (at best) and downright lying (at worst) about its intentions for the border. She also takes issue with this head scratcher: that the United States Border Patrol (USBP) is a federal law enforcement agency under the United States' Customs and Border Protection agency *and* yet is being attacked by those in the highest ranks of American politics. Sandra is aghast as she listens to the rhetoric that is endangering those employed to keep America safe, like her husband, who makes approximately $100,000 annually.

"My husband has been an agent for thirteen years, since Obama. Presently, he hates his job. Morale is the lowest amongst the border patrol agent community it has ever been," says Sandra. Nonetheless, he continues at his post because he believes in this country—in the need to protect the border, to stop the invasion, cartels, drugs, and guns from harming Americans.

Laredo is the number-one inland port along the U.S.–Mexico border.[84] It's home to Interstate 35. In June 2022, more than sixty-seven illegal migrants were traveling from Mexico, Guatemala, El Salvador, and Honduras in the back of a sweltering tractor-trailer. Forty-eight of them died in San Antonio, close to Interstate 35. Rescuers were able to pull sixteen people out of the truck who were still alive and conscious, including four minors.[85] Sandra puts it like this, "If you think the war is on drugs, you're stuck in the '80s." She maintains that the cartels make over $3,000 a head offloading humans, and make more money from the rape slave trade than from drugs.[86]

Just two days before Christmas in 2018, Sandra received a call. Congress was adjourning and taking a two-week hiatus. Her husband and all other Department of Security employees would be furloughed. "The authority figure relaying the information stated there was no word on when a paycheck would be sent," says Sandra.

Sandra was beside herself. She has a large family, and Christmas is a celebratory and expensive occasion. On tenterhooks, she waited for forthcoming news. Days and then weeks went by. Her eldest son, sensing the fraught economic situation, tried to ameliorate the dejection, specifically his panicked mom's. He told her that the siblings had decided they didn't need presents, and if any had already been bought, they should be returned to save money. This was Sandra's Christmas.

Sandra explained to her kids, "It's Mommy and Daddy's problem." She told her son, "G-d provides, and this is the season for miracles." They got in the car and drove to take photos with Santa.

Sandra channeled her angst and made a decision. "After putting on a brave face and getting through the holiday, I became an advocate," she says.

There are more than sixty thousand employees in U.S. Customs and Border Protection, which is part of the Department of Homeland Security (DHS). The border patrol is its mobile, uniformed law enforcement arm, responsible for securing U.S. borders between ports of entry. It's one of the world's largest law enforcement organizations and is tasked with keeping terrorists and their weapons out of America while facilitating lawful international travel and trade.[87] Sandra knew that her family wasn't the only one grappling with the fear of lost income and character assassination in the court of public opinion at the behest of the Biden administration, Ocasio-Cortez, other Democrats, and the mainstream media.

Sandra reached out to her border patrol agent community. Her immediate goal was to keep morale up by uniting people facing the new burdens along with the ones already inflicted on them by the government's response to COVID. Border patrol agents are among the most attacked law enforcers in the country. There are daily hazards, ranging from navigating desperate people trying to infiltrate the border, to contending with depraved drug cartel members, to working in unforgiving temperatures and on dangerous terrain.

Sandra says she was told, "Someone will feed your family. Such and such business will waive the cable bill." The problem was, her family didn't qualify for benefits but still had bills to pay. "All of DHS, with over two hundred forty thousand employees and nine executive departments totaling eight hundred thousand employees, was living through this nightmare of uncertainty. Only those with a badge on the front line were working without pay," says Sandra.

For six agonizing weeks, from December 22, 2018, to January 25, 2019, no paycheck came and Sandra's husband's employment was precarious. The reason for the furlough was that Congress was fighting over the budget and wouldn't agree to President Trump's demands for funding the wall.

"I was a student mom when my youngest was a newborn, and my husband was working and not getting paid. Sitting there at the kitchen table, helpless, like all these other families, I felt G-d say, 'This is why I called you, to not give up and to fight for these families and expose the truth'" recalls Sandra. The stress was profound, and one night in January 2019, her husband came home at the end of a shift at three a.m. Tempers were running hot, and

Sandra remembers him saying in the middle of a fight, "I don't like you now," to which she responded, "The feeling is mutual." As Sandra's husband took off his gear, she let him know that G-d wanted her to run for Congress. "He looked at me like I was crazy," Sandra says. "I didn't have money, influence, or resources, but I said, 'I talked with G-d. Trust me.'"

Sandra viewed her compulsion to run as a calling. It was a moment of clarity amid turmoil. She prayed and talked to G-d and said, "If you open the door, I'll walk through." She didn't feel like she had a choice to ignore the opportunity. "Our silence is our compliance," she says. She embraced her individual responsibility to service. "The corruption at the border, the Second Amendment under direct threat from the Democrats, health care, and not abolishing abortion are issues that preclude me from sitting back and staying quiet," says Sandra.

As fate would have it, a state Republican executive committeeman reached out to Sandra. They spoke about the Left, Ocasio-Cortez, and racism, particularly about how it's been watered down to mean nothing, as it's used now as a tactic to silence the Right or even those on the Left who threaten the hierarchy of professional victims. Sandra was still smarting over Ocasio-Cortez's accusations of racism regarding border patrol agents and how they have white privilege, when all the while Sandra's husband was Hispanic and she, a white woman, had no privilege. "I'm a mom of four Hispanic kids. We live paycheck to paycheck. Where's our privilege? I have no privilege. We work hard and are familiar with sacrifice and service," she says.

Sandra told the state Republican executive committeeman her intention. She wanted to run for Congress against Democratic congressman Henry Cuellar, who had been in Congress since 2005 and in public office since 1987. Sandra's beef with Cuellar: "He is loved by both sides of the aisle because he has no backbone." Republican United States senator John Cornyn worked with Cuellar in November 2020. U.S. House speaker Nancy Pelosi also was a strong supporter of Cuellar's. Cuellar refers to himself as a "moderate-centrist," but as of September 2022, he voted in line with Biden's stated positions 94.3 percent of the time.[88]

Sandra was hyperfocused on the border, and not only because of the strain that illegals put on American taxpayers, the flouting of the law, and the nefarious way in which the Left and globalists use illegals like pawns to "undo" America. It was because as a mother, as someone married to a border patrol agent and with knowledge of the horrors of human trafficking, child trafficking, she couldn't stay silent.

"'Human trafficking' is a Hollywood term. Internally, the border patrol community calls it the rape slave trade," says Sandra. "Women have bills that must be paid, so coming out of Ecuador, El Salvador, and other South American countries, the majority of women have been raped throughout the entirety of their journey to America. By the time they cross the river, they've signed a contract giving away everything. My border is Laredo. I'm good friends with the police chief from Houston. He gets a phone call; a woman from the South America triangle explains the agreement with the cartel. She owes twenty thousand dollars, compounded with a daily six percent interest, like a mortgage payment. Now, she's amassed upwards of one million dollars of 'debt' for food, housing, et cetera, and the number keeps mounting. She's explaining it to the police chief like one would explain a mortgage. The further she gets in the country, the higher her bill, because the cartel pays for her journey."

Sandra also takes issue with the term "border security," saying it's intentionally watered down and belies the true horrors. Border patrol agents deal with, among other things, forced human trafficking, meaning it occurs when a person is induced by force, fraud or coercion.[89] People are bred to be sold and sacrificed to the number-one consumer, the United States, says Sandra, adding: "We end human tracking when we end the consumership of it in America."

However, as Sandra explained to the state Republican executive committeeman, it's not just about the problems at the border; they don't exist in a vacuum. It's about everything that the chaos touches. It's about piling those problems onto an already fallen school system—overloading it with the unforgiving task of dealing with illegals. Bringing in people with different languages and cultures, people who are wholly unaware of and disconnected from American history and traditions, creates the perfect cover for the newly woke educational complex to further neglect American history. Illegals in schools are accelerating the slide down to the abyss of revisionism and outright erasure of historical facts.

The crisis at the border and its effect on Laredo have been so profound that in August 2021, then mayor Pete Saenz, a Democrat, was in a panic. Due to a swell in McAllen and the Rio Grande Valley, illegal immigrants were making their way to Laredo. Saenz said, "We've had no other choice but to basically transport these folks further north because we can't handle it here." His form of governance was to pass on the problem. Saenz added, "We need solutions, short-term solutions. Keep in mind this is a federal issue created by failed federal policies, and they're expecting us smaller communities to bail them out."[90] But short-term solutions aren't going to cut it. While Saenz's actions and outlook were feeble, they're an indictment of the Democratic policies that Sandra calls out. Even Cuellar, a Democrat, is demanding action from the Biden administration, saying, "Imagine you're a mayor and you're limited with hospital beds, and you have someone from Laredo versus somebody that might not be from here. It puts them in a very difficult situation."[91]

The Left continually attacks the border agents instead of the root cause: Biden and the globalists' attempts to transform America yet inability to deal with the influx—proving their utter incompetence. Texas governor Greg Abbott posted a press release on his website in July 2022 that reads in part: "Governor Greg Abbott today issued a statement in response to the recent accusations by New York City Mayor Eric Adams attacking Texas' border busing mission to help local border communities: 'Mayor Adams' problem is not with Texas. It is with President Biden's refusal to stop this border crisis and secure our southern border.'"[92]

This statement was in response to New York City Mayor Adams, who essentially called Governor Abbott a racist for sending illeglas to sanctuary cities like New York City. Adams said this is done to "hurt Black-run cities."[93] Here's the issue with Adams' racist grift: there's no legislation anywhere in America declaring any large urban center a "sanctuary city." It's a scam to level cities and vanish "white supremacy"—but it didn't work. Adams intended for the impact of "sanctuary cities" to fall on the "white supremacists." They voted for their feet. 300,000 so-called "white supremacists" left, taking with them $16 billion in taxes from the Big Apple. If Adams thought the illegals negatively affected whites, he would remain silent. Now, those left holding the bag are the middle and lower classes, and yes, black people.

"My scope came full circle, including fighting with the school board in Laredo, Webb County," says Sandra. The city of Laredo is the county seat of Webb County, located on the north bank of the Rio Grande in South Texas, across from Nuevo Laredo, Tamaulipas, Mexico. It is a hotbed of activity and is deeply impacted by the nightmare at the border. The committeeman Sandra spoke with said he wasn't surprised by the hierarchy that Sandra's platform issues would tackle, that she had developed a reputation throughout Texas as a mama bear.

"People asked me when I ran, why I started with Congress," says Sandra. "It's because corruption is so bad and comes from the top down. We need to break the cycle of insanity, from the courthouse to the Big House to our home."

Sandra talks about what parents saw during the COVID pandemic. Not just the five-minute hall pass some parents were allotted in order to briefly get in order to gain access into school, but the Zoom sessions and the assignments, or lack thereof. "My son was in constitutional law class, and the teacher told my sophomore that no one needs to own a gun and the Second Amendment is toilet paper," she says. Naturally, this didn't sit well with the wife of a border patrol agent. "My testimony for gun rights has been used by Gun Owners of America as a model before the Texas Legislature in 2020. So to hear a constitutional law teacher say it's not worth the price of toilet paper, I have a problem. He's indoctrinating children with no counterargument. My teenage sons were embarrassed when I came barreling into their classroom. But this is the garbage spewed. Kids should never know what teachers feel politically, because teachers are in a position of power," says Sandra.

Since the 2016 presidential election and certainly throughout the time of COVID, educators have been exposed as amplifying their weighted views on polarizing subjects. Issues including politics, sexuality, gender, America, abortion, racism, the climate, activism, and challenges to the nuclear family have taken up most of the oxygen. This has created undo strife in classrooms already under duress due to declining educational standards, two years of limited face time in school, and Marxist CRT. It has caused quantifiable psychological problems among students faced with either going along to get along or being subjected to severe punishment, such as being ostracized, receiving harsh grades, and being refused entry into higher education institutions.[94]

"My kids have no clue about how I feel on most subjects. I teach them both sides so they can form their own opinions, which we can then discuss," says Sandra. "They only found out when I ran for Congress where I stand on issues. My kids choose the right path because they're informed and able to make educated decisions."

The hardest part of the COVID pandemic for Sandra was watching kids get yanked out of school without a real justification. No school, then virtual school, then CRT, then mask mandates… it was all too much to bear.

"I pulled my eldest kid from school—a byproduct of COVID, CRT, and mandates," says Sandra. She adds that in August 2021, right before school started, "I got notified that the school board is enforcing mask mandates. Aside from my disgust, Governor

Abbott signed an executive order prohibiting governmental entities in Texas from requiring or mandating masks."

Sandra was scorched earth. She went to the school board meeting and streamed it on Facebook Live under the heading "Don't mess with my kid." It got twenty thousand views. Due to COVID protocols, only half of the school board was present, the other half was on Zoom, and two people were allowed in the room at a time due to "spacing"—a term that will live on in COVID infamy. "I go in and am told I have three minutes, which they then shorten to two minutes. I said, 'I won't be silenced,'" Sandra says. She explains that a state law called the Open Meetings Act is changing the amount of time allotted to speakers without notification.[95] "I go in with guns blazing, proverbially," she says. "In two minutes, I say, 'When was the last time any of you were in the classroom? You're adding more to the plate of teachers. It's unhealthy; there's medical research showing case after case of children getting bacterial infections from masks. Kids need germs to strengthen their immune system.'"

Sandra describes how when her two minutes were up, the school board members just stared. They're not allowed to respond to public testimony. Her biggest takeaway: only fifteen parents had the courage to stand up for their children. "There was a lack of courage," she emphasizes.

The saddest revelation to Sandra was that removing the mask mandate had garnered plenty of support—but only in private. "People are afraid to stand up to the system, even when they know it's wrong, because they fear repercussions," she says. The Webb County school board ignored the parents and went ahead with the mask mandate. When Sandra asked, "You're going to go ahead with the unlawful order? What will you do to kids who won't mask?" the response was that there would be consequences. "Then the board walked away," says Sandra.

Some warriors fought back. Another parent, a paralegal, sued the school board using testimony from Sandra, and won on the grounds that the school board had overstepped its bounds. It was one of the first lawsuits in the state. Texas attorney general Ken Paxton helped.

But the situation was far from over. Three days later, on the first day of school, Sandra, escorting her sixteen-year-old junior, was intercepted before getting to the entrance. The vice principal said they couldn't come in without a mask. Sandra, undeterred, held the governor's order in her hands, and her smartphone was streaming live on Facebook; she was prepared to fight. "You're going to tell Governor Abbott that my son can't come to school? It's not up to you," she said defiantly. The response: this was what the school board had decided. Her son was not allowed in the building.

Sandra's son was proud. He learned two important lessons: that his mom would fight for him at all costs, and that no one should mess with her.

Sandra continued to defy the mandate. She brought her second son to middle school, saw the principal, and said, "Are we going to have a problem?" The response: "Ma'am, no, we have an isolation room." Sandra's son sat by himself until noon. The principal requested a meeting, had her son join, and offered the following solution: Sandra could fill out a medical form declaring that her son suffered from asthma, which precluded him from masking, and would have to get it notarized. "You want me to get a form filled out and notarized so he can follow the law while y'all break it?" asked Sandra. She was presented with another option: a religious exemption that also had to be notarized. Sandra, unmoved, said, "This form is negating my First Amendment right to explain my religion."

Sandra and her husband had a roundtable discussion with their two teenage sons. They agreed that the school board's mandates were unconstitutional. But something else was vexing them: "On top of mandates, education was appalling and disgusting," she notes.

The moral corruption of the youth was evident to Sandra when she received a phone call from another mom, who said that a sixth-grade girl in Laredo was going to be thrown a baby shower on the school premises. "Because of the culture we've created as parents via consumption, watching TV, [and] social media, right and wrong isn't being taught. We have twelve-year-olds getting impregnated by cartel members, and it's being celebrated at school. The students are even organizing the party. Bringing a daycare facility into the school was discussed; some high schools have one so that moms can attend classes. "Babies having babies creates the welfare circle of life," says Sandra. She details the calamity of an impressionable twelve-year-old's mind's being misguided. The girl claimed she was in love with the cartel member, who was eighteen years old and did not get arrested.

This is the culture that Sandra understands, and the one that New York City's Ocasio-Cortez misrepresents. Sandra says that in Laredo, some kids look up to the cartel members and desire to be one when they're older. They're swayed by the money and power. Our current society has put a premium on dishonest "work" that shuns hard work, education, and staying on the straight and narrow. Sandra says, "I've heard middle schoolers tell teachers, 'I don't have to do a motherfucking thing because when I get done with this bullshit, I'm going to [the] cartel.' Mexico isn't the problem. The problem is on this side of the river, right here."

Even though Sandra lost her bid for Congress, her platform and drive continue to grow. She's the host of *Texas Fully Loaded*, a radio show and podcast that discusses politics, Texas, and life. "I love making people uncomfortable; we're all uncomfortable together," says Sandra.

Her mission might sound grandiose, but it's torchbearers like Sandra who are impacting policy and effectuating change. She is determined to end the rape slave trade and to protect children. It makes no difference to her whether they're the children being illegally smuggled into America or American kids being perverted by the Left and the educational complex. Sandra is convinced that mama bears aren't going to take these evils anymore. Like many of the moms going from blue to red or red to redder, she believes the educational complex is the root of the rot.

Sandra was prescient. Two critical events have recently occurred that have struck fear into the Democratic Party, especially into Alexandria Ocasio-Cortez. The first is that Hispanic Republican Party registration numbers have increased. In the November 2022 midterm elections, the GOP halved the Democrats' margin with Hispanic voters; it's now D+21. Tone-deaf to the Hispanic flight from the Left, Ocasio-Cortez tweeted, "Pardon immigrants. President Biden's pardon only applied to citizens with federal marijuana charges. Many immigrants applying for citizenship could continue to face deportation or other adverse consequences for possessing a substance that is now legal in many states." What she fails to grasp is that Hispanics are Texas' largest demographic group, accounting for 40.2 percent of the state's population.[96] And they are increasingly voting against invasion at the border, because it threatens their physical and economic safety.

The second critical event, which is a referendum on the first, is that in November 2022, then minority leader of the United States House of Representatives Kevin McCarthy came out swinging against Homeland Security secretary Alejandro Mayorkas. Why? Because of growing pressure to blunt what is destroying America, which can no longer be ignored despite what Ocasio-Cortez purports. At a news conference in El Paso, McCarthy said, "We will use the power of the purse and the power of subpoena. Let me be clear: those responsible for this disaster will be held accountable. If Secretary Mayorkas does not resign, House Republicans will investigate every order, every action and every failure to determine whether we can begin impeachment inquiries."[97] He was capitalizing on the growing trend that Americans are against the entry of illegals into America; otherwise, he wouldn't take the risk.

Sandra also is still swinging. "My fire is to get moms to stand up for their families regardless of what their financial situation is," she says. "This is true freedom. It's personal agency. We the people shouldn't rely on the government." She is correct. It's moms like Sandra, who stood on the front lines at the beginning and took incoming shots, who have helped light a fire on the Right. And that fire will continue to grow, thanks to the increasing might of Hispanic voters who believe in Republican principles.

# CHAPTER 5:
# ASRA NOMANI

**SENIOR FELLOW AT THE INDEPENDENT WOMEN'S NETWORK, AUTHOR, AND SENIOR CONTRIBUTOR TO THE WEB MAGAZINE *THE FEDERALIST*. FIFTY-SEVEN-YEAR-OLD SINGLE MOTHER WITH ONE TWENTY-YEAR-OLD SON. LIVES IN VIRGINIA. HAD BEEN A LIFELONG DEMOCRAT BUT NOW VOTES MOSTLY REPUBLICAN AND IDENTIFIES AS AN INDEPENDENT.**

L ots of people take part in grassroots movements. Not a lot of people lead them. Asra Nomani, Muslim single mom of one son, laid the groundwork for what has struck fear into the hearts of the teachers' unions, anti–parental rights school boards, and the members of the Biden administration, who have been watching from the sidelines, powerless, as their proxies have been challenged and humiliated. Asra saw into the future; she knew that CRT would be the death knell for education and for the values that hold America together. She has fought radical ideology for most of her life and has been sounding the most recent alarm since June 2020.

Born in Bombay, India, Asra came with her older brother to America in 1967, when she was four years old, to join her parents. The family settled in New Jersey, where her father was earning a PhD at Rutgers University, and then moved to Morgantown, West Virginia, when she was still young.

Education is critical to Asra; it was the impetus for her family's relocation to the United States and, as for so many first-generation immigrants, the pathway to upward mobility. Usually, immigrants don't have inherited wealth, assets, property, or a social network on which to rely. Education is their golden ticket. America represents the dream, the land of abundance and opportunity, minus the rigid social hierarchy that older countries still have that takes a Herculean effort to escape. As a young first-generation immigrant who had witnessed her parents struggle, both in their land of origin and then upon their arrival in the United States, to create a better life for their offspring through what *only* education can bring, Asra could not sit back and just watch education be reduced.

Asra received a Bachelor of Arts degree in liberal studies from West Virginia University in 1986. By mid-August 1988, she had become a correspondent at the *Wall Street Journal*. While working, she received a Master of Arts degree in international communications from American University in 1990. She was prolific in her career—writing, researching, and covering topics that made the most of her analytical mind.

The year 2002 was significant for Asra, professionally and personally. While on assignment in Karachi, Pakistan, her friend and *Wall Street Journal* colleague, Jewish American reporter Daniel Pearl, was abducted and murdered by Islamic militants in January. Asra began to devote her life to exposing and eradicating Islamic extremism.

Also in 2002, Asra gave birth to her only child, a son, Shibli. "It was not only a taboo but a crime in my Muslim faith for me to have a baby without being married, but I made a choice as a Muslim woman to bring my son into the world," she says. Understanding Asra's choice to forge ahead despite the religious shame relentlessly heaped upon her by the community makes it crystal clear why fighting on her son's behalf before a school board and an educational complex trying to inject racist and sexist radical CRT teachings was never a question for her.

After Shibli was born, Asra cobbled her life together as a single mother. She was fortunate to have supportive parents who coparented her son and was able to continue working as a writer. In 2003, she published her first book, *Tantrika: Traveling the Road of Divine Love*, an introspective look at being Muslim. On June 1, 2003, her first op-ed in the *Washington Post* was published. Following her first book's success, she signed a contract to write a second, *Standing Alone in Mecca: An American Muslim Woman's Struggle for the Soul of Islam*, and took her son on a pilgrimage to Mecca.

It was there that she overcame the shame she had allowed herself to carry for months, as if it were her day of judgment. On the pilgrimage itself, she had lied, or lied by omission, never revealing that she wasn't married. Then in Mecca, she stood and said, "I will not lie on my judgment day, so I will not lie on earth. I will live without shame, and I will raise my son free of any indoctrination that judges or shames. I will raise him free."

Asra is a mother before anything else. She gave up her career at the *Wall Street Journal* to concentrate on raising her son. "I was committed as a single mother to defying the statistics assigned to children of single mothers and was very much aware of the stigma attached to single motherhood. I wanted to defy those odds and the stereotype," she says.

In July 2007, Asra and Shibli moved to Maryland and then D.C., where Asra taught journalism at Georgetown University. It was a short-lived setup. By December 2008, she had packed up their home and moved to Virginia. The state had just helped vote Obama in as president by a 6.3 percent margin of victory. "I prided myself on the fact that my home state of West Virginia had split from Virginia over slavery," Asra says. "As a minority, I was hesitant to live in Virginia, but then finally felt that they were progressive enough for me and my own progressive politics."

From 2009 to 2016, Asra worked as a cultural trainer for the United States military, the FBI, and the U.S. State Department. She was a bridge, familiar with the ways of the West and East and able to decode and translate behavior and cultural mores. She had studied cross-cultural communication, and now taught it to the military deploying to Afghanistan. "The West is mostly linear culturally and challenges authority. The East is most often relational. A U.S. Marine has to learn how to defer to the 'white beard,' or elder, in an Afghan village. A young white man from the South may understand this mentality better than a Black drill sergeant trained in his linear ways," notes Asra. But assigning white supremacy to the characteristics of a linear culture would be an overly simplistic and misguided assessment. "The anti-racists stole simple ideas in cross-cultural communications to push their agenda and indoctrination," Asra says.

Multiple factors, such as geography, age, job, and culture, define whether a person is detail- and task-oriented, precise in keeping appointment dates and times. This doesn't have anything to do with white supremacy, but is a byproduct of a linear culture attributed to many factors irrespective of race, maintains Asra. She points to Oprah Winfrey as an example. Oprah is black and precise; she's very specific about how many seats are in the audience, how they must be filled, what time her show airs, the content and control of her brand. Whites can be this way as well depending on the job; an accountant might have a linear mindset, but when the accountant goes home, he or she might just sit on the porch and tune out obligations. The point Asra stresses is that there's been a misappropriation of terms, like "white supremacy," to hijack certain characteristics that don't depend on race.

While Asra was busy as a cultural trainer in 2013, she also began working on her third book. It would take her nearly a decade to complete. She incorporated her experiences as a Muslim woman familiar with indoctrination, as someone who was aiding the military in understanding and undermining extremism and, years later, as a witness to what the school boards were doing. The book, called *Woke Army: The Red-Green Alliance That Is Destroying America's Freedom*, was published in February 2023.

In 2017, Shibli was accepted into Thomas Jefferson High School for Science and Technology in Fairfax County, Virginia—the top-ranked public high school in the nation, as a freshman.[98]

"Shibli worked hard to get into TJ, and it was a moment of triumph for our family. We had a lot of economic challenges raising Shibli in one of the most expensive counties in America," says Asra.[99] (The median household income in Fairfax County is \$112,436.)[100] Shibli excelled in math and science. His interests and academic seriousness didn't happen by accident but by design. Asra, with a master's degree and a job teaching young adults at the college level, was a formidable role model. She took education seriously. She even helped advocate for a gifted-and-talented program in Fairfax County. Everything Asra did—working, not working, relocating—was to make sure her son stayed on the straight and narrow.

Investing time and effort in the community, Asra added another line item to her résumé, becoming the volunteer editor of *This Week at TJ*, the official newsletter of the TJ PTSA (Thomas Jefferson Parent-Teacher-Student Association). Asra and her son worked hard and are proof that attaining the American Dream is possible. For the first time in her life, Asra was surrounded by other first-generation immigrants, as most of the parents at TJ fit this description. Everything was humming—until it wasn't.

In May 2020, after George Floyd was killed, everything changed. The PTSA president took a strong racial-justice position for the first time ever, arguing that there weren't enough blacks and Hispanics at the school. Democrats used money as a way to enforce their woke and racist initiatives, effectively bribing schools with money and refusing funds to holdouts unwilling to go along with the plan. TJ gets funding add-ons from the state general assembly as a so-called governor's school, with advanced academics and selective admissions. In 2020, Virginia's secretary of education, Atif Qarni (a Democrat), said that governor's schools had to increase "diversity" among their student bodies in order to be eligible for the additional money. The members of Fairfax County's school board, all twelve of whom were Democrats, played into his bluff.

The merit-based system at TJ was dismantled. This happened despite the fact that a merit-based system is the fairest system, enabling people from all walks of life to be judged and rewarded based *only* on intellectual prowess, with this prowess being a result of a) being academically gifted, b) being hardworking, and/or c) having a responsible parent(s). Later, the Biden administration also would deal a blow to the idea of working hard, the basis for societal advancement.

Pacific Legal Foundation represented TJ parents in a federal lawsuit against the school board, saying, "Up until 2020, admission to TJ was merit-based and race-blind; requirements included a standardized test, grade-point average, completion of certain math classes, and teacher recommendations. The school board and superintendent completely did away with the test, starting with the 2021–22 school year."[101]

"On June 7, 2020, my birthday, I received an email from the school that was like a stab in the heart. Our now-disgraced principal, Ann Bonitatibus, told us she wanted to match the racial demographic of the county. Obviously, Asians would be screwed. Her aim was to increase black and Hispanic enrollment on the backs of Asian students," says Asra. Pacific Legal Foundation predicted drastic reductions in the number of Asian American students at the school, and sent the school board a warning letter that it was engaging in unconstitutional racial discrimination against Asian American students.

Asra viewed the racial-justice position as dehumanizing on its face. It wasn't just to admit students based on immutable characteristics such as race. She also took it as an insult to her family and the Asian American community's lived experience. "We have overcome so much and then succeeded in this country. My mom worked as a babysitter to raise money for my brother and me to join her here in America. She wept every night waiting for our arrival. I happily ate my free lunch. My brother was embarrassed, bullied, and picked on. We were poor. Ann Bonitatibus just erased all that," notes Asra.

Worse, leaders on the Left insisting on a woke agenda are embarrassingly ignorant to the history pertaining to the identity groups they disingenuously champion, and simultaneously cause harm in more ways than one. Asra brings up the name of TJ's sports teams, the Colonials, as an example. The principal adopted the position that the term represented colonization. Colonialism is something the Left has made a hot topic, bemoaning it yet ignoring its complexity. Asra is well versed on the subject of colonialism; her father is five foot three due to malnutrition he suffered and survived during the Bengal famine of 1943, which spread through British India. Yet her parents don't hold a grudge against Britain or India; they understand history and never blamed the nation-state. Asra's father marched with Gandhi, who was inspired by the American Colonials, who had removed the yoke of colonization from the British. Asra found Ann Bonitatibus' virtue signaling offensive.

In May 2020, Asra and Shibli, along with their cat and two dogs, moved into Asra's parents' home. They all lived together for one month before shit hit the fan.

"On June seventh, I woke up," Asra says. She quit the PTSA and resigned from the newsletter, which she viewed as a vehicle for propaganda spread by parents who had turned into woke activists. One day, while her mother was making dal and basmati rice, Asra went downstairs to the basement, sat in a makeshift office she had created, and prepared for an online school board meeting. Members of this school board control a $3,500,000,000 budget for the 2023–2024 school year (up from $3 billion budget from the previous year)—similar to the budget of a small country.[102] Despite this astronomical sum, in 2023, new Superintendent Dr. Michelle C. Reid of Fairfax County Public Schools (FCPS) requested an additional $159.6 million from the Fairfax County Board of Supervisors. It's the second-largest employer in the state of Virginia. The school board should have been in the power seat. But Goliath was about to meet David.

Asra was allotted three minutes to speak. "I warned them of 'Woke Inc.,' CRT, and activists hijacking the school and school system," she says. "At first they ignored me. Then they treated me like a terrorist threat. They cut my mic. I had no hesitation in this parents' battle. Been there, done that. I was put on trial at my mosque for walking through the front door. That was no different from the treatment and viewpoint of the school board. That's what I brought with me. I studied ideological extremism for fifteen years and understood it immediately when I saw CRT—and recognized in it an indoctrination at school emanating from the school board, much like I'd seen dangerous indoctrination from my mosque."

After the meeting, this methodical, analytical, investigative researcher and reporter became an expert in CRT. She studied up on its "godfather," Harvard Law School tenured professor Derrick Bell. She read his seminal book. She interviewed James Lindsay, coauthor of the nonfiction book *Cynical Theories: How Activist Scholarship Made Everything About Race, Gender, and Identity—and Why This Harms Everybody.* Asra also spoke with Chien Kwok, a father and leader at PLACE, a New York City organization advocating on improving the academic rigor and standards of K–12 public school curricula. Asra recalls Chien saying, about his PLACE team of parent advocates, "The Left will always use kids. We [our group] have a rule; we won't use kids."

The Fairfax County school board, as mentioned, was composed of twelve Democrats. Democratic governor Ralph Northam's administration and Fairfax County Democrats used TJ's admissions as part of their campaign on "equity," installing Secretary of Education Atif Qarni in 2017, shortly after Northam was elected. A budget was put in place with language specifying that within the annual report, diversity goals must be met. "Asians are considered a minority when playing the victim. When they refuse, they lose minority status in the eyes of the Left. If they don't wear the cloak of victimhood, they're considered white-adjacent and resource hoarders, spending thousands on test prep and called racist and toxic. Jews are a minority so long as they reject the state of Israel and support a Palestinian state. Otherwise, they're white," says Asra.

Contention ratcheted up in Fairfax. Asra describes the great shaming of America. Activists and special interest groups exploited George Floyd's death to shame America, intentionally leaving out the racially diverse police associated with his death so as to not undermine the Left's political agenda. The shame was then inserted into the school system in Fairfax County, Virginia. Asra, accustomed to following the money while working at the *Wall Street Journal*, points out that the shaming of America was critical for companies now eligible for a windfall of money, exceeding billions, *if* they got on board with the Left's woke agenda. When George Floyd died in 2020, Virginia's education secretary made a secret task force composed of the principal, two board members, the superintendent, and other Democratic leaders; Asra found out about it in August of that year. By then, the CRT agenda and woke policies the school board was implementing were all-encompassing and too poisonous to ignore.

Asra and some other parents joined together to form one of the first, if not *the* first, parent group in the nation to organize against CRT, forming the Coalition for TJ. Many of those involved had the most to lose; some parents were green card holders, immigrants, and new citizens. They were the very population that liberal Democrats are supposed to care about, but in this case they became the inconvenient minority. These fearless parents lit the match in Fairfax County, and the fire would soon be felt around the nation.

They used Facebook, Twitter, and Instagram and held protests against the war on merit that was toppling the country. They strategically didn't mention CRT, knowing that it went over the heads of most people. The term was new in 2020, and the public was in the throes of COVID and all the disasters that overreaching Democratic leaders and unelected bureaucrats had caused in their efforts to "fight the virus." The Coalition for TJ used simple concepts the public could wrap its head around to illustrate the problem of employing anything other than merit in school admissions.

The parents' movement fanned out like a prairie fire. "It was so raw and real, the injustice we felt from the school board. It was a window into what everyone else experienced around the country. Ignored moms included those in the Chinese, Indian, Korean, and Bangladeshi communities, which culturally have high respect for people in power," Asra says. "We are taught to respect people in positions of authority. Our parents were so polite, kind, and tried to honor school board members and political leaders, but they were treated like dirt. I felt a personal responsibility to represent families, as a first-generation immigrant, journalist, and teacher. These folks were given three minutes to ask questions and voice concerns and basically told to shut up." The Left's ultimate gaslighting technique, eaten up by an unwitting public, was to claim that CRT, DEI (diversity, equity, inclusion), and SEL (social-emotional learning) were about social justice and being "anti-racist." Asra and the parents that formed the Coalition for TJ *were* minorities and had been treated like shit. They, nonwhites, had been likened to white supremacists. Atif Qarni even had banned Asra from speaking at a town hall, because Asra is a Muslim feminist. Qarni is "a bully and a jerk," says Asra.

The Coalition for TJ opposed an initial lottery system for admission to the school. Asra was scolded for saying she's an "Asian tiger mom." She was told that the term degrades Asian moms, painting them as aggressive. Asra disagreed and leaned in. She was told by the moderator of a group email that she was using the language of racists. So Asra adjusted. "The only way to combat being marginalized is to brand ourselves with something fierce and affirming," she says. "I started referring to ourselves as mama bears and papa bears and insisted that the school system is treating us like pariahs."

The lesson for Asra was that CRT's ideology uses the same oppression and suppression techniques on moms as does radical Islam; this is the connective tissue. Wokeism sabotages children by making them feel guilty for sins of their forebearers, then blameful toward their family for oppressing and suppressing them. Leftists who force wokeism work in tandem with Islamists to indoctrinate and mainstream criticizing the state of Israel. Asra says she knew something was off in 2019 when she attended a fundraiser for American Muslims for Palestine, a controversial organization that supports Hamas and is anti-Israel. There, she saw a candidate for school board, Abrar Omeish, promise she would push to change the curriculum to be more pro-Palestine.

Omeish became an at-large member of the Fairfax County school board, and sure enough, she fomented hatred and division, stating that Israel practices "apartheid" and "colonization," "desecrates the Holy Land," and "kills Palestinians." Imagine such an openly biased and hateful ideologue speaking this way about any other minority group. Imagine how the Jews and any reasonable parents and students would react to being gaslit into believing that the Left and people like Omeish care about inclusivity and diversity. "Spending twenty years challenging Islamism because it indoctrinates children showed me we had to challenge

CRT, which also strives to claim the hearts and minds of children," says Asra.

Through the fall of 2020, Asra continued to speak virtually before the school board. Then in March 2021, in-person meetings resumed. In what became a viral video, Asra called out a school board member for reducing the concept of Asian appreciation to loving the hibachi, a Japanese portable cooking apparatus. Then, the school board chairwoman shut off her mic. Asra, though nauseated, kept going before the school board at future meetings.

Asra believes we must be unapologetic as parents. She understands that administering a healthy dose of shame is often an effective means of teaching—not to humiliate but to course-correct, as in relying on catechisms such as, "Our family doesn't do that. It's not our value system." But she cautions that we cannot absorb the feeling of shame so intensely that we allow it to silence us. "I overcame shame by having my son," she says. "My mother empowered me to not have shame due to my boyfriend's inability to take responsibility. My mom said, 'You live in West Virginia, not Pakistan. Have pride; don't live in shame.' The Muslim community wanted me to lie. But I refused. I decided I would raise my son without shame, and with honesty and truth."

Up until June 2020, Asra had identified as a Progressive. She's pro-choice for cases of up to three months of pregnancy. She believes in capitalism but maintains that it isn't the answer for everyone—for example, in the case of her brother, who has a long-term disability, lives in Section 8 housing and is on Medicaid. Her parents are on a fixed income and depends on government benefits to assist her brother. But the Left has repelled so many empathetic people like Asra. "I don't agree with men in girls' sports," she says, referencing the current trend of transgender people competing in gender-based sports events; it's one subject on which she disagrees with the Left.

In 2021, Asra got involved with a group of parents in the governor's race in Virginia. These parents were mainly immigrants who had never engaged in politics or hosted debates before. The Left messed up; none of the Democratic candidates participated in debates that the parents organized.

Of note also is that Suparna Dutta, one of the other moms in the Coalition for TJ, became a leader of an effort called Educators for Youngkin Coalition. In a story that speaks to the American dream and American greatness, Suparna went from "just" a mom to being placed by Governor Youngkin on the Virginia Board of Education. (Virginia's Democratic state senators later killed the nomination in a character assignation campaign that labeled Suparna with the "white supremacist" smear.)

But back to Asra. If the school board members thought they could shut up Asra simply by turning off her mic, they had another thing coming. They were about to learn that you don't mess with mama bears protecting their cubs. The Coalition for TJ, represented by Pacific Legal Foundation, filed a lawsuit against the Fairfax County school board in 2021 over the new admission policy. In February 2022, federal judge Claude Hilton ruled in Coalition for TJ's favor.

It remains the most significant victory nationwide thus far for parents pushing back on CRT. Judge Hilton agreed that the new admissions policy was illegal and unconstitutional based on the Fourteenth Amendment, which specified that everyone has equal protection under the law. CRT is the antithesis of the

Fourteenth Amendment, because it creates a new and fluctuating hierarchy of human value. For now, according to the Left's hierarchy, Asians are below blacks, and transgender Asians are above straight Asians—all of which flies in the face of the Fourteenth Amendment. Coalition for TJ won the major federal ruling on the basis that the Fairfax County school board had acted in a way that was patently unconstitutional, anti-Asian, and discriminatory.

The victory was short-lived, however.

The school board *couldn't* accept the loss; it would have been a massive impediment to the Left's and globalists' designs for "reimagining" the nation and crushing the constitutional republic. The Fairfax County school board appealed and won a stay on the decision in the Fourth Circuit Court of Appeals, two to one. The school could continue its new woke admissions practices, essentially concentrating on color quotas while the case was on appeal.

TJ, as mentioned, is a public high school. But the highest court in the land, the U.S. Supreme Court, agreed in October 2022 to hear cases regarding the lawfulness of race-conscious admissions at both Harvard University and the University of North Carolina at Chapel Hill, which, depending on the outcome, will set precedent. The plaintiffs in the Harvard suit claim that the university deliberately discriminated against Asian American applicants because of their race, and that it considers race in ways that violate Title VI of the Civil Rights Act of 1964. According to its own website, Harvard holds the position that those demanding nonracist merit-based admissions are racists. "In November 2014, an organization created by anti-race conscious admissions activist Edward Blum calling itself Students for Fair Admissions

(SFFA) sued Harvard, alleging that the University discriminates against Asian-Americans and seeking to prevent Harvard College and other colleges and universities from using a wide-ranging and thorough admissions process that considers the whole person."[103]

SFFA states in its Harvard petition that "an Asian American in the fourth-lowest decile has virtually no chance of being admitted to Harvard (0.9 percent); but an African American in that decile has a higher chance of admission (12.8 percent) than an Asian American in the *top* decile (12.7 percent)."[104] Critics of Harvard's practices say its treatment of Asians is similar to the ways in which it prevented Jewish enrollment in the past.

Read between the lines of the claims made by academically superior schools, including many of the Ivy League ones, and you'll see why grade schools have shapeshifted away from core curriculum. As per the *Washington Post*, Olufemi Ogundele, UC-Berkeley's dean of admissions, said "he wishes the university could do more to represent the breadth of the nation's most populous state. 'There is no replacement for being able to consider race…It just does not exist. And we're trying to do some dynamic things here. I'm digging into context and all of these details. But there's no alternative there.'"

The article continued, "UC policy calls for each campus to encompass 'the broad diversity of cultural, racial, geographic, and socioeconomic backgrounds characteristic of California.' Here at UC-Berkeley, the admissions team does not entirely ignore racial identity if applicants bring it up in an essay. Whatever they choose to write about, Ogundele said, 'we should hear them out for who they are.' But the law known as Proposition 209 bars admissions officers from putting a thumb on the scale for race or ethnicity."[105]

Translation: without special considerations and admittance based on race, the schools won't make their racial quotas. How does this impact a school's professors and curriculum, ensuring that those lacking the necessary academic skills to get into once-prestigious institutions can graduate? And how does this impact business owners and the workforce when those students leave the school?

Asra believes that both Coalition for TJ's case and the ones before the Supreme Court will establish important precedents disallowing school admissions discrimination.

She also is optimistic that the Left will lose its ideological war, but at a great cost to America and Americans. She believes that the war will destroy a generation, and that there will be profound academic loss. The casualties will at first be the children, but as they grow and graduate—or not—there will be a ripple effect on crime, quality of life, and government assistance—and thus on the economy and employment. Dumbed-down schools are a short-cut to mental health struggles, and it seems like every child has to deal with psychological issues connected to identity based on the trajectory of where schools are headed. "Ultimately CRT and wokeism will be defeated, because the Left's ideas are such losing ideas and they can never succeed. Marxism and Communism fell. So too will wokeism," Asra says.

"I keep fighting because I love kids," she continues. "Even though my son has graduated from K–12 schools, I care so much about our young ones. I wish I could go back to when my son was four years old. It was such a glorious time. I resent and oppose ideologues and armchair activists. They aren't developmental psychologists or childhood experts. They're just criminally messing with our kids." She believes the only way to win this war is in a civil court of law, because civil rights issues are being violated. Parents are winning in the court of public opinion now, and they must win in the court of law. This can only happen if parents engage." On this, Asra holds firm, saying, "We can't let the Left hijack children."

Asra lays out a plan by which parents can take back their children's education. It's straightforward but demanding: parents must be responsible and held accountable. It's a myth that school is just for the children; it's for the parents as well. Parents must be part-time teachers and ensure that their children are at a minimum grade-level proficient in all of the subjects. They must repudiate CRT, DEI, and SEL, designed to waste class time and to allow teachers to shirk their responsibility to teach reading, writing, and arithmetic. That the educational complex has been permitted to erase advanced academics is an indictment of the teachers' undeniable inability to teach; either the teachers or the students are subpar, but either way, the system is broken.

Let's remember that CRT, DEI, and SEL are experience-based rather than data-based, that the Left values lived experience over data. "It's common sense to reject CRT," says Asra. And yet there are approximately 250 consulting groups selling CRT to school districts.[106]

Parents can never take their feet off the pedals, Asra says. Being busy, depressed, or confused no longer is an adequate excuse; those moms fighting tirelessly to save our nation's children are all grappling with their own personal challenges. They can't be expected to carry the load alone.

And it's not just being depressed or busy that's preventing parents from getting involved. The Left and globalists don't fight fair, and another one of their insidious tactics is drug legalization efforts—because stoned parents are not involved parents. Asra notes that the drug crisis in West Virginia has resulted in grandparents raising kids because the parents are too stoned to do it themselves.

Drugs also create zombies who are vulnerable to ideologies, which affects not just the parents but the children themselves. "Kids' cognitive skills decline with drugs, killing them spiritually, keeping them stuck in victimhood instead of triumph and resilience," Asra says. "Then nefarious actors reward kids with more badges of victimhood, which garners applause." This is one more reason the Left is working to legalize drugs.

Asra points to the importance of spiritual strength in combating this drug-pushing effort, along with the Left's other wicked machinations. Spiritual strength can help turn negative experiences, such as drug use, into lessons, and it washes away the need to blame others for inherited trauma. A lack of faith, on the other hand, erodes the self—and self-development is critical to being balanced and successful. "The enemy is anyone messing with a child's sense of self. Exploiting racism, gender, and sexuality to confuse, gaslight, and undermine children is spiritually empty, if not criminal," says Asra.

Asra sees the two sides of the educational war as being very clear, with no middle ground. And she feels free to fight without confusion or shame. "I've gone through years of being shamed by my community. I would get paralyzed, and I would feel unworthy of speaking up," she says. She sees her school board using the same extremist tactic: shaming parents and kids and shutting them up.

Working all those years on *Woke Army* prepared Asra to take the slings and arrows in the current educational battle. The school board "tried to shame me, shut me up, and humiliate me," she says. "My book is about exposing a network that waged a character assassination campaign against truth tellers. It's about fighting back against fake names and fake websites."

Some of those slings and arrows have even come in court. Coalition for TJ had a court date in Richmond, Virginia, in September 2022. "An unfriendly panel of two-to-one Democrat versus Republican made fun of our lawyer, likening the case to the Indian Wars, and made mention of speaking with a forked tongue. You can't make this up," says Asra. The coalition is expected to receive an electronic judgment by summer 2023, and then likely will file to go to the United States Supreme Court.

On October 31, 2022, Asra was at the United States Supreme Court regarding the Harvard case. "The three liberal judges were so ignorant about the Asian community; it made me feel invisible. By midday, the conservative judges spoke, and they were fierce; Chief Justice John Roberts pushed back hard, and Justice Clarence Thomas was scorched earth," notes Asra.

Leaving the courthouse tired but emboldened, she made a video documenting what had happened, with some commentary added. It went viral. A group called Foundational Black Americans, people believing they're the descendants of aboriginal blacks predating America, responsible for building America, then called Asra a racist and an upper-caste Hindu. They said immigrants like her take their jobs, echoing the "replacement theory."

Replacement theory is that white Americans and Europeans are purposefully being replaced through immigration. [107] Initially, those on the Left brushed this concept aside and called it a conspiracy. Then, when this "theory" started gaining traction, the Left pivoted from calling it a conspiracy to calling those discussing it racists.

Despite the shellfire, Asra isn't backing down. Her hope is for a clear mandate against woke politics. While the 2024 presidential election is still a little ways off as I write this, one thing is clear: politicians are taking note of moms like Asra. Governor Youngkin won his election *only* because he made a sharp pivot from having a run-of-the-mill sleepy campaign to fully repudiating CRT.

Despite having been a classic liberal, Asra voted for Trump in 2016 and 2020. The next presidential candidate to earn her vote must take a strong stance against CRT, as well, and must promise to uphold merit-based school admissions and parental rights.

Asra's mission is valiant: she doesn't want even one more child to suffer due to the negligence of school administrators. Critics accusing concerned moms of storming school board meetings fail to understand that moms are fighting not just that single board's policies but for the future of both their children and the nation. These supermoms see that America's beauty, goodness, and inherent equality exists because the country's foundation is tied to a meritocracy.

# CHAPTER 6:
# KIMBERLY FLETCHER

**FOUNDER OF MOMS FOR AMERICA.
FIFTY-SEVEN-YEAR-OLD MARRIED MOTHER
WITH EIGHT CHILDREN, WHOSE AGES
RANGE FROM NINETEEN TO THIRTY-SIX.
LIVES IN BRANSON, MISSOURI. "I'M A
REGISTERED REPUBLICAN BUT DON'T
BELONG TO ANY PARTY," SHE SAYS.**

The homeschooling trend is picking up across the nation, thanks to the COVID pandemic's exposing the educational complex's failures. More parents than ever are now contemplating joining what prior to 2020 was a very small club. Kimberly Fletcher is a mom of eight who isn't a psychic, just an extremely tuned-in individual. She saw before most others the true dangers of the federal government's chokehold on public schools and started homeschooling her children long before it became a national conversation.

Homeschooling eight children is an undertaking that few would imagine is possible, let alone believe that a homeschooling parent would have time to do anything else. However, Kimberly isn't content with saving only her own kids; she's hell-bent on saving America's kids, and that starts with helping their moms. In 2004, she launched Moms for America, "a national movement of mothers reclaiming our country for truth, family, freedom, and the Constitution," according to the group's website. With more than half a million members, Moms for America connects, empowers, and teaches mothers what they can do to protect their children from the part of the Left's attempted Marxist makeover of America that targets children.

There are approximately fifty-one million people under the age of eighteen through the public schools.[108] There are approximately another five million people under the age of eighteen in private schools, institutions that are not primarily supported by public funds and that are grouped into the following categories by school orientation: Catholic, other religious, and nonsectarian (not religiously affiliated).[109]

Wanting to protect America and America's families comes naturally to Kimberly. "I was always patriotic and raised in a patriotic family," she says. When she was growing up, being patriotic wasn't considered alt-right; it was simply being American. And while Kimberly says that her patriotism happened by default and was ingrained in her from birth, she didn't understand its importance until 9/11. "My husband was stationed at the Pentagon as an IT officer with top secret security clearance, and by a miracle, on that infamous day he came home," she says. This was a turning point for Kimberly, who says, "I committed to being a patriot, not just patriotic."

The terrorist attacks on 9/11 came from outside America, perpetrated by those who hate what America represents: freedom. And Kimberly saw how it united Americans across race, religion, and gender, and reconnected them to patriotism, church, and family. The effects, unfortunately, were temporary. When President George Bush said on the one-year anniversary of 9/11 that a year of mourning was over, "division started again, and I was brokenhearted," Kimberly says.

Globalist powers and backward oppressive regimes have now cleverly figured out a better way to ensure America's demise than sending hijackers: using Americans to destroy themselves from within. BLM, antifa, and "climate warriors" sprouted from Marxist ideologies. Marxism is a social, political, and economic philosophy calling for a revolution to overturn capitalism in favor of Communism. The Left and globalists foment BLM, antifa, and "climate warriors," who commit widespread terror involving financial devastation, murder, assault, looting, and vandalism, because it sows chaos within America. Yet these groups and their leaders aren't thwarted; they're rewarded. Conversely, concerned moms *have* achieved notoriety; the Biden administration has struck fear in concerned parents' hearts who dare to ask questions at school board meetings or write inquiring emails to the principals of their children's school ever since they were likened to "domestic terrorists."[110] These moms are part of Kimberly's Moms for America.

Kimberly believes that the rot started in the early 1900s, saying that era "ushered in compulsory education, the federal reserve, and the Sixteenth and Seventeenth Amendments. Four powerful seeds planted generations ago have led us to our current decline and were the effective beginning of the end." She says these seeds are diametrically opposed to America's founding principles.

With compulsory education, children must go to school, public, private, or homeschool. The lines are becoming increasingly blurred as to what extent Big Government has injected itself into education overall, turning it into Big Education.

Public schools are government-run schools regulated by federal, state and local law—the ties to government are clear.[111]

Here's where things get tricky. Private schools, generally assumed to be islands unto themselves, are quickly losing independence. Historically, they weren't funded by government and the teachers weren't part of a union. This began to change during COVID, minus explanations and parental input. Government wanted more power over the kids.

There's an invisible hand controlling private school boards of trustees. It's called NAIS (National Association of Independent Schools) and a long list of other third-party accreditors. As per NYSAIS, "This revision to the NYSAIS Manual for Accreditation includes several new and revised criteria for accreditation in the areas of Diversity, Equity, and Inclusion (DEI) following an extensive review of the instruments used by schools to undertake the comprehensive self-study by the NYSAIS Commission on Accreditation and Board of Trustees with support from members of the NYSAIS Diversity Committee."

In case private school parents are wondering why things changed without any parental referendum, be advised—this is the new mission for private school dictated by NYSAIS. "Include the mission of the school and any other statements of purpose, core values, philosophy, and diversity used to support the mission statement." Moreover, under the heading labeled "Baseline Criteria," NYSAIS wrote, "These criteria are rated by both the school and the visiting committee with a 'yes' or a 'no.' The school provides a program of instruction that is substantially equivalent to that which is afforded in the local public schools. Courses are offered in mandated subjects. The school day and year are substantially equivalent to those in public schools. If the school has a secondary program, the school is registered by the New York State Education Department."[112]

The NAIS agenda is to break down the wall between public and private schools. This was cemented with the Substantially Equivalent Instruction for Nonpublic School Students, which was adopted at the September 2022 board of regents meeting.[113] In case private school parents wondered why during COVID, Floyd, and BLM, private schools weren't acting independent but like public schools in many ways, attention; your child(ren)'s private school has likely opted into accreditation. If they have, independent schools are not private in the sense of the definition; they don't have autonomy over how they govern their individual schools because they've abdicated this right by belonging to accreditors, which is a stamp of approval from the NYSAIS, an affiliate of NAIS. To be clear, having an accreditor is optional. Meaning, if these private schools want to remain a self-governing body (accountable to parents and the board of trustees) and eschew all the woke craziness, they can by not opting into an accreditor.[114]

Alas, it seems like that ship has sailed. Private schools are unionizing. Once they do, the teachers unions' members are taking over the libraries.

A recent article from *Times Union* alerts parents to the gameplan. "The powerful statewide teachers union is seeking to organize libraries and private schools to bring dozens of new groups into its 700,000-member organization."[115] The federal government's proxy, the teachers unions, are coming for private schools *and* the libraries.

Here is a short example of just some of the books found in public school libraries: *A Kids Book About Being Transgender*; *Becoming Nicole: The Transformation of an American Family*; *Gender Identity for Kids: A Book About Finding Yourself, Understanding Others, and Respecting Everybody!*; and Ibram Kendi's *Antiracist Baby*, to name a few.

Private school parents, the days of your children having traditionally trained educators are numbered. The days that private school children will read and discuss classic literature are coming to an end.

Here's the billion-dollar question: why did private schools opt into accreditation? Their track record of success is settled science by every metric. They have a waiting list out the door *because* they employ traditionally trained teachers insistent on rigorous academics, classroom decorum, and accountability, like attendance and completion of homework. The class syllabus focuses on reading, writing, and arithmetic. Tests are routine, helping educators, parents, and students track progress and isolate weak spots. There *were* accelerated, honor, and advanced placement classes. Finally, Private schools *were* feeders to ivy league institutions before "equity" kicked merit to the curb.

Here's the answer. "The goal of accreditation is to ensure that institutions of higher education meet acceptable levels of quality. Accreditation in the United States involves non-governmental entities (accrediting organizations) as well as federal and state government agencies."[116] This means private grade-schools were likely bulldozed by "institutions of higher education," heavily financed by the government, to fall in line so that applicants are *already* primed for the onslaught of Marxism in these esteemed universities. It's easier for professors to work with already primed students than those who are critical thinkers, in command of American and world history and the perils of Communism, Socialism, and Marxism.

Lastly, there's homeschooling. Depending on the state, laws vary. But by way of example, in New York state, parents who wish to homeschool their children must provide written notice of intent to the school district superintendent. The school district then responds to the family and provides a copy of the home instruction regulations as well as an individualized home instruction plan (IHIP) form to complete.[117]

Whether public, private, or homeschool, Big Government is poised to take over education and as a result, there isn't much choice. School choice only works if there are genuine differences and the differences among the three options are becoming harder to parse, although there is certainly more freedom in homeschooling.

Essentially, since the early 1900s, American children have been raised by the government. Kimberly says it's a methodical plan that captures the youth and one that all dictators understand and employ, from Hitler to Mao to Stalin. "We're living in their Germany, China, and Russia," says Kimberly. As Mao said, "The young people are the most active and vital force in society," which is why the Left is looking to control them in its effort to create a new society that disables American dominance and has the country joining a globalist coalition.[118] This is being done via any means necessary: "social justice," "climate change," and abortion. They're all items in the tool kit used to manipulate and create a divide.

The Sixteenth Amendment goes against the Constitution and uses taxpayers' money to fight parents and subject them to the government. The Seventeenth Amendment has taken away the states' individual authority to protect themselves from the federal government. Finally, the federal reserve solidifies the entire package. "It is a legacy of destruction," Kimberly says. The contradiction is that parents believe they're living freely, but the educational complex is at total odds with this notion.

Kimberly links America's Left to Marxism; she sees overlap in their views on family and G-d. Indoctrination is possible only with a shaky family base. Mao shut down schools so that all the focus could be on the revolution. Books were burned, statues were toppled, everything traditional was destroyed. Sound familiar? The kids became monsters in the Red Guard. "People think they were men—they were elementary school kids," says Kimberly. Hitler created Adolph Hitler Schools. Sunday was "funday," in Hitler's Germany, intentionally to disconnect children from faith and going to church with their parents. Stalin, Hitler, and Mao used kids to create Communist revolutions by turning on their families.

Why is Marxist and Communist history in other parts of the world important? Because the same experiment has failed many times, resulting in the deaths of hundreds of millions, and now is being foisted upon Americans by Marxism-embracing Democrats. The Democratic Party harbors those who hate America and reject history. "We're supposed to learn from history so we don't repeat mistakes," says Kimberly. The problem is, many of those doing the bidding in America for globalists don't know history, and the educational complex is intentionally teaching revisionism. This is why Moms for America's mission is "to empower moms to raise patriots and promote liberty for the healing of America." They are working to keep the principles our country was founded on in 1776 from regressing further into the memory hole.

The educational aspect has been the driving force behind Moms for America, because of what Kimberly learned while she was raising her own children. She experienced major growth between 2001 and 2003. While she was pregnant with her eighth child, her fourth son developed a physical condition that precluded him from going into school. She researched homeschooling and, after trying it out for just three days, was sold on the concept. In a quest to teach her son, Kimberly became a student. Together they learned about battles and parts of history that she'd never been exposed to, and she felt robbed. They studied the American government and how it works in depth, along with the Constitution, the Declaration of Independence, and the Founding Fathers. They delved into different movements that helped shape the country—why they worked, why they failed, and how they were derived. "I read everything I could get my hands on about America, history, and heritage," says Kimberly.

In 2003, Kimberly learned about her school district in Spotsylvania, Virginia, a bedroom community one hour away from Washington, D.C. "My friend kept telling me about horrible things that were happening in school. I would complain about them, and my friend retorted, 'Run for the school board or stop complaining.'" In 2003, Kimberly ran for school board.

The *Washington Post* interviewed Kimberly and it was an eye-opener. It was her first experience with biased media; the story was focused on a homeschool mom running for school board, as if paying taxes didn't earn her a say in what was happening in her district. "A school district determines the economy of the entire community," Kimberly says. "Thirty-five to forty percent of property taxes goes toward public education nationwide."[119] Translation: all people who pay property tax have a right to discuss and give input regarding the educational system, whether they have kids in it or not. It's why, in theory, school board meetings are meant to be open community forums. During the time of COVID, this changed. School board meetings switched to being on Zoom, parents were muted, and those who spoke out against shutdowns were silenced and ridiculed. The meetings became even more contentious when the educational complex brought in CRT. Those on the school board perceived the parents' and community's upset, and took actions to profoundly limit the community's presence and participation.

Kimberly was pregnant during her run for the school board, and was experiencing pregnancy-related sickness. Nonetheless, she worked through it, getting signatures to get her name on the school board ballot, studying up on the role, and asking the superintendent for a budget. "I was blown away by the amount of waste," she says. "They claim to never have enough money, yet the misappropriation of funds is unbelievable. The refrain is, if you don't give more money to the schools, you don't care about kids. When will it be enough? It's never enough."

In a bizarre turn of events, Kimberly lost the election but won on getting all four of the line items pertaining to wasteful spending that she had campaigned on reversed. And a seed germinated: she wanted to become more actively involved in her community. Kimberly learned while running for school board that she's a natural at grassroots engagement: economically savvy, good at messaging, and strategically gifted.

As Kimberly's husband is an officer in the Air Force, they move every three years. In May 2004, they set up their home in Dayton, Ohio. One of Kimberly's first stops was the Republican county office. She offered to help, citing her acumen in grassroots organizing. From this moment on, the Fletchers became the poster family in Dayton for the upcoming Bush election. As they became media magnets, Kimberly recognized the need for media training. She threw herself into this endeavor with the same full-throttle commitment she's had with homeschooling and running for the school board. She learned the importance of repetition. "My kids said, 'We care about American values and principles' every time they engaged with the community and media," she says.

Kimberly incorporated civic engagement into her children's homeschooling lessons. Moreover, she also taught them about entrepreneurship. They brought handmade items to rallies, and those items garnered attention. The Fletchers began to mass produce and sell them.

Kimberly was building a network, crafting her skills in media and communication, and she focused on issues that resonated with her community. She became familiar with conservative political commentator Sean Hannity, bought his book, and started listening to his radio show; she liked that he opened his show up to callers, finding the inclusivity appealing. Every time Kimberly called in to Hannity's show, she was featured.

"I didn't know that I was supposed to be afraid," she says. "I just knew something was wrong in the country that needed repairing. I didn't know G-d was preparing me to start a national organization. Everything led me there—the homeschooling, running for school board, rally involvement, media training. I was learning, constantly learning."

The day before the November 2004 election, Hannity joined a rally in Dayton to motivate the crowd and do a "get out the vote" effort. He spotted Kimberly and pulled her onstage. Kimberly's influence continued to grow. So did her skills at isolating weak spots in Republican messaging and figuring out how to engage with moms in ways that both political parties were neglecting.

A canvassing volunteer asked Kimberly for help in Trotwood, a town that's 85 percent black and had historically voted overwhelmingly for Democrats; Republicans had written off the town as a lost cause. Not Kimberly. "I went with my seven- and three-year-olds," she says, "and in the pouring rain made sure all the precincts were covered and polling stations monitored. After some time, my youngest asked, 'Are we giving up?' and I replied, 'No, baby. Pull out Christian voter guides. We'll hand that out, not the Bush stuff.'"

Everything changed based on Kimberly's pivot. "I realized the power of information and that moms put social issues on the top of their priority list," she says. "Also, I learned moms don't vote because they're scared to vote wrong. They need information. They're so busy with their households, they don't necessarily have time to read about current events and understand how policy shapes their day-to-day lives."

The lessons Kimberly learned in Trotwood were the impetus behind Moms for America. "We needed an organization that supported moms, conservative women of faith, G-d, family, and freedom lovers," she says. No party is going to save the kids, she felt; it's the mothers coming to the rescue. But first, they must unite.

The intention behind Moms for America is reviving sisterhood, says Kimberly. Regrettably, many elected officials seem to care about moms only during an election. Kimberly wished to create an organization that always cared for mothers.

In the middle of October 2004, Kimberly told her mom about her plan (despite having fears of inadequacy around being "just" a mom) to start a national organization. Her mother suggested calling it Homemakers for America, which Kimberly thought no one would take seriously. Her mom replied, "Maybe that's the problem." Building a home is the foundation for everything, posits Kimberly.

"My generation was the bridge connecting those that knew and those that no longer do" regarding time-honored traditions as well as gender roles, Kimberly says. She references the first march that Moms for America held, in 2017, a counter to the worldwide Women's March, which was filled with pink vagina-hat screamers. Kimberly says she received calls from many moms who had attended the other event and felt disgusted and misled. To protest Trump's inauguration, as a symbol of solidarity, people wearing pink knitted beanies with cat ears, called "pussy hats," participated in the Women's March on Washington, on President Donald Trump's first full day in office.[120] Kimberly maintains that the premise of the Women's March is a rejection of women and the beauty of what only women's bodies are genetically wired to do: procreate, gestate, and lactate.

When Kimberly began her organization in 2004, she had twenty-six moms onboard. But it didn't take long for that number to skyrocket. In May 2005, Kimberly called in to Sean Hannity's show and announced live that she had a national organization, called Homemakers for America. Hannity told his audience that Kimberly had been pivotal in the 2004 presidential election. Within hours, she had amassed five thousand members from all fifty states and was flooded with donations totaling $15,000. This is the power of having a vision, setting goals, networking, never giving up, strategizing, and successfully getting out messaging.

Kimberly buckled down; her organization continued to grow, and she continued to help educate the moms. They got involved in the 2008 presidential election. When Obama won, Kimberly's worst fears about the globalist cabal were realized. Being a woman of faith, she viewed it as a necessary eye-opener. For years, Kimberly had been warning others about the dangers of electing those with anti-America sentiments and the destruction it would cause to Americans.

The Obama years ushered in policies and misguided beliefs championed by America's detractors that are still causing harm today. From Obamacare to "social justice" to climate change to the $1 trillion omnibus bill, the policies were tied to Communism and thus tied to failure.

Rather than give up, Kimberly rose up. She understood that to create change, the focus needs to be localized. Also, it must be centered around education. Between 2008 and 2012, Kimberly leaned into what she loved: America and empowering moms. She became one of the original members of the Dayton Tea Party, along with founder Rob Scott. And in 2008, eight thousand grassroots activists stood shoulder to shoulder, and the Dayton Tea Party exploded. Kimberly also helped organize Ohio liberty group networks. "I realized, being *just* angry isn't effective," she says. "We need to focus on education and local issues if we want to win."

Kimberly learned other lessons as well through her involvement with the Tea Party. She learned, for example, that forty years ago, certain states were flaming red, and Democrats were wondering how to change that; they were strategically targeting states with a high number of electoral votes. They analyzed how many neighborhoods and then counties were necessary to win each state, and came up with a plan.

In 2010, the Democrats' plan was to take Texas by identifying "problem" areas and going after minorities. They set up nonprofits, resources, and programs aimed at recruiting those looking for a path to citizenship. "The Democrats do this for three years and become a trusted source while spreading propaganda," Kimberly says. "Blacks are led to believe Republicans are white supremacists, Asians are led to believe Republicans want to hold them back, and Hispanics are told they'll be deported by Republicans. Then, door-knockers are recruited from the minority groups, paid to stand at polls, instructed to vote for selected candidates, harvest voters, and mules are hired to ballot-dump. Our tax dollars pay for it." Kimberly goes on to say that ACORN (The Association of Community Organizations for Reform Now), Planned Parenthood, and the teachers' unions grift taxpayers' money, because there is no accountability.

Kimberly is so knowledgeable that blindly supporting the Republicans is out of the question. She acknowledges that both parties work together and have morphed into a uni-party and that this is a bitter disappointment to her. "You must vote for people and principles and ignore the party," she says.

Homemakers for America changed its name to Moms for America in 2018, a big year for Kimberly. As steadily as her national organization was growing, overcoming the destroyed brand of "homemaker" was challenging. Feminists went to work on the term, belittling the role, making it appear old-fashioned and undesirable. There's nothing insignificant about building a strong foundation that serves as the cradle for the future, says Kimberly. But many on the Left discredit moms, putting forward the lie that the most important things are outside the home, even though we have seen time and time again criminals, drug addicts, homeless people, sex offenders, and people with similar profiles who are products of unstable homes. Kimberly points out the Left has even gone so far as to get rid of the time-honored Mother's Day tradition, erasing a day of celebration and recognition for the foundation of our society.[121] Ultimately, the bigger picture prevailed; Kimberly changed the name Homemakers for America to Moms for America to remove the term that might prevent mothers from joining.

By 2018, Moms for America had one hundred fifty thousand members and had launched Mom Vote. The group tested messaging in five congressional districts, two in North Carolina and three in Minnesota. All five conservative candidates won. Wherever Kimberly and Moms for America did outreach and messaging, there was an increase in women voter turnout. "The vast majority of conservative moms don't vote," says Kimberly. "We want moms to understand why their vote is so important. We take into account their reasons to not vote, then message and help them understand if they abstain, their values aren't represented and their voices aren't heard."

Moms for America used the same approach in 2020 for the presidential election. "Moms came out en masse," Kimberly says. "The message was, 'We are asking you to vote not for Trump but for freedom.'" They voted for freedom. They didn't like mask mandates and the COVID shutdowns. The moms liked even less that they were told to shut up and deemed unworthy of explanations. Moms for America offered them community, education, inspiration, and a forum for exchanging ideas.

Then, it happened. Moms for America became too threatening, too much of a game changer, and too much of a means to topple the Left's control over moms. "Right after the 2020 election, during the Stop the Steal movement, Twitter deplatformed Moms for America," Kimberly says. It was a referendum; Kimberly's beliefs were contagious and had to be silenced. Moms for America was part of the initial wave of people convinced that the presidential election had been stolen, and who weren't going to stay silent about it. Stop the Steal started the day after the election, and the day after that, Moms for America mobilized. Two days later, all fifty states had Moms for America representatives in myriad rallies.

Moms were reaching out to Kimberly, confused and mad, wanting to know why their votes didn't matter as they came out in droves. They didn't believe the media or the election results. They were being asked again to not see what they saw, to doubt their eyes. It was the masks, "vaccines," BLM, and CRT all over again; they were told they were crazy and that what was so undeniable was impossible. They had seen the size and energy of the Make America Great Again movement. They had seen the fumbling basement campaign of Biden. They had seen the election called before high percentages of battleground states had been called and after Trump had won states in which Biden previously had been declared the winner. Then there were the drop boxes, viral videos of suitcases being pulled out stuffed with just enough ballots to swing the outcome, poll watchers and workers caught on film interfering, and scoffs at the mainstream media's narrative that the 2020 election was the most secure one in history. For questioning the "vaccine," their children were either encouraged or mandated to take, moms were labeled "vaccine deniers." For questioning CRT being forced on their kids, they were labeled "racist conspiracy theorists." Now, for questioning the 2020 election inconsistencies, they were called "election deniers." "Our moms got involved in election integrity hearings in Nevada, Wisconsin, Arizona, and Missouri for ballot recounts," says Kimberly.

Kimberly has been entrenched in politics for decades. As someone who has run for school board, commandeered grassroots campaigns whose support has propelled candidates across the finish line, and started a national organization, she has seen all the unscrupulous tricks the Democrats have used. However, she's a woman of faith. Kimberly knows the power of the moms and that they can move mountains. "I've seen the belly of the beast," she says. "I was at the Kavanaugh hearings, and until moms showed up, he didn't have the votes. When we became a countervoice, he made it onto the Supreme Court."

Kimberly brings up the mainstream media's depiction of BLM riots and the January 6 event at the Capitol. The media stood in front of burning buildings, the result of BLM rioters, and called it a "peaceful protest" but called January 6 an "insurrection."[122] "Everyone was singing and praying. But the media decided on a narrative before the descent to the Capitol, which was already a hot mess before President Trump spoke to his supporters," Kimberly says. She went to the Capitol that day and notes that she saw no police. "I was there," she says. "Mayor Bowser released an emergency text to the district announcing a curfew because of an attack on the Capitol before anyone broke in and Ashli Babbitt was shot. There was no violence. It was heehaw, a bunch of people who had never been to the U.S. Capitol who thought you could walk around and it would be okay."

Kimberly brings up the mainstream media's interference with the 2020 election, the fear porn regarding COVID and new viruses meant to scare people to death. She recognizes the power of the media and how they push a narrative to hypnotize the masses, making people doubt their common sense and intuition and reject personal freedoms.

Because Kimberly has witnessed abundant foul play, she's unsure if there will even be a 2024 presidential election. She believes that the powerful forces wanting America to be engulfed in chaos will stop at nothing to allow America to have a free and fair election. "When parents look around, take stock of the current situation, and can't believe what's happening in their kids' schools or on TV, they need to understand, we're at war. It's G-d versus the devil. And the devil is Communism," she says. Kimberly is certain that G-d will win but believes there will be casualties. She insists that as a mom, she will do everything to make sure kids are not casualties. "I am a lioness," she says. "A Sherman tank is how I identify if you mess with my kids."

Kimberly believes we can turn this around and snuff out Marxism in America in one generation. The proof is that Marxists destroyed America in one generation, she says, adding that the way to heal is through the mothers' taking control of their respective homes. But she believes that the school system in its current state is beyond hope.

"I don't believe the school system can be saved," she says. "Kids are in school Monday through Friday, for approximately seven hours a day, taught to hate their parents, country, and themselves." She still believes that turning over the school boards is vital, saying that the school boards determine the economy of the entire community, which affects housing prices. However, she feels that school choice is necessary to create checks and balances by way of competition. Moms need to have choices, because with choices comes responsibility.

Kimberly outlines three steps she believes will improve education. The first is dissolving the Department of Education, as having the federal government oversee schools has no upside for parents. The second is making teachers aware that they needn't belong to a union. The third is defunding associations and affiliates in every state; the training they receive is indoctrination. As soon as affiliates infiltrate the school board, the association comes to "help," she says. She highlights their agenda of constantly demanding more money to fund training, dues for school board members, and the fight against parental rights. "We don't need cheerleaders for the broken system," Kimberly says.

Kimberly is buoyed by the response by certain businesses to the failed educational complex and CRT ideology. And why is it that businesses are getting involved? Because everything comes down to money. "Companies are starting their own colleges due to the declining caliber of graduates churned out into the workforce after leaving government schools and woke higher education institutions," Kimberly says. "Entitled, lazy, unprepared, injustice collectors pose substantial threats to the work environment, from gratuitous lawsuits to unnecessary distractions." In addition, she believes that workplace productivity will decline, courtesy of graduates who have received a degraded education, puffed-up grades, and false encouragement for lackluster performance, and that these graduates will dress like unprofessional slobs. *Business Insider* discusses a study that Yale University conducted in 2014, focusing on 128 men between the ages of eighteen and thirty-two who participated in mock negotiations of buying and selling.[123] "Those dressed poorly (in sweatpants and plastic sandals) averaged a theoretical profit of $680,000, while the group dressed in suits amassed an average profit of $2.1 million. The group dressed neutrally averaged a $1.58 million profit." By extension, companies *can't* tolerate Marxism dressed up as CRT or wokeism, because it's financially unsustainable. Technical schools are also making gains as they draw more interest amid businesses struggling to hire skilled workers, and enrollment is picking up. A report by the National Student Clearinghouse Research Center shows that in the spring of 2022, nationwide enrollment at two-year institutions in construction trades increased by 19.3 percent because practical skills are in demand.[124]

Kimberly sees technical schools as part of the path forward in that because they're condensed into two years and intensely focused on practical skills, aren't as vulnerable to woke ideology, and because they generally cost less than four years of learning at university, don't leave students in financial debt.

Again, Kimberly is quick to point out that regardless of what corrections are made to the school system, there's no substitute for the moms. They're the linchpin that will determine whether Americans live free or under the face diaper of Marxism.

Moms for America continues to grow. It has partnered with the National School Board Leadership Council to put students first and be accountable to the community as well as the school boards within the community. The goal is to reach as many moms as possible and empower them with tools and resources to take back their children's education from the schools and bring it to the kitchen table. The mission remains the same: to nurture a new generation of patriots.

Moms for America's goal is to have five thousand cottage meetings, intimate educational gatherings, in the next three years and one thousand field moms engaging in their respective counties with the sheriff and people critical to the county. The organization plans to train school board ambassadors in America's sixteen thousand eight hundred school districts on how to foster relationships within the community. It aims to relate how the school boards policies will impact the residents. Kimberly maintains that this is how to turn the tide.[125]

Finally, by 2024, in time for the presidential election, Moms for America intends to have two million moms in its organization. The group will have a Moms Report Card scoring every member of Congress, holding them accountable no matter which party they represent. "This is a spiritual war," says Kimberly. She adds, "mothers are the fiercest warriors and are instinctively protective." She believes that G-d created women to nurture, teach, love, and maintain culture. She feels feminists have lowered the bar, and now it needs to be raised. Feminists also have diminished fathers. Kimberly recognizes the importance of dads and points proudly to her husband—her rock and partner—while saying, "I have the greatest respect for single moms. When one suddenly has to be everything, it's [a] Herculean [effort]."

Kimberly is respectful regarding the varying challenges mothers face. It's one way that Moms for America is different from other organizations that inadvertently pull mothers outside the home. "When a mom says she's busy, we say, 'That's great; raise and nurture good solid humans at home,'" she says. Although America leads in charity and is the most welcoming to foreigners and foreign ideas, it seems that too many American moms have neglected being charitable to themselves and to their family.[126] This is what Kimberly and Moms for America are seeking to change. "Am I willing to live in a cave? I don't want to but I will," Kimberly says, referring to escaping tyranny and being able to protect her children. "That's how much I care about freedom," says Kimberly. Based on the November 2022 elections, Kimberly isn't alone in her views. According to exit polls, married women favored the GOP over the Democrats by a margin of 14 percent.[127]

# CHAPTER 7:
# SARA GONZALES

**HOST OF *THE NEWS & WHY IT MATTERS* ON STREAMING SERVICE BLAZE TV. LIVES IN TEXAS AND LAUNCHED THAT STATE'S CHAPTER OF DEFEND OUR KIDS, WHICH AIMS TO GET DRAG SHOWS FOR KIDS SHUT DOWN. MARRIED WITH TWO BOYS, AGES TEN AND TWO; AGE WITHHELD. REGISTERED INDEPENDENT BUT VOTES REPUBLICAN.**

Sara Gonzales, mother of two, is one of the many moms who have felt acutely betrayed by the media. Unlike many of those other moms, however, she's *in* the media. Sara is the host of *The News & Why It Matters* on Blaze TV, a conservative streaming service founded in 2018. Contrary to those working at Leftist mainstream media outlets and even some centrist ones whose audience has dwindled, resulting in mass firings and lineup shake-ups, Sara can boast of a growing audience for the show she hosts. She isn't afraid to tackle controversial issues that initially are ignored and suppressed by the other networks and taking heads, like the FDA-unapproved "vaccine" and gender dysmorphia.

Sara, along with a lot of the collective public, has noticed that many media outlets, journalists, investigative reporters, and news corporations are full of it. Desperate for honest reporting on numerous events gripping the nation—COVID, BLM, CRT, crime, the economy, the current and former presidents, Russia's war in Ukraine, the southern U.S. border, education—people have long been loyally turning to household media names. However, at some point people started to realize that the "facts" weren't adding up. Those on the ground saw a reality that was egregiously misrepresented or ignored by those meant to present the facts. Information was weighted, wrong, and dripped out in intervals as if to measure the public's tolerance for it. Lie after lie. Public outrage was severe; many people stopped tuning in to their usual sources and started looking to alternate ones.

Sara once owned an insurance brokerage firm, a far cry from being part of a media company. But her beginnings laid the groundwork for her current profession. She was born in Houston, Texas, and her family moved to Dallas when she was five years of age. "I'm an only child, and my mother taught me core values, which is the moral system I have now," she says. Sara's biological father was an alcoholic and drug addict whom her mother left when Sara was a young child. Her stepfather adopted Sara as an adult, significant to her because it underscores the importance of the family unit. Family values have shaped Sara, and she mentions that her family's nightly dinners around the table, minus distractions like TV and the phone, set the tone when she was growing up. "I was raised in a spiritual, religious household," she says. And her parents expected her to work hard.

Sara holds a degree in criminology and minored in forensic psychology, two fields that have helped her understand what is transpiring in America: the subversion of the rule of law, the flouting of the unconstitutional mandates, and the societal impact of sexualizing children. The psychosis behind these things is worthy of study by a forensic psychologist. Sara also took classes in law and politics at university.

In 2015, Sara started blogging for the website RedState as a hobby. She was prolific and noticeable, and joined Blaze Media almost at its inception. Not long after she joined, her responsibilities shifted from writing to reporting. As Sara built her résumé and excelled, her interests expanded, and she told the Blaze higher-ups that she wanted to share her opinions verbally instead of in print. "I proved I could handle my own show," she says. Now she has over a thousand shows under her belt, her show's ratings keep increasing, and the number of new viewers is steadily growing.

"People are craving a news source that gets the audience and doesn't talk down to it," says Sara. The format of her show is a roundtable of rotating guests, with Sara as host. "We are a family getting together talking about average American issues," she says. It's similar to when she was growing up and her family gathered around the dinner table to discuss the events of the day.

"There's a lot of people in the flyover states and not elitist bubbles living in ivory towers," Sara says. The pejorative term "flyover country" refers to the vast swath of America that's not near the Atlantic or Pacific Coast. While New York, Washington, D.C., and California tend to garner the most attention because they're either the hubs of where policy is decided, require the most amount of federal money, or have the largest population, many of the people keeping America afloat live in between the two coasts.

The leading industries in the United States are petroleum, steel, motor vehicles, aerospace, telecommunications, chemicals, electronics, food processing, consumer goods, lumber, and mining—and many of these industries have headquarters or facilities outside of New York, California, and D.C.[128] Among those keeping America running, many are sick of funding the policies of Democratic politicians as they rack up failure after failure—with results spilling beyond their Democratic enclaves into once thriving and traditionally safe states, benefitting from smaller populations determined to uphold traditional values. The entire nation is paying the price of these failures, suffering tenuous financial offsets by carrying Democrat run states and their collapsing educational system and pro criminal policies. Sara speaks to these people.

"Mainstream media is a dying cause. It can't course-correct. Too much damage has been done by CNN and MSNBC," Sara says. "Those platforms care about a narrative and not the truth." As reported in August 2022, for the first time since 2016, CNN has been hemorrhaging viewers, losing $1 billion in profit for the first time in years.[129] Its new cable news boss, Chris Licht, has scrambled to rework the lineups for both prime-time and morning shows.[130] CNN has lost 90 percent of its viewers in 2022.[131] During the same time frame, MSNBC has also taken a massive hit, losing 46 percent of viewers.[132] Even centrist Fox News has taken a hit but continues to dominate the other networks.[133] As per a

September 27, 2022, *Forbes* article, Fox has an average prime time audience of about 2.2 million viewers.[134] MSNBC is a distant second with about 1.3 million viewers. CNN is trailing, with seven hundred seventeen thousand viewers. For prime time, Fox News is first, with two hundred ninety-four thousand viewers; followed by CNN, with one hundred fifty thousand viewers; and in last place is MSNBC, with one hundred twenty-seven thousand viewers.

This is a referendum; *even* the Democratic base watching CNN and MSNBC seemingly isn't very interested in the spin, bias, suppression, and science fiction. They are likely not looking to be indoctrinated and forced into accepting interpretations that don't line up with reality. According to a Gallup poll, "Just 7 percent of Americans have 'a great deal' of trust and confidence in the media and 27 percent have 'a fair amount.'[135] Meanwhile, 28 percent of U.S. adults say they do not have very much confidence and 38 percent have none at all in newspapers, TV and radio. Notably, this is the first time that the percentage of Americans with no trust at all in the media is higher than the percentage with a great deal or a fair amount combined."

Sara points out that alternative media and social media platforms are growing because of the public's thirst for information and distrust in the formerly trusted platforms. "A positive for society is, people can now get a full video as opposed to a deceptive video sliced and diced and misrepresented by mainstream media," she says. This points to why there has been mistrust: people don't want to be fed a narrative and treated like dolts who can't believe their eyes; they want to draw their own conclusions based on facts and evidence. They can now look up information on their own and add to the conversation by becoming citizen journalists and reporters.

"This is why we at Blaze have been successful. We tell the truth and don't care about political narrative. The truth always comes out," says Sara. "Blaze never once told me I'm not allowed to say something." She is proud that Blaze is at the forefront of sharing the truth regarding COVID and that it remains inquisitive, resisting the urge that so many other outlets have to push a narrative. She goes on to say that even conservative platforms fall prey to feeding a certain narrative. She notes that Blaze's predictions concerning COVID and the "vaccine" have been accurate, and that this has bolstered faith among its viewers. A primary concern of the audience based on feedback is the amount of control that the government has usurped during the COVID pandemic. This leads Sara to ask, "When has the government taken power for a temporary period of time and then given it back?" Then she answers her own question: "Never."

The government told people to stop working and close businesses, and nothing good has come from this—and the reality is, the virus wasn't the cause of the government's actions; the reaction to the virus is to blame, says Sara. If a virus is bad enough, people will decide to stay home for themselves, she says. This wasn't the case with COVID. "We at Blaze were cautious about government overreach," she says.

However, being over the target, as Sara is, has consequences. Questioning the COVID vaccine and the government's push for people to use it resulted in Blaze getting demonetized for a month by YouTube. Sara recalls the event that caused the reaction: "I read the results of a study that concluded the vaccine was changing women's menstrual cycle." She asked her CEO to remind her of what she said as she couldn't remember the specific episode or specific comments that elicited such a reaction. That being said, she was supported by her media company and praised for never backing down. "Blaze understands we need hosts willing to tell the truth."

Sara tackles issues like medical tyranny, which her audience prioritizes and mainstream media largely ignores. This includes tyranny related to the COVID "vaccine." Once the FDA-unapproved experimental COVID "vaccine" became available, the government and various other parties—specifically Democratic leaders, unelected bureaucrats, the World Health Organization, and the Centers for Disease Control—led a robust effort to coerce the public into getting jabbed once or twice and then jabbed again with "boosters." Side effects, efficacy, and natural immunity were barely discussed. Nonetheless, people who refused had to deal with fallout including being fired, disallowed to dine in restaurants, turned away from museums, banned from travel, barred from gyms, and blocked from going to school.

Perhaps the mainstream media shied away from critiquing the COVID "vaccine" because cable networks profit from Big Pharma. As per an *Adweek* article published on April 4, 2018, "CNN…came out on top in terms of top brand ad revenue for one category in particular: pharmaceuticals.[136] According to data from Alphonso, a research firm that tracks TV audience to help brands better target their customers, CNN had 6,487 EQ units of commercial time among its top pharmaceutical brand advertisers, bringing in a spend of $19.9 million; Fox News had 5,279 EQ units among its top 10 brands for a $16.2 million spend; and

MSNBC had 4,737 EQ units for a spend of $8.1 million." There seemed to be a conflict of interest.

Sara highlights her own experience concerning medical tyranny. She gave birth during the pandemic and found it traumatizing. Her youngest son was born in September 2020 amid the hysteria. "Hospitals went crazy," says Sara. Creating and expanding a family are supposed to be celebratory events, but giving birth in a hospital during the pandemic involved separation, projections of death and disease, and anxiety. Sara and her husband rejected the new hospital rules. In her third trimester, "I decided I didn't trust the hospital and didn't want to risk having our baby taken because I tested positive for COVID," she says. "I felt so uncomfortable and scared to go to a hospital to deliver a baby in 2020, despite all of America's medical advancements."

Sara was faced with a choice: delivering in the safety of a hospital equipped with doctors, nurses, staff, cutting-edge machines, and medicine, or a birthing center with a tub. She chose the tub and a midwife instead of risking trigger-happy quarantine-supporting practitioners who might separate her from her newborn. "It was a sad state of affairs that I was driven to this point. Medical tyranny was terrible," says Sara.

And it was a scary experience. At the birthing center, she started hemorrhaging and given a shot of Pitocin, a hormone used to control bleeding.

However, as concerning as medical tyranny has become, Sara says there's no issue more important to her audience then the sexualization of our nation's children. Sara discusses the Biden administration's move to introduce children to sexual concepts. "It's the pronouns taught to kindergartners, schools encouraging students to sexually identify, and drag queen reading hour that have mobilized a critical mass of parents. The sexualization of children is hit on so many angles," says Sara. Some in academia even use the term "minor-attracted person" instead of "pedophile." Esteemed professors give speeches on how we should use this term to avoid stigmatizing grown adults, says Sara.

As per a November 5, 2021, *New York Post* article, a Virginia university assistant professor, Allyn Walker, age thirty-four, a transgender person who uses the pronouns "they/them," said it wasn't immoral for adults to be sexually attracted to kids.[137] "A firestorm erupted over the educator's controversial argument that pedophiles should be referred to as "minor-attracted persons," the article says.

Sara says, "Normalizing pedophilia is insane. Prior to BLM being used by nefarious foreign agents and the globalist Biden administration as a means to usher in CRT, this was settled science. Now, there are very sick people in very powerful positions spending an inordinate amount of time with children with the motivation of fucking them up. To create empathy for the person sexually attracted to a child leads to untoward problems, which is the point. Rape is destigmatized. Babies start having babies, then comes the improbability of going to school, followed by the probability of not being able to secure a decent job, with the final destination being on the government dole. Once there, one is a slave to government. There are substantial benefits for federal and local leaders who believe America is a terrible place to sow discord. Creating chaos is done by weakening the children."

At New York City private school Dalton, parents found out that first graders were being taught sex education by "health and wellness" educator Justine Ang Fonte. Topics included masturbation (touching themselves for pleasure), consent, and gender-related subjects such as gender assigned at birth, gender identity, and gender expression. A horrified mother told the *New York Post*, "We are furious." Another parent told the publication, "We were horrified to learn this was shown to our first-grade 6- and 7-year-old kids without our knowledge or consent. But it's so hard to fight back because you'll get canceled and your child will suffer."[138]

Columbia Grammar & Preparatory School also hosted Fonte's "porn literacy" workshops. As per the *New York Post*, "120 co-ed juniors learned 'three big male vulnerabilities'; statistics on the 'orgasm gap' showing straight women have far fewer orgasms with their partners than gay men or women; and photos of partially nude women, some in bondage, to analyze 'what is porn and what is art. Fonte's presentation included a list of the most-searched pornographic terms of 2019, including 'creampie,' 'anal,' 'gangbang,' 'stepmom' and more."[139]

The fixation from the Left to sexualize kids is pervasive, and not only in New York City. In Texas, organizers of the SXSW EDU conference announced the featured speakers for their March 2023 event: three Drag Queen Story Hour board members who would dress in drag and describe the "Fight for Queer Herstories." In Ohio, during the summer of 2019, Near West Theatre and Veranda L'Ni hosted a drag queen story hour as part of the national effort to organize storytimes with larger-than-life drag queens, according to Near West Theatre. In Minnesota, a Planned Parenthood–sponsored program focusing on the three R's—rights, respect, and responsibility—was taught at a Minnesota school, as reported in online publication MEAWW.[140] The three R's sound great in theory, but turned out to be a perverted nightmare. "Parents accused a school district of asking teenagers to play transgender and homosexual characters. They've also been accused of telling children as young as 4 to refer to a female as 'a person with a vulva' as part of their curriculum. Parents have complained that the curriculum includes sexually explicit content which involves situations where teenagers are 'turned on,' 'hooking up,' and 'doing awesome things' to each other."[141] Parents were outraged and took up the matter with the board.

An April 11, 2022, *Daily Mail* article describes how some fifth-graders in New Jersey are being taught that puberty blockers are a means to "manage" adolescence and that masturbating "a few times a day" is a healthy way to relieve stress.[142] These types of lessons are part of a broader K–12 health-and-sex-education curriculum adopted by the New Jersey Board of Education. Fifth-graders are taught "it's all about the hormones," and fed a propaganda animated video pertaining to puberty and transgender youth.[143]

Accounts of schools' sexualizing children are prolific and widespread. Sara notes that the news moves at such a fast pace that it's difficult for many to fully grasp what's happening and the extent of manufactured destruction. "Americans don't have time to consume all the news," she says. "I digest it for them and give the stories that matter the most." Often, what school boards do affects the nation as a whole, as it trickles down and ignites public outcry, says Sara. On her show, she provides insight and options to consider.

"So many people thank me for what I'm saying. I'm a mouthpiece for the common-sense sector of society. Mainstream media have overlooked these people, their fears and their realities. It's an honor for me to provide a platform whereby everyday people can tune in and connect," says Sara.

Some people aren't so grateful, however. "I get death threats all the time. A man was just prosecuted in North Carolina due to death threats he made against me. I get hate messages all the time and told to kill myself regularly. The profile of the haters is always the same: pronouns in profile and all the virtue-signaling flags," says Sara. This virtue-signaling is a trend she highlights, how certain people on social media are committed to everything and yet committed to nothing, as each emoji or meme cancels out the other. For instance, supporting BLM cancels out supporting overwhelmingly white Orthodox Ukraine. Using the hashtag for "Stop Asian Hate" cancels out simultaneously supporting defunding the police; they cannot coexist, as crime stats prove. For example, Asian hate crime is up nationwide 339 percent since 2022, As per NBC News, "The significant surge is part of an overall 11 percent increase in suspected hate crimes reported to police across a dozen of America's largest cities."[144] Los Angeles took top place for the most hate crimes of any U.S. city this century in 2021—New York comes in just behind.[145] Guess what these cities have in common.

Sara notes the hypocrisy of those regarding themselves as tolerant: they get to hide behind social media, acting as keyboard warriors, but in reality they are the most hateful and intolerant portion of society. "They wish horrible things on my children" says Sara, but, "anytime I get these messages, I'm fueled to continue. I'm making the right people mad, and this is how I know I'm effectuating change."

Sara is creating a stir. In October 2022, she posted a video to her Instagram that went viral. The video was taken at an all-ages drag queen brunch in Plano, Texas. It shows a little girl sitting among women of varying ages at a table. An obese man in makeup and a short gray wig twerks, gyrates, lifts his skirt, and exposes his skintight white underwear with bulge popping out and grabs money being tossed to him, all the while lip-synching lyrics from "Pussy" by Lady.

In a second video Sara posted from the same event that also went viral, a dominatrix enters the scene with a whip and dry humps the floor. Other giant drag queens enter the mix, one of whom goes up to the young girl, who is being propped up by one of the women in her group, and encourages the little girl to give money to him by wagging his fake breasts in her face. Adults laugh and applaud the little girl; the scene is interrupted only when another drag queen distributes sex toys, which he makes clear are "for all genders."

Sara Gonzales' fight against child abuse has gained so much attention that she was on Fox News' *Tucker Carlson Tonight* show on November 1, 2022. In reference to the videos discussed above, Carlson thanks Sara for being one of the few public figures to speak out against the sexual exploitation of minors. She tells him, "Now the Left is gaslighting me into thinking I'm somehow the crazy one for having a problem with this." This pertains to Sara's critics, who blast her for belonging to a party that cares about parental rights. Sara tells Carlson, "Parental rights doesn't apply to child abuse. This is the sexual abuse of children, which the Left and right used to agree upon, but the Left has become so radicalized, it's no longer the case." She goes on to say, "A subsector of adults within these organizations know this is wrong but don't have the courage to speak up. Anyone that doesn't speak out is just as culpable, Republican or Democrat."

Just like globalists and the Left have used BLM to hobble America, they have weaponized the female sex in America. Women are not only shaped differently than men, they have wholly different bodily functions. Women menstruate, carry babies, and lactate. This used to be settled science a child understood. Now, it has been turned into grotesque caricatures; the Left posits that anyone can be a woman as long as lipstick and boobs are smacked on, as if being a woman is transactional—able to be purchased from a drugstore or a plastic surgeon. Those supporting this anti-science lunacy are the same people pretending to care about women's rights, using *Roe v. Wade* for political expediency. They don't care about women or women's rights. Supreme Court justice and Harvard graduate Ketanji Brown Jackson recently said she couldn't even identify a woman, stating in the line that was heard around the globe, "I'm not a biologist."[146] The Left implies that anyone or anything can be a woman.

Parents tuning in to Sara's show are right to be disgusted and panicked. It's little wonder that children's sexuality is the number-one concern of her audience, because as the Left understands, everything hinges on upending it. Family division is caused, and procreation is threatened. Moreover, medical calamities from transitioning do occur (physical and emotional), like depression and anxiety, though, because this is such a new topic, it has been "poorly explored."[147] Since cheerleaders from the Biden administration to the teachers unions are moving at breakneck speed to encourage such a permanent change to civilization, one might think slowing the breaks until the public ascertains just exactly what the extent of the side effects are from transitioning from gender to gender have been fully understood. Alas, transitioning is a cottage industry of new government jobs and task forces as well as Big Pharma concoctions necessitating more drug dependency.

So, how did we get here as a society, and what options do parents have? Sara is blunt: "Parents are so quick to rely on convenience factors: iPads, video games, and TV. Parents don't have to interact. It's obvious that kids are starved for attention." Identifying as any or all of the infinite fringe identity groups is like a sugar high. Coming out as a nonbinary, transgender, or furry [person who identifies as an animal] elicits endless praise. Words like "brave," "courageous," and "authentic" are lavished upon youth made schizophrenic by two years of insanity from those they're supposed to trust (teachers) and those they idolize (morally deranged celebrities).

The numbers speak volumes. As per an article on Spectrum News, UCLA School of Law's Williams Institute, a think tank that conducts research on sexual orientation and gender identity law and public policy, estimates there are 1.6 million transgender people age thirteen and older in the U.S.[148] The percentage of adults identifying as transgender has remained consistent at 0.6 percent since 2017. However, there's been a sharp rise in transgender people ages thirteen to twenty-four in just five years. "The study found that 1.4 percent of 13- to 17-year-olds and 1.3 percent of 18- to 24-year-olds identify as transgender. Five years ago, both of those numbers stood at 0.7 percent."

Here's why Sara is hitting hard on the topic of paramount importance to her viewers.

According to a May 19, 2021, *Forbes* article, "52 percent of all transgender and nonbinary young people in the U.S. seriously contemplated killing themselves." Our nation's youth, driven crazy with lockdowns, mandated drugs, online platforms accused of being "vectors of transmission" and merchants of death, educationally left adrift and bored, and told they're racists or victims, are now disenfranchised, angry, and confused. Some have been convinced to deny science and take hormone blockers or mutilate parts of their bodies, and then they feel even worse.[149]

Sara understands that kids need their parents to be actively involved. "I understand the nature of what being a parent is about and not farming it out to a tablet. G-d put me in charge of raising my children, and I'm not dismissing them to methods of convenience," she says.

She discusses the pitfalls of social media and how it has taken the place of parents in many ways, given that kids take their cues from what they see and hear. Nonetheless, she's optimistic. "We can get back to normalcy, but it might take the COVIDs of the world to open our eyes so that we, as parents, remember our responsibility and power and assist our kids into being productive members of society," she says.

Sara isn't being flip or downplaying the challenges of being a parent; she *is* a parent. She doesn't come from inherited wealth or a problem-free life. She's intimately aware of juggling multiple children, having a career, economizing, and spending time researching in order to be armed with accurate information to make good decisions.

During the COVID pandemic, she had a newborn, a job, and a child not returning to charter school. "I jumped to homeschool for my older son going into third grade," says Sara. The remote learning and mandates were anathema. "Over my dead body," she says. Speaking from personal experience, she notes that not only is homeschooling not expensive, but it's manageable. "The idea that government institutions want parents to believe it's too hard and need to go to government-run schools is so unfortunate," she says ruefully. Her eldest son is now in a private Christian school, but she vetted it thoroughly to make sure it aligned with her values.

Sara believes moms have a real chance to turn the decline of America around, but they have to show up. "There's nothing like messing with a mama bear," she says. "It awakens an instinct, the, 'Hell no, you're not doing this with my kids' battle cry." Moms have to remember: we hold the cards; we have the privilege to go to the ballot box and vote in our values, she insists. Sara references the overturning of a school board in deep-blue San Francisco and says that if it can happen there, it can happen anywhere.

Sara notes optimistically that right now, *because* of all the man-made chaos, it is a capitalist's wet dream. "This is a time ripe for massive creation of new nonwoke content," she says. She praises The Daily Wire for doing a great job and investing in children's content, adding that trailblazers are paving the way, that entrepreneurial spirits will prevail, and that parallel economies that cater to deplatformed conservatives are emerging.

Sara puts her money where her mouth is and consciously avoids brands that erase women and sexualize children. She started a makeup line, American Beauty by Sara, to provide an alternative for women who want to feel and look feminine and do not want to see female products featured on men. For example, makeup company CoverGirl had as their first CoverBoy, James

Charles, representing the company. Charles is the face of "So Lashy" and wants us to "celebrate lash equality." CoverGirl's mascara for all lash types will continue to be added into advertisements and commercials.[150] CoverGirl isn't alone. More and more makeup companies are hiring men to model full faces of makeup.[151] Ironic, as women are the consumers driving the beauty market. "I was tired of the radical part of society taking over the beauty industry. Tired of men in dresses. I'm leaning in and hope others take initiatives to spend their hard-earned money on people and companies that represent their values," Sara says. Her products are sold exclusively on her website, and she intentionally won't expand to partner with companies (like Sephora) that have cut ties with conservative influencers.

Whether it's joining Blaze in its infancy or starting her own makeup line, Sara has proven prescient. She's on the right side of the issues, activated and activating others, during that spark-plug special moment in history we have witnessed before, at the start of every revolution, when only a select few have the courage to lead. Sara will never back down from the fight. Because of moms like her, we're winning the culture war, which has almost exclusively been dominated by the Left.

Sara's show attracts approximately 60 percent men and 40 percent women viewers. She notes that a ton of moms are loyal watchers, and that this demographic is growing. Little wonder that the tagline on Blaze's website is "news and entertainment for people who love America." Just this proclamation alone might feel cutting-edge, given how the Left has fully embraced its hatred of America. It's little wonder why overtly biased media platforms have shrunk; hearing negative people support poisonous concepts is off-putting. Moreover, the Left's "I hate America" movement, which is what "reimagining" America boils down to, has been only about destruction. The growth we have seen with the Left is in the number of unelected bureaucrats acting as its proxies.

The COVID response locked down and bankrupted the masses. BLM vandalized, burned, assaulted, murdered, and looted. CRT ruined education and children. Sara, on the other hand, looks to lift people up, inspire them, and invite them into the fold. "I want to know when I leave this earth, I have done all I can to make our society a better place. It's my highest priority. I'll never stop advocating. I owe it to my children," she says.

# CHAPTER 8:
# MADELINE BRAME

**NEW YORK CHAIRWOMAN OF THE VICTIMS
RIGHTS REFORM COUNCIL AND STATE
DIRECTOR OF BLEXIT, LIVING IN NEW
YORK. SIXTY-YEAR-OLD SINGLE MOM
OF FIVE GROWN CHILDREN; THE THREE
LIVING ARE AGES THIRTY-FOUR, THIRTY,
AND TWENTY. SHE WAS A DEMOCRAT FOR
FORTY YEARS AND HAS JUST REGISTERED
WITH THE CONSERVATIVE PARTY USA.**

Madeline Brame, age sixty, isn't your typical grandmother. She's lost children, struggled with addiction, been in and out of prison, and has a tacit understanding of how the criminal justice system is broken and what needs to be done to optimize it for both the taxpayers and those in need of rehabilitation. She leans into various issues with the candor of a woman who has learned from her mistakes and is determined to bring her lived experiences to the legislature.

Madeline was born in 1962 in Suffolk County, New York. The youngest girl and the sixth of the seven kids her single mother raised, she was, in her own words, "a different type of kid." Her home life was strict; her mom was a reverend, a spiritual leader, and a firm taskmaster corralling a large family for which she was the sole provider. G-d, family, patriotism, and hard work were the guiding principles—all the hallmarks that should lead to stability and a life on the straight and narrow.

When I interviewed Madeline, she was multitasking at a barbecue with friends and family—watching grandkids in the pool, making sure her son had eaten, and so on. She presented the typical image of mother and doting grandmother. But this image belies heartache. She's been forcibly separated from her children and been a fixture in penal and rehabilitation facilities. After reuniting with her kids, she experienced the ultimate betrayal: New York City's criminal "justice" system allowed her son's murderer to go free. These experiences fuel the power and force she brings to her mission: politically activating minorities and getting them to vote against policies and candidates they've traditionally supported who've let them down. While she lacks credentials and a degree in political science, finance, or journalism, she proves there's no direct path to being in politics or being political.

Since 2019, Madeline has been the New York state director of BLEXIT, whose mission is to uplift and empower minorities to realize the American Dream. Since 2020, she has been New York state chairwoman of the Victims Rights Reform Council, which works to give victims of crime a voice. Her efforts were born from her need to correct past failures and provide a safer future for society at large.

At BLEXIT, she manages a team of six carrying out the mission. She is working to help change the narrative in the black community by focusing on five pillars: school choice, criminal justice reform, small business and entrepreneurship, the arts, and ancient African history, bringing the group's message to the community through rallies, information sharing, and education.

There are approximately 19.5 million people in New York state. White people account for nearly 66 percent, black people nearly 16 percent, and Asians a little over 7 percent. According to Pew Research Center survey data spanning more than two decades, the Democratic Party maintains a wide and longstanding advantage among black, Hispanic, and Asian American registered voters. Madeline, a Democrat for forty years until recently, is determined to change this scenario.

At the Victims Rights Reform Council (VRRC), she's hellbent on making sure no mother ever has to go through what she has experienced: losing a son to murder and being hamstrung by authorities—and through the criminal "justice" process alone.

To understand how Madeline became a community influencer, an activist, a sounding board for Republican candidates, and a critic of Democratic public office holders, it's essential to know about her formative years. Hers is a cautionary tale as well as a hopeful one: no matter how far kids stray, they always come back home. Home to their roots and values. As Madeline says time and time again, "It's lived life experiences that have shaped my positions on policy, as well as the standards set forth by my mom."

Madeline's life has not followed an easy path, and she rebelled early on. The town in which she was born, North Bellport, was segregated, halved by railroad tracks—rich white people on one side and blacks on the other, except for Madeline's family; they lived on the south side along with the rich white people. "It felt normal, and we were accepted," she says. They participated in the same events and activities as their white neighbors. "I didn't experience racism as a child, and my mother taught us we're all equal," says Madeline. She had white and black friends; they were invited to her house, and she was invited to theirs.

Madeline describes the other side of the railroad as being a predominantly black community in a lower socioeconomic bracket, a place where bad things would happen. "My uncles and grandparents called [residents there] the 'N' word, a vestige from the forties and fifties that privileged blacks used to seem superior," says Madeline. They looked down on the poorer blacks on welfare or in trouble with the law. Her mom, however, wouldn't accept the use of the N word, going so far as to throw her own father, Madeline's grandfather, out of our house for trying to instill the same values in the younger generation as he had instilled in Madeline's mom and uncles.

Madeline's best friend lived on the other side of the tracks. Curious about the forbidden, Madeline would sneak out to walk her friend home. She describes the dichotomy between her neighborhood and the other side as straightlaced versus exciting. The people in the black community looked and dressed colorfully, listened to different music, and had different lifestyles. Madeline found it intoxicating.

She graduated high school by the skin of her teeth; she wasn't a great student and was frequently bored in school. To her mother's chagrin, when Madeline was seventeen she started dating a star basketball player who got drafted to a team in Puerto Rico.

Her mother begged her to stay in New York, but Madeline's rebellious nature prevailed, and she left home.

The basketball player (whose name Madeline won't divulge) was the Puerto Rican version of Michael Jordan. For eight years, from 1980 to 1988, he and Madeline were based in Puerto Rico and traveled together throughout South America. They never married; it was another example of breaking the so-called rules and bucking tradition.

She gave birth to her first son, Hason, in Puerto Rico in 1983. Her son's father then got traded to a team in Mexico, due to a drug problem that had arisen. Similar to other professional athletes at the time, such as boxers Hector Camacho and George Foreman, he was partying too much, and it spiraled out of control. He and Madeline were just nineteen and caught up in cocaine and alcohol.

When they'd left New York, their high school friends were "just" smoking weed. Returning home for a visit, they saw how the scene had drastically changed. "The same friends were now sitting around the table with glass pipes filled with smoke and freebasing," says Madeline. She had crossed an invisible line, like that of those railroad tracks slicing through diametrically opposed worlds. "In Puerto Rico, we sniffed coke off of spoons and glass tables, and it was high-end," says Madeline. But in New York, the "other side" was doing low-end drugs—a kind of boundary pushing that Madeline found irresistible.

Madeline's home life began to unravel in earnest. Provided that her partner's game wasn't negatively affected, the team management overlooked his cocaine use. He could score fifty-five points in a single basketball game. In fact, he scored thirty-five points off Michael Jordan in the Pan American Games of 1985, and during this period was considered the superior player. But the drugs were destroying his ability to play the game. In 1988, he was traded to a team in Mexico because he failed a drug test. When the Puerto Rico national basketball team was on its way to Seoul, Korea, for the Olympics, he was pulled off the plane.

He and Madeline stayed in Mexico for a year. While there, she became pregnant with her second son, Rasi. Soon after, they moved back to New York.

The year 1988 was a bad one for Madeline. She broke up with her sons' father while she was pregnant, as their drug habit was full-blown and all-consuming. "My partner fed me coke like it was candy, which I consumed while pregnant," Madeline says. And tragically, both her sons were affected by it. After she gave birth to Rasi, her partner's grandparents took both of the boys and placed them with an aunt in Puerto Rico. Madeline felt like she shouldered the blame for the drug use, despite the fact that her sons' father had introduced her to drugs and financially kept the habit alive.

For nine years, Madeline didn't see her boys. She continued to numb herself with drugs and sank further into darkness in New York, becoming completely addicted. To support her habit, she turned to drug dealing and prostitution. Her addiction was costly; she'd spend $500 to $700 a day on average. Some days were so bad that she'd consume $2,000 worth of crack.

"My mother, the reverend, was so distraught, she'd come to crack houses in search of me, send my brothers inside to pull me out," Madeline recalls. She went to such lengths to avoid her family and stay high that she would hide in the closet. She was racked with guilt, shame, and feelings of worthlessness.

Then Madeline's sons' father went back to Puerto Rico later in 1988. Life for him continued; he remarried, had several kids, and continued to use drugs. She was cut off from him and his side of the family, and was not allowed to see her children.

More problems for Madeline were on the horizon. She was arrested and charged with criminal sale of a controlled substance in the first degree. Her sentence was three years to life. She completed three years in jail and was then handed a nineteen-year parole sentence. "Unable to stay clean, I violated parole repeatedly, continuing to relapse," Madeline confesses. Each time, her mother turned her into the authorities, preferring to see her struggling daughter behind bars alive than out on the streets dead.

Madeline got pregnant in 1990 with her daughter Monet during a period of sobriety. Then another son, Ravon, was born in 1991. She knew she was ill equipped at the time to take care of them and gave temporary custody to a family friend. Ravon lived to be only twenty-six; he tragically died in 2020 from an accidental overdose of fentanyl-laced cocaine.

"I wasn't aware there was a court system able to assist in getting back my children," laments Madeline. The court order in effect mandated her to pay child support to Monet and Ravon in addition to the cost of medical care for the older boys. Only one of fifteen hundred women in the state of New York had been saddled with this burden at the time—she was being used as an example. Madeline provided for her kids while still being denied access to them. "It was years of struggle, but I never gave up," she says.

That being said, she continued to relapse regarding drug use, and each time returned to prostitution.

Seven times, Madeline violated parole. It wasn't until the last sentence that she was able to break the cycle. She was offered a spot in a long-term inpatient drug rehab program at Samaritan Village in Ellenville, New York, and now had access to fresh air, good food, proper medical treatment, and parenting and budgeting workshops. Madeline completed her treatment at Samaritan Village in 1994, after three years there.

As Madeline details her metamorphosis, it's easy to spot the role played by the values her mother had instilled in her—faith, hard work, and personal accountability.

Since completing her time in prison, Madeline has seen the vulnerable spots in the criminal justice system that criminals exploit. However, she's quick to mention that in its present form, the system is set up to fail. One needs only to look at recidivism rates to know this is true. Historically, the rate at which those who have been to prison return there within three years of release.[152] Madeline mentions the pointless government platforms and initiatives that drain taxpayers' money and yield a low return on investment. Jail and rehabilitation facilities are revolving doors stocked with repeat offenders.[153]

Madeline is a firm believer in tough love. Her numerous run-ins with the law and dealings with the criminal justice system have made her an expert, not only on what the policy problems are but what cost-effective measures policies should include to combat the waste of taxpayer money and criminality itself. She champions long-term inpatient facilities for drug and alcohol rehab. Drawing upon personal experience, she is adamant that twenty-eight days of inpatient care isn't adequate to help those in need. Long-term treatment methods popular in the 1990s, known as ATI (alternatives to incarceration) yielded better results than short-term stays and were a better use of taxpayer money.[154]

Monet and Ravon were three and four years of age, respectively, when Madeline left Samaritan Village, a drug treatment facility, and reentered public life. Her children had been living with a friend, which became another nightmare. "My friend didn't want to give me back my children," says Madeline. She believes that the friend wanted to keep the girls due to the benefit of Section 8 housing they enabled.

The federal government's Section 8 housing choice voucher (HCV) program enables those in the lowest-income households in the country to rent or purchase decent, safe housing in the private housing market by providing rental and homeownership assistance. The entire time Madeline's friend was keeping the children, Madeline's mother joined her in fighting to reclaim them, but they were both clueless about how to navigate the family court system.

For six straight years, Madeline worked to stay clean and employed; reuniting with her kids was the driving force. "My kids were angry with me until they got older and appreciated my determination," she says.

I interviewed Madeline's second son, Rasi, wondering how he had fared given his mother's prolonged periods of abandonment, drug use, prostitution, and criminality. Did he harbor anger or resentment? Had his heart been broken?

"It took me a while to even understand what happened," says Rasi, who is now a father of two. He discusses coming to grips with feelings of abandonment. He also details how he and Madeline reconnected, which happened organically. Rasi is gracious, saying that the challenges of parenting are constant and amorphous. He says there's a closeness now between him and his mom, built on honesty and understanding, though he acknowledges having resentment when he was younger.

"When I had my first child, I realized I still had a problem with my mother," Rasi says. All the anger bubbled to the surface, and due to his feelings of abandonment, he was hesitant to let Madeline have a relationship with his son. He says acceptance came through Madeline's honesty and visible commitment to family. Now Rasi uses his parents' lives—their mistakes, their successes—to inform not only how he is raising his children but how he is living his own life.

"I have met three strong women in my life: my grandmother, my mom, and my kids' mother," says Rasi. He gushes about the love and respect he feels toward Madeline. He emphasizes family values and says that these values compose the bedrock that he instills in his fourteen-year-old son and six-year-old daughter.

Madeline, like her mother and forebears, is a fierce patriot. The men in her family date back to the Buffalo Soldiers, who were members of the Tenth Cavalry Regiment of the United States Army, formed on September 21, 1866, at Fort Leavenworth, Kansas. The name was given to the Black Cavalry by Native American tribes fighting in the Indian Wars. Similar to how soldiers are taught, "we were raised with discipline and structure," Madeline says. "You live and act a certain way. There's no in between or gray."

Madeline got her kids back when they turned eighteen. Then in 2002 Madeline had another son, Ayumi. She was living in a one-bedroom apartment in the Bronx but made sure her kids knew her door was always open. She was no longer using drugs and was employed and thriving, and her children started visiting regularly. The family bond strengthened, and in 2005 her eldest son, Hason, moved into her home.

In 2010, Hason joined the army. He wanted to leave the Bronx—the area where they lived in the Bronx was dangerous and rife with gang activity. Madeline was ecstatic.

In 2012, Hason was stationed in Fort Riley, Kansas, until he was deployed to Afghanistan. In Afghanistan he completed two tours, six months apiece. He sustained an injury scaling a wall in Kandahar but he still served for another four years and then retired with medals, and accommodations for fighting valiantly. He had received enemy fire from the Taliban and returned it, securing two kills. But at age thirty-four, his career in the military was over.

On October 19, 2018, Madeline's whole world changed forever. Hason, a war vet who had survived the Taliban, couldn't survive the New York City streets. He became another victim of failed Democratic policies that started in earnest under the former Mayor de Blasio's administration, such as unequal distribution of serious violent crimes.[155] By 2020, murder and shootings had been steadily going up and three of Manhattan's twenty-two precincts, all three in Harlem, saw killings rise over 100 percent.[156] Hason was murdered in Harlem—stabbed, beaten, kicked, punched, and left to bleed out on the street. Madeline says the district attorney, Jessica Troy, told her that the murderer "is a homicidal maniac.

Unfortunately, Hason was killed at the wrong time." This was during a period when laws, like arresting and prosecuting criminals, were flouted in Democratic enclaves like New York.

The murder of Hason and what happened next birthed Madeline's fight for justice and efforts to mobilize citizen engagement.

Due to bail reform in New York in 2019, holding murderers accountable in the state is a Herculean effort. Judges have been stripped of discretion in determining the seriousness of the crime. Defunding the New York Police Department has also led to a crime spike; New York has the second-highest violent crime rate in the Northeast.[157] Due to one-party Democratic rule, under which bail reform was implemented and the NYPD was defunded, criminals have become emboldened and far too many victims are left without recourse knowing that arrests are down, crimes are up, charges are downgraded, jails are being emptied, judges are faced with the conundrum of bail reform laws, and far too often, repeat offenders are released onto the streets to strike again.

For this reason, moms like Madeline are switching parties; they don't feel safe and don't want to live as victims or bury their children.

In 2020, Madeline joined the Victims Rights Reform Council, a 501(c)(3) nonprofit organization. She challenges the criminal justice system and bail reform, and fights against the Left's dangerous policies. She's a nightmare for the Democrats—a former Democrat and a black G-d-fearing patriot who doesn't believe blacks should be treated any differently than people of other races, that they should be held accountable for their actions. VRRC advocates and lobbies for legislation to strengthen and protect the rights of victims of all crimes. It fights to have victims' rights advocates act as court buddies, helping families navigate the court system, understand legal terminology, and interpret laws and rulings. It also provides resources for victims to secure housing, as well as offers social and grief services and provides a community of support. "Only another mother that has lost a child due to homicide can understand the pain, and only a mother living in a place where the rule of law is subverted can understand the anger," says Madeline.

*Because* of Madeline's criminal history, she's pro-law enforcement. "Some people belong in a penitentiary for the rest of their lives," says Madeline. But she believes others can be helped in ways that don't necessitate incarceration. "I've been to Rikers twice—'Rosie's House,'" she says. (Rikers Island contains NYC's largest jail, and its Rose M. Singer Center is where the women reside.) "A lot of people fare better in Rikers than on the street." Inmates get a warm and clean bed, laundry services, three meals a day, access to a fully staffed medical team, dental and mental health care, GED programs, Alcoholics Anonymous and Narcotics Anonymous programs, religious services, and recreation facilities. They can even get mail and visitors, can get high, can work, and can go shopping at the commissary. "And let me tell you about recidivism. It's so high because doing time is comfortable," Madeline says matter of factly.

Despite myriad prison reform initiatives, the rate of recidivism in the United States is still a whopping 70 percent within five years of release. New York state releases approximately twenty-five thousand inmates annually. Over 50 percent are back inside within three years, placing New York among the states with the worst recidivism rates in the nation.[158] Bail reform caused decarceration across New York state, and the prison population dropped even further as COVID was used as a means to go soft on crime. Presently, the incarcerated population has decreased by 30 percent over the ten-year period from 2011 to 2021.[159]

The First Step Act, a criminal justice law supposedly intended to remedy some of the systemic issues in the American federal prison system, is a failure. Not only has it not blunted the recidivism rate, but because of the defunded NYPD, the removal of qualified immunity for the NYPD, and a DA that is reluctant to prosecute, arrest numbers have declined while crime soars.[160]

Madeline has the current Manhattan DA, Alvin Bragg, who is backed by the billionaire George Soros, in her sights. She's embittered that the original DAs overseeing Hason's case quit after Bragg was elected, due to his embrace of "restorative justice." "As soon as they were able to manipulate the bail reform law, I knew there would be no justice," says Madeline. She saw prosecutors that were no longer allowed to do their jobs and maintain their oath of office leave in droves.[161]

Madeline believes people aren't arrested; they're rescued. Incarceration provides an opportunity for a person to be removed from a bad situation. She also contends that those who support being soft on crime and tearing down jails wouldn't want people engaging in criminal activity in their backyards. "Bail reform is hurting the Black community; the very people they're releasing return to their community and continue to commit more crime," says Madeline. She insists that many black people don't support bail reform, didn't ask for it, and are not the majority protesting on behalf of BLM, which she also maintains has done nothing for the black community and has not ameliorated race relations but actually made them worse.

"I'm against criminal and social justice reform, restorative justice, bail reform, and raising the age [to be tried as an adult]," says Madeline. She says former New York City mayor Rudolph Giuliani understood what was needed to curb the violence and protect the people, and that crime statistics related to his policies are proof.

Madeline is adamant that people with drug and alcohol problems should be immediately mandated to participate in an in-person program for twenty-four to thirty-six months. DA Bragg's tolerance of petty larceny enables drug users, as this crime is specific to "dope fiend behavior," Madeline says, and she knows this from experience. A brazen, incompetent thief wants to get caught, she says, and the crime is a cry for help.

Madeline calls for a mindset adjustment and hopes that Democrats adopt it before they lose a loved one to the policies their votes precipitate. She sees it like this: career criminals and dangerous people belong in a penitentiary and must be removed from society. While behind bars, they must be required to take anger management and behavioral modification programs, like inmates did in the '90s, she says. She insists that if the perpetrator is a teenage boy, authorities must come down hard on him the first time. "This is tough love. A slap on the wrist is encouragement, and he'll continue committing similar crimes until ratcheting up his behavior," Madeline says. "One must slam him the first time. And this is key: hold the parent responsible, especially if receiving services like Section 8, food stamps, cash benefits, or any taxpayer money to take care of children." She is firm in her belief that one must go straight into the four walls of the home. She dismisses the notion that it would be an invasion of privacy, saying taxpayers must take a stand. "If taxpayers are paying [even] just one dollar to support a household, then what goes on inside that home becomes the taxpayers' business," says Madeline.

As part of an environment in which Democratic leaders are legalizing weed and embracing hard drugs via concerted messaging that targets youth—including subway advertisements that remove the shame from addiction and public service announcements on how to check hard drugs safely for fentanyl—Madeline has strong anti-drug opinions rooted in lived experience. She is categorically against legalizing weed, which she started abusing at the age of twelve. She warns about what many recovering addicts have learned: it's a gateway drug that can lead to harder ones, especially among adolescent users. Madeline is particularly opposed to alcohol, believing that it's even more harmful than drugs, because it's legal, it's publicly accepted, and it claims more dependents than other substances. She repeats a refrain from AA: the use of any substance used as a crutch to function that alters the mood and mind is an addiction.

In New York, blacks compose 43 percent of people in jail (a place for those awaiting trial or held for minor crimes) and 48 percent of people in prison (a place for criminals convicted of serious crimes). Madeline posits that the government led a robust effort to remove black men from their homes via the removal of G-d, dependency on welfare, and the saturation of crack and cocaine into their neighborhoods. Madeline points out the gaslighting campaign that the Left now uses to pretend it's antiracist by legalizing drugs—and not only legalizing them but glamorizing them as well, encouraging addiction, dependency, and loss. Drugs have long been a tool in the tool kit to oppress and suppress black and brown communities, says Madeline.

Educating people is a big part of Madeline's work. Even when she describes her stay at the long-term in-treatment program, she attributes her turnaround to the information she picked up during therapy and the knowledge she soaked up in workshops. She concedes that the members of the black and brown community largely aren't tuned in politically because they feel disenfranchised and are preoccupied with simply trying to survive. Madeline looks to impart on minorities the importance of local races, such as for PTAs, school boards, and city councils. Find out who the sheriff is, who the superintendent of the public school is, says Madeline. Elections for positions such as these affect us on the ground level.

In 2022, Madeline testified at a hearing on reimagining public safety held by the House Judiciary Committee's Crime, Terrorism, and Homeland Security Subcommittee. Both Congressman Andy Biggs, Republican of Arizona, and New York congressman Jerrold Nadler wrote to thank Madeline for her time and thoughts on the pitfalls of defunding police. She spoke out against bail reform, how it negatively impacts the black community and wastes taxpayers' money.

She also has done rallies with candidates and elected politicians such as Lee Zeldin, Andrew and Rudy Giuliani, Joe Pinion, Michael Henry, and Andy Biggs.

Madeline's call to action to black moms is to not view themselves as victims. She admits she hasn't been the perfect mother and has made plenty of mistakes. But if she can pull herself up, there's no excuse for anyone else, she believes. Madeline talks about sacrifice, investment, and staying on one's kids night and day to make sure they're responsible and accountable and that they go to school. She also recognizes the value for children in making mistakes: letting kids be accountable and not saving them will allow them to grow into healthy, responsible adults. She posits that children have been taught to embrace entitlement, and says they're entitled to nothing. Madeline believes there's a social contract both parents and kids have neglected, involving chores, schoolwork, and summer jobs.

Madeline is optimistic about the future. She has been seeing a change in the narrative and more of the black and brown community registering to vote Republican. Despite the fact that New York's Democratic rulers yammer on about the threat of white supremacy, which according to Compstat (the computerization and quantification program used by police departments) is nonexistent, members of the black and brown community are waking up to the reality that their real issue vis-à-vis crime is black-on-black crime. NYPD numbers show that blacks composed 67 percent of its murder victims, 64 percent of its murder suspects, and 62 percent of those arrested for murder in 2021. The Left's policies are simply not working for or protecting blacks.

New York governor Kathy Hochul banked on upset over the United States Supreme Court's reversal of *Roe v. Wade* to carry her to victory. On this, too, Madeline speaks about her lived experiences. She had an abortion at nineteen. Besides losing Hason to murder, it was one of the worst things she experienced. "I went in crying, came out crying, and have regrets to this day," she says. She didn't abort her two pregnancies resulting from prostitution because she was too high and far along, and is thankful for that.

She notes that abortion disproportionately affects the black community and wants there to be a focus on alternatives.[162] She says there's little talk about abstinence, because it borders religion and church.

Madeline thought New York gubernatorial candidate Lee Zeldin would prevail, given that the lagging economy and soaring crime rates rank as the top two voter concerns.[163] More than one million voters across forty-three states have switched to the Republican Party over the last year, according to voter registration data.[164] As per a Siena College Research Institute poll, concerns over public safety in New York cut across political affiliation, age, gender, race, and geography.[165] Crime was the dominant campaign issue in the 2022 gubernatorial election; 74 percent of New York voters called crime a "very serious" concern.[166] This includes 61 percent of Democratic voters as well as 69 percent of Republicans and 61 percent of independents. The real point of interest here is that in New York, Democrats make up approximately 53 percent of voters, while Republicans make up 28 percent, and going by the numbers, the Democrats are more outraged about crime than the Republicans are.

Madeline notes that real, aka "kitchen counter," issues had a strong impact on local government and the mainstream media's two-directional emotional play on abortion and race even though Zeldin lost to Hochul because Zeldin surpassed the magic 30 percent of NYC votes that even Pataki didn't reach. She thinks people have had enough. "I was a Democrat for forty years because I was told that's what Black people had to be," she says. "I have now switched my registration to Conservative, because this is where my values align: G-d, family, and country."

Madeline, like many moms, never dreamed of getting involved in politics. She did so because of her kids. And she switched political parties because the Left is anti-family on topics from education to crime to abortion. Madeline is proving that some of the most effective political operatives are those who have never held office before; they're indefatigable moms who stand to have everything to lose and are owned by no one and nothing.

# CHAPTER 9:
# YIATIN CHU

**PRESIDENT OF ASIAN WAVE ALLIANCE, COFOUNDER OF PARENT LEADERS FOR ACCELERATED CURRICULUM AND EDUCATION (PLACE), AND BOARD MEMBER OF THE FOUNDATION AGAINST INTOLERANCE AND RACISM (FAIR). AGE FIFTY-FIVE AND MARRIED, WITH TWO DAUGHTERS, AGES TWENTY-FOUR AND ELEVEN. LIVES IN NEW YORK CITY. REGISTERED DEMOCRAT BUT VOTED FOR REPUBLICAN LEE ZELDIN IN THE 2022 NEW YORK GUBERNATORIAL ELECTION.**

One of the biggest stories to come out of the 2022 midterm elections is that Democratic enclave and ground zero for lefty lunacy New York City helped save the nation and give Republicans the majority in the House. Moreover, the impossible almost happened: New York state almost flipped from blue to red, and that's thanks to New York City. Republican gubernatorial candidate Lee Zeldin got 47.3 percent of the vote, and Democrat Kathy Hochul got 52.7 percent.[167] New York City *outperformed* in an election that pollsters thought was a sure thing. In the Big Apple, Zeldin got a higher percentage of votes (30 percent) than former Republican New York governor George Pataki had gotten (28 percent).[168]

It's because of Democratic moms like Yiatin Chu, who is the president of the Asian Wave Alliance, a nonpartisan political club; cofounder of Parent Leaders for Accelerated Curriculum and Education (PLACE NYC), which fights for quality education; and board member of the Foundation Against Intolerance and Racism (FAIR). Yiatin, who is a mom of two, put her kids, her family, and her physical and economic safety before her party. She voted for Republican Lee Zeldin in the 2022 New York gubernatorial election.

Yiatin isn't alone. She's part of the growing swell of Asian New York City residents who have had it with the Left's war on women and the failed Democratic policies. While Democratic policies are indiscriminately hurting people from all walks of life, they're taking an especially heavy toll on the Asian community. As of June 6, 2022, in New York City, the NYPD reported a 361 percent increase in anti-Asian hate crimes over the course of the year.[169] And this number doesn't take into account another kind of hate Asians face: discriminatory admissions policies ranging from grade school–level gifted-and-talented programs to higher education institutions, including Ivy League universities.

Yiatin was born in Taiwan. Due to instability on account of diplomatic and political setbacks in the early 1970s, that country suffered from economic and cultural isolation. Yiatin's parents were worried and looked to leave. Yiatin's dad, an engineer, went to Singapore for a job when she was three. Her mom, a teacher, held down the fort. Two years later, Yiatin and her mom joined her father in Singapore, where Yiatin then attended school.

In 1976, when Yiatin was eight years old, the family moved to New York City. "We came with nothing, knew nothing, had no relations but for an aunt, and started from nothing—the typical immigrant story," she says.

First, Yiatin's family lived in a studio apartment in the Murray Hill section of Manhattan, then they moved to Stuyvesant Town in the same borough; finally, they saved enough money to buy a home in Whitestone, Queens. They lived a comfortable life despite the fact that Yiatin and her two younger sisters were "latchkey kids."

Yiatin's first foray into the American education system was at P.S. 32 in Queens. She attended that school for just two months upon arriving in New York, then she attended P.S. 116 in Murray Hill. Both schools were challenging because she didn't speak English. The main languages in Singapore are English and Chinese, but the education is Chinese dominant. After moving to Whitestone, Yiatin went to J.H.S. 194. Whatever Yiatin and her parents were doing worked, because she tested into the Bronx High School of Science, a public specialized high school ranked forty-one nationwide and ranked fifth in New York State.[170] Schools are ranked based on the students' performance on state-required tests and graduation rates, and how well the school prepares graduates for college. To get in, a student must pass the SHSAT (Specialized High Schools Admissions Test), administered to eighth- and ninth-grade students residing in New York

City; the test is used to determine admission to all but one of the city's nine specialized high schools. Admission to Bronx Science is highly competitive. Approximately twenty-five thousand students take the SHSAT annually.[171] Out of these, only eight hundred are accepted into Bronx Science, meaning the acceptance rate is below 3 percent.[172]

Yiatin might not have realized it then, but her experiences from birth to Bronx Science led to her future advocacy efforts: living in Taiwan and fleeing for a better life to Singapore, moving to America, watching her parents excel in the American experiment (starting with nothing and making enough to buy a home), entering a school system without knowing the language, and then testing into one of the most prestigious schools.

Yiatin continued to excel; she went to college and then earned an MBA. She married at twenty-seven, had her first child by thirty, and separated from her husband in her midthirties. At forty-two, Yiatin remarried and took a step back from her job to concentrate on expanding her family; she had a second child.

"I had a serious job, worked a lot, and had a difficult time getting pregnant with my second. I resigned on the best terms in June, and the following month, I was pregnant," says Yiatin. By the time her second child was just over two years old, Yiatin was rehired by her former boss. However, her time there would be limited to just a few more years.

"When my youngest daughter started kindergarten, I decided to be a stay-at-home mom," says Yiatin. As any parent knows, no two children are the same, and no two periods in time are identical. Yiatin's two children had very different educational experiences despite the family's residing in the same city during their academic years.

Yiatin's firstborn daughter went to the Anderson School, a citywide K–8 public gifted-and-talented (G&T) school in Manhattan. The National Association for Gifted Children defines "gifted students" as being those who perform or have the capacity to perform at higher levels. On Anderson's website, it describes its origin: "a group of visionary and tenacious parents who saw the need to accommodate young students with high academic potential." The competition for admission is unbelievably tough. Just fifty students are admitted to Anderson's kindergarten, and a handful are admitted in the first through third grades. The Anderson School is ranked sixth among New York State's elementary schools and eleventh among the city's middle schools.[173]

Clearly, G&T schools are in high demand. They celebrate academic excellence and create for people like Yiatin—an immigrant who came to America with no money—and her firstborn child a means to get ahead regardless of ethnicity, religion, or sex. It's for reasons like this that people come to America—because hard work is rewarded.

Yiatin's eldest daughter graduated from the Anderson School and got accepted into Stuyvesant High School, which also requires passing the SHSAT. Every March, Stuyvesant accepts eight hundred to eight hundred fifty applicants with the highest SHSAT scores out of approximately thirty thousand eighth and ninth graders who apply.[174] It's ranked as the third top public high school in New York State and number thirty-six in national rankings.[175] Around 20 percent of the graduates go on to either one of the Ivy League schools or MIT, Stanford, or the University of Chicago.[176]

The enrolled children aren't the only ones participating in schools like Anderson and Stuyvesant; the families do too. A commitment to hard work is nurtured at home, given that the competition is fierce to both get in and stay at these institutions, which are rigorous and rewarding.

Yiatin's youngest daughter's path wasn't as straightforward, and her academic climate wasn't the same as her older daughter's. The playing field had started to change dramatically for the worse during the time between each girl's academic beginning, courtesy of Democratic policies that no longer promoted hard work but punished it instead.

While Yiatin had her youngest daughter try for one of the G&T schools, "she didn't get a spot like thousands of others who tested well. She went through standardized testing before former New York City mayor Bill de Blasio got rid of it in 2021," says Yiatin.

Her youngest went to kindergarten at a zoned school, P.S. 340, located in District 2 of Manhattan's Chelsea neighborhood. She was doing more work than what the school was able to offer academically, and Yiatin and her husband were frustrated. One day, parents were invited to a "publishing party," at which they could read what the kids had written in class. Yiatin noticed her daughter's ten short stories juxtaposed with all the other kids' one little story. "I said, 'You know what? This isn't the right school for her.' It was progressive, and there was no homework. We didn't want to put her in private because of the expense and because my husband and I went to public school. We're big believers in public school education," says Yiatin. Her daughter stayed at P.S. 340 until midyear of second grade.

Yiatin and her husband looked for schools with an open spot; midyear is tricky. They found a Title 1 dual-language school on Manhattan's Lower East Side, P.S. 184M. It was majority low-income and 70 percent Asian.[177] Yiatin looked at one of the bulletin boards; the writing was in Chinese script. She spoke to the family coordinator and was warned that there was homework.

"Within a month, I transferred my daughter to P.S. 184M, and my advocacy was spurred," Yiatin states. The first move she made was to volunteer at the school's library. This is a great way for moms to get involved at a local level and realize their true potential to make an impact. Think about what's going on in today's climate. Classics like Margaret Mitchell's *Gone with the Wind*, Shakespeare's *Twelfth Night*, and Dr. Seuss' *The Cat in the Hat*, to name a few, have been banned in some schools because they violate the Left's woke standards. Conversely, sexually explicit, racist, and rudimentary revisionist books are purchased with taxpayers' money and stocked front and center in many school libraries. Volunteering at the school library or even running for the library board, which anyone residing within the service area of their public library can do, is a relatively easy way for a mom to test the waters of advocacy. Library boards of trustees determine the mission of the libraries, set policies that govern the libraries, hire and evaluate library directors, and oversee library management.

The parents at P.S. 184M were inquisitive; they wanted to learn more about the new mom. They asked Yiatin questions like, "Do you know what's going on?" and "What do you think of the mayor [de Blasio's] wanting to get rid of the test?"

"I was into makeup and YouTube. I knew nothing," says Yiatin. She asked them what was going on and to explain. They told her how the Asian community was fighting de Blasio over his attempt to remove testing to get into specialized high schools. A fellow mom relayed that a Chinese parent group based in Queens and Brooklyn planned to testify at the mayoral hearing against de Blasio and cite their issues with NYC schools chancellor Richard Carranza.

The sinister reason for wanting to remove the G&T program and testing for specialized schools is that the Left has embraced and rebranded Marxism as "diversity," "equity," and "inclusion." It sounds more palatable and conveniently distances itself from an ideology that has led to carnage. Communist regimes are responsible for the greatest bloodbath over ideological in history, killing more than a hundred million people in the last century.[178] Marxism was the precursor to Communism. Karl Marx espoused the work of German philosopher G. W. F. Hegel, who said something that American Democratic elected officials have put into action: "The State is the Divine Idea as it exists on earth."[179] Hegel, Marx, Lenin, Stalin, Hitler, and Mao rejected G-d and deified the state. Getting rid of the G&T program is getting rid of capitalism, exceptionalism, and true diversity—diversity of academic prowess that leads to competition and innovation. Capitalism is the backbone of a thriving society. But the whole point is, the Left and globalist interventionists don't want America to thrive.

The de Blasio administration claimed that G&T, of which there are 15,979 children in the city's eighty-six programs, were racist because blacks were underrepresented. The irony is, removing these programs *is* racist, because the move targets

Asians—who, to the Left's chagrin, are "overrepresented." The program *is* disproportionately white and Asian; students of these races make up 73 percent of the student body, while 21 percent are black and Hispanic.[180] But this speaks to the elephant in the room that makes too many dishonest people uncomfortable to confront.

First, everything starts at home: a nuclear family, rules and respect, accountability, responsibility, and a drug-free environment are key. Myriad research shows that children experiencing instability at home demonstrate poorer academic and social outcomes than their residentially stable peers. This includes having poorer vocabulary skills, behavioral problems, grade-retention issues, increased high school dropout rates, and lower adult educational attainment.[181] Rather than attack a test, this is the issue to address in communities that are underrepresented in G&T schools.

Second, these tests are the *least* racist methods; they categorically have nothing to do with race. They're color-blind.

Third, rather than burn the system down, why not build it up by creating more G&T programs? As evidence shows, they're in high demand and would benefit Americans and thus America. Oh, wait.

By the time Yiatin joined the Chinese parents group in June 2018, eight months after it formed, things had ramped up. Initially, she was hesitant, feeling uninformed on the issues. But the group was convincing and needed an English speaker to help with the speeches and testify, and Yiatin was motivated. "Asian parents have never been as organized and as activated as they were when it came to education. It's like the third rail; there's a lot that Asian immigrants put up with, but messing with their children's education isn't one of them," says Yiatin. When de Blasio went after their kids, he went after the pathway to the American Dream.

On March 15, 2019, the parents group went to the mayoral hearing and read their statement. They had a back-and-forth with Senator John Liu, who presided over the hearing, and with the chair of NYC education and some other public officials. "John Liu and I went to high school together. He came down from his seat, was gracious, said hello, and promised to let us testify early," says Yiatin. She engaged with reporters and found she was building a reputation. "People started to know who I was, and I was building a network of parents that preceded me," says Yiatin. After testifying, she met Wai Wah Chin, a respected figure in New York City, a mom, and the founding president of Chinese American Citizens Alliance of Greater New York (CACAGNY).

"Previously, the only people I knew were the parents at my school," Yiatin says. "My social circle was people I grew up with and my family. I wasn't involved with the parent community in Queens and Brooklyn. It was strange; I didn't know what to expect. I went to my corporate job, then took care of my family, and didn't get involved outside my inner circle. Getting involved brought me more relationships, but admittedly, I knew very little about this growing group of advocates. We know each other through a pointed context. These are the ties that bind; we're all so committed and spend more time on the cause than with our respective families."

Yiatin refers to herself as an accidental advocate who initially did a favor for a friend. She got sucked in, learned about the issues, and learned about what had transpired and changed in New York City in the forty years since the G&T program's birth in 1973 and since the formation of the specialized high schools. De Blasio wanted to get rid of the SHSAT, arguing it impedes racial diversity at the schools.[182] By 2018, eight of the G&T high schools used this single test. The 542 other high schools in New York City relied on grades or geography for admission.

Yiatin describes the problem with the Democrats' plan to remove the test as being specifically detrimental to Asians, because they rely on public education more than any other community. Approximately 50 percent of white children go to private schools in New York City, 20 percent of blacks go to charter schools, and 85 percent of Hispanics go to public school.[183] But 94 percent of Asians go to public school, so they're overwhelmingly reliant on the system. Furthermore, because the Asian community in New York City has such high poverty rates, they can't access charter schools, because those schools are not in close proximity to where they live. Finally, and most important, the Asians know there's a single high school test for which they can prepare. Skin color, lack of social capital, and undesirable financial conditions do not serve as impediments for them to prepare, take, and dominate the specialized test. "It's free from discrimination. The SHSAT is a hard test but a simple process with a clear outcome: do well and get in," says Yiatin.

Other schools involve not just test scores or grades but interviews, portfolio reviews, and open houses—it's an onerous process for immigrant families. There are many steps, and the process is confusing, not to mention expensive, explains Yiatin. "The Chinese community knows about these specialized schools and rely on education, so they pay attention," she says.

There's been a lot of change in New York City over the past forty years, including shifts in demographics and immigration patterns, and a ubiquitous and profound dumbing down of education. There used to be a lot more G&T programs, and kids would be "tracked." "Tracking" refers to a method formerly employed by numerous secondary schools to group students according to their ability, IQ, and achievement level. Students were placed on high, middle, or low tracks in an effort to provide them with a level of curriculum and instruction that was appropriate to their needs. In the '80s and early '90s, however, an anti-tracking movement began—even though, Yiatin says, "research says tracking produces good outcomes."[184] Some of the benefits of tracking include individualized learning plans, prevention of apathy, encouragement of competition, and having a group of students at similar talent levels and who can advance at a similar pace. Tracking is beneficial for the student and the teacher. To truly advance development among students, it's vital to understand them and their shortcomings, strengths, weaknesses, behavior, and attitude toward their studies.

"When I got involved in advocating for keeping the specialized testing, I saw no Blacks and Hispanics coming out to say, 'Get rid of the test.' Blacks and browns go to charters, realizing public schools aren't good. I think the parents that do care seek out the better alternatives and, along with their children, do the work. For some of the areas that don't have great public schools, they choose Catholic schools, which are less expensive than secular private schools. This is why charters have opened and have a waitlist," says Yiatin.

Yiatin added starting a political club to her educational advocacy efforts. The mission is to help the Asian community become more involved in politics via voting and understanding legislation that impacts the community. "I hope to get away from identity politics. We've been burned and need to get smarter about who we elect into office," she says.

In September 2019, Yiatin, along with a group of parent volunteers, cofounded PLACE. She became copresident in April 2020. Her duties include visiting with elected officials, going to Albany to lobby, and endorsing candidates. Educational advocacy is tied to politics, and PLACE understands it must work with elected officials.

PLACE's first real race was the New York City mayoral election in 2021. The mayor, at the end of the day, controls education. New York City was granted mayoral control of the city's school system in 2002, meaning, the mayor has the power to appoint the city's schools chancellor and a majority of the board of education, known as the Panel for Educational Policy.[185] Being that education hits close to home for this group of parent volunteers, it made sense that PLACE activated for this specific race. It did a lot of work and held a large event for the mayoral candidates to discuss education. Ultimately, PLACE endorsed Democrat Eric Adams. "He said all the things we were happy to hear. He'd expand gifted and talented, leave the specialized testing for high schools in place, and champion academic excellence," says Yiatin. PLACE didn't endorse Curtis Sliwa, a Republican, because it didn't see him as a serious candidate. "We realized that in New York City, it's hard to elect anyone but a Democrat," Yiatin says.

When it came time for the general election, a vocal group of Republican Chinese parents were unhappy with PLACE's endorsement of Adams. Yiatin maintains that PLACE isn't an Asian organization, saying, "I'm Asian, copresident, but the Asian community couldn't compartmentalize our choice." The Asian community supported Republican candidate Sliwa for mayor. Yiatin was verbally attacked because her community values her decisions.

Asked whether she is currently happy with Mayor Adams, Yiatin sighs. "PLACE is giving Adams time to work things out. For the first six months, we hoped he'd undo de Blasio policies. He didn't. The school system is big, and there's a back-end process," she says. Yiatin is forgiving, stating it would have taken a lot of inertia for Adams to unwind the situation created by de Blasio's policies. That being said, "We're disappointed. We engaged with his team, and they haven't reversed the bad policies. We are trying to engage with the administration based on what the families that are still here and haven't moved want," says Yiatin.

The chancellor of the New York City Department of Education, currently David Banks, presides over the largest school system in the nation.[186] He's a longstanding friend of Mayor Adams. Based on the current state of New York City schools, both of these men have been abysmal failures. Together, they admit, the schools are "hemorrhaging students."[187]

The reasons for this are myriad and exclusively tied to Democratic policies. Crime has skyrocketed in New York City, thanks to a defunded and demoralized NYPD and a woke Manhattan Democratic DA (Alvin Bragg) who leans into social justice. NYPD figures show that major crime increased by 36 percent in 2022 compared to the same time the year before. The result is that many families and business owners have fled. NYC has clinched the number-one spot in outmigration, beating San Francisco. Since the COVID pandemic began, New York City has lost at least one hundred sixty thousand households—and a household can include multiple people.[188] The homeless crisis hasn't seen such epic proportions since the Great Depression, making the streets inhospitable for families. Encampments create unbearable quality-of-life concerns, such as rampant waste, drug use, and property devaluation.

Then there's the issue of the schools themselves. Not only did they suffer due to tyrannical shutdowns at the behest of Democratic rulers, but the students suffered due to mask mandates as well. And woke ideology in the form of CRT compounded the effects of two years of degraded school time. On top of the havoc created by closing the schools—which caused significant learning loss, an uptick in abuse and suicide, emotional and psychological damage, obesity, and health side effects from masks, vaccines, and boosters—the actual education itself is a joke. It's no longer focused on the core curriculum but on race, sex, and activism, and the standards have been lowered because the standards are viewed as a form of white supremacy.

Yiatin says, "The deep state is ingrained in the educational structure brought about by the de Blasio and Carranza philosophy."

As people began looking to Yiatin increasingly for help with more than just educational advocacy, she began to think about something beyond PLACE. People trusted how she evaluated the political landscape and were looking to build bridges outside of the Asian community. So shortly after the mayoral election, in February 2022, she cofounded the Asian Wave Alliance (AWA). She and the other cofounders, parents who also were advocates for education, held several meetings, discussed bylaws, and talked about the ways in which politics can be divisive.

They culled together their varied experiences and viewpoints. They were all Asian, but each was different. "To endure debates and disagreements, we had to agree on how the club functions and works together," she said. "Many of us have done community organizing beyond advocacy, [such as] fighting homeless shelters, and have experience outside education. We bring in all the issues that are tough upon the Asian community," says Yiatin.

The Chinese community is the largest within the Asian community in New York City. And NYC has the highest Asian population of any U.S. city, 6 percent. About 40 percent live in the borough of Queens.[189] For this reason, the majority of AWA's focus is on the Chinese communities in Brooklyn and Queens. "The top issues for the Asian community are crime and public safety. There's an attack seemingly every day. Next is public education. Following that, economic prosperity. Tenant, landlord, property taxes, small-time landlords, small property owners—this deeply impacts Asians, as they're the highest percent of homeowners. They invest their nest egg in real estate, not stocks, as an investment to generate income. Finally, they care about immigrant services and want to take care of seniors," says Yiatin.

Yiatin speaks plainly, saying the Democrats have a stronghold on the Asian community regarding welfare and social services, because Asian communities are largely low-income. The majority of low-income students in NYC are Asian and rely on some sort of social service.[190] This is how the Democrats have recruited immigrants, and they continue to do outreach to new ones—helping with the forms and providing translation services. That means that NYC immigrants' first contact with the United States is through nonprofits funded by elected Democratic officials.

Yiatin discusses the frustration, saying, "Asians can't bite the hand that feeds them with services through public funding, but end up screwing themselves with the strings attached pertaining to education. The DOE diversity program sets aside 65 percent of public school kids in low income (so Asians have voted Democrat even though their policies hurt the Asian community). Middle and high schools give priority to low income. Immigrants secure jobs in Manhattan and have a two-income household, so they're at a huge disadvantage for top schools. Immigrants that have done okay, made a life, are disadvantaged. If it was merit, okay, but the lottery has changed the game and families are moving out, going to Catholic and parochial schools."

The problem parents like Yiatin face is that the system is trying to break those who work hard. It insults the immigrant families who are breaking their backs to provide and who set a good example for their kids. It breaks the kids by sending the message that their hard work is scorned.

Despite all this, Yiatin is hopeful. "One must be optimistic to be an advocate. We're volunteers squeezing out family time and sacrificing," she says. The demographics of the city and the attacks on the Asian community act as motivators. Things are so bad that even culturally subdued Asians are waking up. "The numbers of the Asian community taking an active role in politics is strengthening," Yiatin says. "This is where I want to move the needle, with turnout and carving out the districts. Pushback from critics is that Asians might vote progressive. I say, this is how democracy works."

Yiatin believes that educating voters is key and that rejecting identity politics is equally important. "People will say we need to elect a Chinese person. I want a majority-Asian district not to elect an Asian but to have a voice we can elect, who will be effective in getting results we respect," she says. "If that person happens to be a minority, it will be nice to see someone in leadership resembling us, but if they don't espouse shared values, that's not a win."

Many Asians still wear masks in New York City. It makes Yiatin feel culturally out of place because she doesn't. "Every time writer Karol Markowicz wrote her weekly article for the *New York Post*, I was so happy," she says, because it made Yiatin feel that there was still a fighter for New York City, highlighting the injustices of the COVID measures. Indeed, there have been few voices that have captured the essence of the horrors that both parents and children have experienced with such accuracy. Yiatin mentions that her youngest daughter at the Title 1 Asian immigrant majority school was the only child in her entire class who decided to unmask; the student body was 70 percent Chinese.[191] Going along with the program, not creating waves, and masking are the norm in the Chinese community. "My husband and I were the only ones unmasked. Moreover, we were anti-masking. When schools lifted the mask mandate, all of my Chinese mom friends and the teachers continued, even when it became optional," Yiatin says.

Yiatin understands that the media have a lot of control over how Asians think in America, a problem they attribute based on their knowledge of how it works in China and how the Chinese government operates. The Chinese Communist Party (CCP) is presently still upholding a zero-COVID policy, and shutdowns nationwide are proving deadly. An apartment building in Urumqi was engulfed in flames, and life-saving efforts were hindered due to COVID restrictions. Protests have erupted, and punishment from the government is severe.[192] This affects the mentality of the Asian community in America.

Yiatin treads lightly regarding COVID. "I don't ask too many questions," she says. "I'm opinionated and don't want to lose friends and family with people clearly on a different page. My husband, however, has created friction. COVID has done this to people." The response to the pandemic, government overreach, and Marxist policies and practices *have* created a shift, even among unlikely bedfellows.

Some of the members of AWA and other Asian moms, many of whom are Democrat, voted Republican in the November 2022 midterm elections. They got involved with causes centered around keeping schools open and lifting mandates. "This was a fight with many vocal moms, most of whom are Democrats. We have changed COVID policies at schools and have fought against CRT and gender confusion. It's so terrible what we have done to kids, I want to cry," says Yiatin.

A few issues unite people during such polarizing times. And Democratic moms in the Democratic stronghold of New York City, immigrant moms, and minority moms who traditionally vote in lockstep with the Left have broken from tradition.

Newly elected New York Democratic governor Hochul, who won in November 2022, might actually be *good* long-term for those valuing freedom. This is because everything is going to get worse short-term, as we are seeing. The crime spike persists, outmigration continues, schools, specifically private, are doubling on CRT and woke ideology, the illegal crisis is expanding and numbers offered from the top to deal with it keep inflating, the drug crisis is ballooning, and as a result of all of this, the financial outlook is miserable. There has also been talk among the Democratic rulers to resurrect the COVID mandates. After two years, DOE chancellor David Banks and his buddy Mayor Adams are still continuing the policy that keeps unvaccinated parents from entering New York City public schools and attending their children's performances and activities on school premises. These parents can't go to open houses, parent-teacher conferences, or PTA meetings. And in February, 2023, almost three years post the beginning of the school closures for COVID, Mayor Adams, with all his knowledge in epidemiology, warns that *all* COVID mandates might come back.[193] And this medical apartheid is only going to ratchet up the moms. Here's why: moms play the long game. We learn about the long game the moment we get pregnant, and it's reinforced throughout our experiences in rearing children.

The next New York City elections will be in November 2024. They're for mayor and city council, both of which are governing bodies that deal directly with education. Moms fought hard for Lee Zeldin in the previous election, and it showed. Since he lost, the moms have never taken their feet off the pedal; they've been strategizing, networking, and widening their net. Government isn't going to save us; the moms will. It's what most of them do—they're protective by nature, and you can't fight nature.

# CHAPTER 10:
# LINDSAY COLE

**FORMER CINCINNATI BENGALS CHEERLEADER AND FORMER CANDIDATE FOR STATE LEGISLATURE; LIVES IN OHIO. CURRENTLY ON THE BOARDS OF DIRECTORS FOR SHELEADS (IN HAMILTON COUNTY, CINCINNATI) AND THE NORTHEAST HAMILTON COUNTY REPUBLICAN CLUB. JUST LEFT BIG PHARMA AFTER BEING A SALES REP IN THE INDUSTRY FOR OVER TWENTY YEARS. FORTY-ONE-YEAR-OLD SINGLE MOM OF TWO KIDS, AGES TEN AND SEVEN. HAS ALWAYS BEEN A REGISTERED REPUBLICAN.**

America has changed profoundly since March 2020—after grappling with COVID, BLM, and a heated presidential election resulting in Biden irrevocably altering the country, all the fifty states been impacted to varying degrees, Coastal states such as New York, Florida, and California are used to the swinging pendulum of politics, culture, and mood. In the heartland, whose name conjures an image of wholesome, Norman Rockwell–style Americana, states like Ohio tend to steer clear of fads. Upholding traditional values has been the mainstay. The concepts of a strong family, economic self-sufficiency rooted in agrarian life, and religious and conservative political ideals are the glue that holds these states, and America itself, together.

Single mom of two Lindsay Cole is exactly what you'd imagine when you picture someone from Ohio. She's patriotic, hardworking, self-sufficient, and kind. The University of Cambridge conducted a study in 2017 analyzing the personality traits of 1.6 million Americans, and concluded that those in the Midwest are the most "friendly" and "conventional,"[194] and Lindsay fits this description. In her work as a professional cheerleader for the Cincinnati Bengals, a Big Pharma sales rep, a candidate for public office, and on the board of directors for conservative-leaning female advocacy groups, Lindsay has been guided by her intuitive and unshakeable Midwestern values. She literally cheers herself and others on to victory.

Running for state legislature in 2022 initially wasn't part of the plan. In 2020 and 2021, Lindsay was dealing with two young kids, COVID-policy problems, a job at a small pharmaceutical company during the FDA-unapproved experimental "vaccine" rollout, and a nasty divorce that was exacerbated by a broken judicial system, on top of being the sole provider for her kids. But it turns out that for her, the time when she was navigating these circumstances was the best time to run for office. Lindsay was heated (not New York City–style in-your-face heated, but a thoughtful and composed Midwest-style heated). She wasn't looking for answers; she was looking to serve in government in order to provide them.

Lindsay comes from a middle-class family and is the youngest of three daughters. Her grandfather fought in World War II. Her father is a navy veteran who fought in Vietnam. Her stepfather was in the army. Service, honor, and protection aren't foreign concepts she's read about in books; they're her reality. Lindsay's parents worked at the U.S. Enrichment Corporation and made a good living, enough to send all three of their girls to college.

With all the current news on how to mess up kids six ways from Sunday, it's easy to forget that lots of people really do have beautiful childhood experiences. It makes it all the more obvious why many of them who are now moms are fighting so hard against the Left's goal of dissuading today's youth from marrying, procreating, and raising the next generation to be set up for success. Innocence, the sort of innocence that children get in safe neighborhoods and from solid family bonds, is being intentionally corrupted at every turn, subliminally and all up in your grill by the people voted into office. There was a time not so long ago, though it feels like another century, when sheltering kids from adult activities was sacrosanct. Most adults understood that an immature brain and an undeveloped body aren't able to process concepts and activities with which even adults struggle.

"Americana is how we were raised. The whole town shut down on Friday for football, and there was a sense of community. This is the bedrock of my faith: love of country, freedom, the white picket fence, and the American Dream," says Lindsay.

Things are different now. Lindsay's hometown of Portsmouth, Ohio, has been devastated by opioid addiction. "The pill mill started here because drug cartels settled in the epicenter between north and south, Canada and Florida," says Lindsay. A "pill mill" is an illegal facility posing as a regular pain clinic. In exchange for cash or other bribes, these facilities prescribe medication without the standard elements: the buyer's medical history, a physical examination, a diagnosis, or medical monitoring. This subject is in Lindsay's wheelhouse, not only because she's seen the change to her community firsthand—normal people full of life and promise turned into begging zombies—but because until recently she was in Big Pharma for twenty years.

"There was no drug or opioid problem when I grew up," Lindsay says. "It was largely middle-class families with their white picket fences in farm country. We had great county schools. The gorgeous Ohio River teemed with boats. On Labor Day, we had the River Days Festival and ships would come from Ashland, Kentucky, to Cincinnati, Ohio. It was wholesome."

Cincinnati is the onetime home of Roy Rogers, who is known as the "King of the Cowboys." He was one of the most popular western film stars, as cofounded the Sons of the Pioneers, which was America's foremost western singing group formed in 1933 by Ohio-born Leonard Franklin Slye—better known as Roy Rogers. It was a thriving town, with department stores such as Mitchellace. "My one-hundred-and-three-year-old grandmother worked there making shoelaces. Now that spot has been turned into a thirty-million-dollar drug rehab center," says Lindsay.

At fourteen years old, Lindsay got her first job; she worked at a local ice cream shop. Then, during her senior year in high school, she was picked to try out for summer staff for the Universal Cheerleaders Association and was accepted. This is how Lindsay made money during the summer, traveling to different college campuses to cheer. While people are picked from all across the nation, the staff is Ohio-heavy. "We're the Buckeye State, for G-d's sake," says Lindsay.

While at Ohio University in Athens from 1999 to 2003, she was a cheerleader with the Bengals organization, which is part of the National Football League. She toured as a cheerleader overseas for the men and women who fight in the armed forces as well as participated in a ten-day tour in Iraq and Kuwait. "And I had a full-time job, which is mandatory when one cheers. I worked during the day and cheered at night and on Sundays," says Lindsay.

Upon graduating, Lindsay took a job with Pfizer as a sales rep. Prior to the COVID pandemic, beginning in March 2020, Pfizer wasn't a household name; it is now. The American multinational pharmaceutical and biotechnology corporation is one of the few that pumped out what has been touted as a vaccine. Some critics, like reporter Alex Berenson, feel this is a mischaracterization. "Think of it—at best—as a therapeutic with a limited window of efficacy and terrible side effect profile that must be dosed IN ADVANCE OF ILLNESS," he tweeted in July 2022.[195]

In 2021, Pfizer reported $7.8 billion in U.S. revenue for its COVID vaccine. The American government has options to buy 1.6 billion Pfizer vaccine doses. Thus far, it has purchased nine hundred million, including five hundred million to be donated to poor countries. In July 2022, the United States government signed a $3.2 billion deal with Pfizer for 105 million more doses of their COVID vaccine.[196]

Lindsay was with Pfizer when Hank McKinnell was president and CEO. "We were the 'big blue machine': Viagra, Celebrex, Lipitor, and other blockbuster products; Zoloft. Training was extensive. There were home studies, regional studies, a Pfizer learning center in White Plains, New York. I studied at night and tested during the day. It was harder than college," says Lindsay. During the process, sales reps like Lindsay were trained on how drugs were brought to market. The training covered things like how expensive the products were, the different phases, and the clinical trials.

"We were schooled on how difficult it is to bring products to market and that most don't pass FDA approval. I'm then watching as the COVID vaccine is fast-tracked to market in less than a year when most products take upwards of twenty years due to enrolling people in trials and [having a] myriad of phases. Most products die between phase two and three because they're not performing well or have adverse effects," she says. Bringing products to market involves a lot of money; this is why pharmaceuticals are so expensive. "I questioned the validity of bringing the COVID vaccine to the masses, that it was fast-tracked, and so many people never questioned taking it. I would never give it to my children," says Lindsay.

"I'm not anti-vaccine," she adds. "But I lost sleep over being required to get something that isn't FDA-approved in order to work. I'm the breadwinner for my children, fighting my ex-husband in divorce court, had already had COVID, and faced a choice that would be disastrous financially for my family. I did as much as I could to stave off getting fired, even looked for other jobs, but the first question was, 'Are you vaxxed?' Finally, I had to give my company a yes or a no."

While a sales rep by day, Lindsay was a professional cheerleader for the NFL between 2007 and 2010. She was one of thirty women selected to join the Cincinnati Bengals squad and root for her hometown. Cheerleading is no joke; competition is fierce, the hours of practice are intense, and the pay is low (the average for Lindsay was eighty-nine dollars per game). The benefits include learning how to work with a team, maintain laser-like focus, and trust skills; cheerleaders also develop serious dedication and learn to handle intense competition. And the games were weekly.

As a woman of faith, Lindsay would say that her time in the pharmaceutical industry as a sales representative—learning how to recruit consumers and message effectively—and cheering worked together to prepare her for what was on the horizon.

Lindsay got married in 2010 and went on to have two children. Irreconcilable differences led to a divorce. The already painful time was compounded by the need to navigate a complicated, lengthy, and expensive legal system. If anything can make you Conservative, it's going through a divorce. Once you've been in the system, you want as little outside interference by people wholly disconnected to your life as possible.

"I've gone through a five-year divorce starting in 2018 that is currently in the appeals process for the last year. It's a broken system. Due to pending litigation and no orders in place, I never received child support that was promised in good faith. Also, shared parenting is encouraged irrespective of personality disorders and mental health. I had an inside look at how different wheels in the cog clog the system—from lawyers to judges to magistrates to parent coordinators to forensics to child support enforcement agencies. They punt the ball to different players, and tensions flare and bills rise in the midst of emotional turmoil precipitated by the dissolution of the family unit," says Lindsay.

In Ohio, as long as there is pending litigation, child support collection agencies won't get involved. The onus is on the plaintiff to do the forward motion. This means that one must spend money in order to get the person who owes it to pay child support when in family court. This is the same situation in appellate court. Lindsay has been banging her head on this rock for years. Her frustration with the broken system, gratuitous red tape, and pigs feeding at the trough has shaped her views on big government and unelected bureaucrats.

Lindsay was going through a divorce, raising two young kids, working full-time in pharmaceutical sales, and keeping her head above water when COVID struck. She felt underwater, angry, and motivated.

"Ohio received a stay-at-home order from Governor [Mike] DeWine, a Republican in name, and Dr. Amy Acton, who wasn't an elected government official," says Lindsay. Acton served as the director for the Ohio Department of Health in 2019 and 2020, and played a main role in Ohio's response to COVID. "A week prior to the stay-at-home issued March 16, 2020, I started at a new job and was supposed to close on my home. Now I'm stuck homeschooling my children, ages seven and four years old," Lindsay says. Both preschool and grade schools were shut down in Ohio as part of the COVID response.

Lindsay's experiences mirror the problems many moms faced during the COVID pandemic, but hers were worse because she was a single mother and the sole provider for her children. According to a Pew Research Center study:

> ...the COVID-19 pandemic has presented challenges and obstacles for many Americans, but one group has been getting a lot of attention lately: moms. Much of the focus has been on the effects of school closings and child care responsibilities on mothers' employment and labor force participation rates, with some suggesting the disruptions caused by the pandemic might have long-lasting consequences for gender equality in the workplace.[197]

The study goes on to say:

> Pew Research Center surveys have highlighted some of the unique challenges facing moms during the pandemic. For example, a survey last October found that, among employed parents who were working from home all or most of the time, mothers were more likely than fathers to say they had a lot of child care responsibilities while working (36 percent vs. 16 percent). Working mothers with children younger than 12 at home were also more likely than fathers (57 percent vs. 47 percent) to say it had been at least somewhat difficult for them to handle child care responsibilities during the coronavirus outbreak.

In other words, nuclear families absolutely had challenges during the pandemic, but single-parent families were in another class in terms of being screwed. They didn't have the option to stop working and *only* stay at home, picking up the brunt of schoolwork and housework; they had to do it all.

In March 2020, Lindsay's son was in first grade at a private Catholic school. "We picked up his school stuff—lesson plans, papers, and notebooks—on the sidewalk amongst a sea of all the other students' school possessions. We made use of the studies curriculum to get him through the rest of the year. I was doing Zoom calls during the day for work, preoccupied, trying to make money, keep my job, and pay the bills. I couldn't get help for kids due to the lockdown, and was frequently interrupting my workday to pay attention as much as possible to my kids. I set up stations for my four-year-old so she could entertain herself, and had my seven-year-old son stuck on a different website that was grade-level-appropriate," says Lindsay. This was their routine for the next three and a half months.

By the end of the academic year in June 2020, Lindsay was mentally overextended. She sought to put behind her the living situation that was riddled with negative associations—COVID, shutdowns, and scarring personal issues—and to put distance between herself and her ex-husband. She was overjoyed to find affluent Terrace Park, a village in Hamilton County, Ohio, situated along the Little Miami River. It's an idyllic town and golf cart community with an elementary school that is its center.

In August 2021, Lindsay's daughter began kindergarten. "The days were shorter than all the other grades, but we were just thankful she was going to school," says Lindsay. This was a common sentiment among mothers back in 2021, who had just experienced their lives' being turned upside down for six months prior to the start of the 2021 academic school year. Their pain, emotional duress, and financial uncertainty were exhausting and often dulled their decision-making capability. Perhaps this was the Democrats' intent. Government control had lowered the bar of expectations pertaining to academic standards to such an extent and exhausted parents, just being able to send their children to school, forget if it was good, felt like a win to some. Parents were willing to overlook indisputable educational decline as well as the usurping of parental rights. It was a key moment in history that many parents presently wish they had handled differently. Because so much had been taken away, getting the smallest sliver back, a return to in-school instruction, felt like a win. It turns out that it was a monumental loss, involving government overreach, the flouting of the Constitution and the Nuremberg Code, zero parental rights, and critical race theory. Shortsightedness made future battles even harder.

The new school year was off to a difficult start. At the age of four, Lindsay' daughter was diagnosed with migraines. In order for her to attend kindergarten on school premises, she was mandated to wear a mask. Lindsay was faced with securing a medical exemption, a laborious task, as doctors weren't keen to go against peer pressure–favoring mandates. "I was struggling to make up for the diminished hours in school, unsuccessful at teaching my daughter to read and write, and contending with my son in hybrid, which meant *only* in school on Tuesday, Thursday, and every other Friday," says Lindsay.

"In 2020, during the BLM riots, signs started cropping up in the yards—lots of signs. It was pervasive," she continues. "They said, 'We accept all', 'BLM,' and 'No hate here.' This is an old village, where the older generation voted Republican, but over the past years, the forty-year-olds have shifted Left. It's also an overwhelmingly white population, clocking in at 98 percent.[198] These are people that would have been appalled if BLM riots infringed upon their way of life, vandalizing property, depreciating real estate, assaulting family and friends, and yet, the message put out was that they were in accord." A Facebook group for Terrace Park moms against racism was started, with 150 moms in the group.

Discontentment with the school system; with COVID misinformation promoted by the government, the mainstream media, and unelected bureaucrats; and with the illogical response to COVID spurred Lindsay into action. She gravitated toward the Women's Northeast Republican Club. It provided a venue to network, ask questions, and explore ways to activate.

"I became more aware of what was going on with the school and community. I connected with the judges and legislators who came in to speak at the club. What activated me, stoked my desire to first get involved at the school level, was a speaker who validated what I was seeing vis-à-vis my own kids and opening my eyes to the widespread issues at every corner within the education complex," says Lindsay.

During a luncheon at the club in mid-April 2021, Lindsay first heard about CRT. It had been made part of the curriculum not only without alerting the parents but undercover, in a genuine attempt to deny its existence. Lindsay recognized the word and its doctrine because the Mariemont City School District, which included her village, Terrace Park, had it in its curriculum. "I started researching CRT online and noticed they kept changing the name to DEI [diversity, equity, inclusion], as if to throw parents off track with an acronym that sounds holy," notes Lindsay.

In school, Lindsay's five-year-old daughter was reading *Let Them March*, a work of historical fiction set during the time of the Birmingham Children's Crusade in 1963, and was sufficiently confused; she alerted her mom. Her young mind couldn't process the graphic and disturbing images rendered in childlike cartoon images meant to appeal to young minds.

Lindsay, concerned, went on the teacher's Facebook page. Under the area that was dedicated to "Kindness Month," she saw the images from *Let Them March* and was shocked. "None of the other parents at that point knew what was going on. We're all in our forties, underwater, going through COVID, just happy our kids are back in school and we can work and keep our jobs, and are clueless as to the age-inappropriate material they're teaching in spurts and out of context, in a narrative that fits the Democrats' agenda, without any regard to the psychological impact on the kids," she says.

In June 2021, Lindsay attended a school board meeting. She was one of the few who stood up and said, "I fight hard to be a part of this community. I could have gone anywhere. I chose this school because of its commitment to education. I'm immeasurably disappointed to find out about the new curriculum that was decided without parental consent. In particular, I take issue with a book showing white police officers hosing black kids in Birmingham, Alabama, titled *Let Them March*. This is on the heels of the kids' being masked all day long. Now they're being taught a pointed and incomplete view of 'social justice' without accurate historical context."

Sitting behind Lindsay were some parents from the Foundation Against Intolerance and Racism (FAIR). It's a nonpartisan organization dedicated to advancing civil rights and liberties for all Americans, and to promoting a common culture based on fairness, understanding, and humanity. "They asked if I wanted to join a chapter to help educate parents as to what is being taught in school. This is when I found out about Terrace Park Moms," says Lindsay.

The Terrace Park Moms group had been active all year before the school board. They were pro-masking and supported the new CRT agenda, which had no empirical record of improving anything—not the students' success or the skills they'd need to get into higher education, secure a job, navigate adulthood, and raise a family, let alone their happiness, race relations, or educational prowess. It was completely new and untested. Yet the Terrace Park Moms and the school boards, the Biden administration, Democratic elected officials, and unelected bureaucrats were all-in. When parents like Lindsay tried getting Freedom of Information Act requests for documents on the curriculum, they were stonewalled by the Terrace Park Moms.

In the fall of 2021, three Terrace Park residents went up against three FAIR members for the school board. All three of the FAIR members lost. Out of nine board members in the Mariemont City School District, there's only one that's conservative. This is problematic, because a school board is supposed to be nonpartisan. In an echo chamber committed to radical and unscientific policies, as CRT and COVID mandates are, blunting further insidious policies and wasteful spending is next to impossible. Moreover, without any pro–parental rights school board members, *all* parents, no matter what they support, don't have a say. The body in charge can be emboldened to act however it wants without any consideration for the parents. "As it was, everything the school board was doing transpired behind closed doors," says Lindsay.

"The principal of Terrace Park Elementary is a white older lady. The principal of Mariemont Elementary is Black. The Black principal was put in charge of DEI for both schools. It is a nine-year program, and we were three years in. It was going on all this time, and none of the parents knew," she adds.

The DEI movement isn't new. Its roots date back to the 1960s civil rights movement, but it was largely unfelt and therefore never discussed until recently. Now it's ubiquitous, overwhelming nearly every institution from the public sector to the private sector: government, art and entertainment, hospitality, the airline industry, the medical industry, the judicial system, housing, sports, drugs, and education. The kicker: redefining all ways of life is based upon the whims of someone whose *only* job requirements for a DEI position are "demonstrated commitment to valuing diversity and contributing to an inclusive working and learning environment. Two years of experience in diversity related programs or equivalent education/experience. High school graduation or equivalent."[199] Reread the previous three sentences. Americans' entire way of life since June 2020, over a bogus narrative that George Floyd was premeditatively killed, motivated by racism, at the hands of white cops, has unequivocally changed America and by all metrics-crime, economy, grade level proficiency at school-for the worse.

Race relations haven't been this contentious since the 1950s. Schools have never performed so badly, according to statistics based upon the lowest levels of grade-level proficiency. Crime has spiked in nearly *every* Democrat-run city.[200] Segregation based on race in all institutions and industries has not been openly encouraged in America since the 1950s. According to the World Happiness Report, America is downright morose: "Relying on the variables of 'real Gross Domestic Product per capita, social support, healthy life expectancy, freedom to make life choices, generosity and perceptions of corruption,' America barely makes it into the top twenty."[201] This was in 2022, when CRT was supposed to fix everything. CNN cites a recent Gallup poll which found that only about one-third of Americans are satisfied with their lives; this is an all-time low.[202] The National Institute for Mental Health estimates that in 2020, "an estimated 21.0 million adults in the United States had at least one major depressive episode."[203] This is a referendum on the Left, in charge and ruining lives based on experimental grievance police and woke policies.

Lindsay notes that Mariemont prides itself on the fact that high school graduates placed in the top 5 percent of all schools in Ohio for overall test scores (math proficiency is top 10 percent, and reading proficiency is top 1 percent) for the 2020–21 school year.[204] But in accordance with the woke agenda since June 2020, colleges have drastically lowered standards. "Being a valedictorian used to mean something. Now what does it mean? Meaningful benchmarks have been removed, merit has gone out the window, and rewards are doled out based on immutable characteristics, Democrat political affiliation, and one upping the next person over grievances and commitment to activism," she says.

Shortly after Lindsay got involved with FAIR, she decided to run for state legislature. She researched, connected with, and interviewed various moms and studied up on the dynamics of the school board. She found out that neighboring schools, like those in Anderson Township, draw their curriculum inspiration from Mariemont. "Mariemont hired an outside consultant from a Cincinnati public school district to come in and instruct teachers about SEL [social-emotional learning], another social justice initiative under the CRT umbrella," says Lindsay. As per the Collaborative for Academic, Social and Emotional Learning (CASEL), which describes itself as the nation's leading organization advancing the development of academic, social and emotional competence for all students, requirements to be a SEL professional are "self-awareness, self-management, social awareness, relationship skills, and responsible decision making."[205] Translation: anyone could be assigned to this position, as it requires zero gradable skills.

This new "job" pays handsomely: Mariemont paid the consultant $31,000 for the course. This is provided by the taxpayers funding the budget for the school board. Since George Floyd's death and the beginning of BLM, the Biden administration, Democratic elected officials, and unelected bureaucrats have created another way to bilk taxpayers and expand baseless jobs with the creation of SEL. More than 90 percent of schools and districts throughout the nation report focusing on developing students' SEL skills.[206] Critics blast SEL. The Hechinger Report, a national nonprofit newsroom dedicated to education, says that "two moms from Sandy, Utah…combing through the district's eighth grade curriculum…[were] alarmed [by what they found].[207] As is mentioned in the report, 'Parents are unaware that concepts like Critical Race Theory and Comprehensive Sex Education are being taught under the guise of Social Emotional Learning programs.'"

"As per the consultant, teachers in Mariemont were encouraged to read certain books by Ibram Kendi," Lindsay says. "One hundred fifty copies were distributed to the teachers as suggested reading. In addition, parents weren't allowed inside the school building, but kids reported back to their parents describing the atmosphere. Each teacher had a flag, 'I am safe,' for the trans kids. For my daughter's first-grade orientation, the teacher said he's thrilled to teach 'social justice' as part of the curriculum."

She notes the double standard: "My son came home from school asking why a classmate can wear a Biden mask but he can't wear a MAGA T-shirt. I wouldn't let him because of the political climate. I don't want him to be a target. But wearing a shirt, flying a flag, connected to a movement kids don't understand with truly dangerous alignments and outcomes is promoted."

Double standards were everywhere. Lindsay ran for legislature shortly after Trump lost in 2020. During that time, she had a lot of friends bound together by similarities: motherhood, age, camaraderie among the children. These relationships were put to the test; politics were proving divisive.

"My very good friend invited six moms over for drinks just before the election. A conversation got heated when Trump came up, and I was asked to defend my choice in voting for him a second time. I was then called a racist. I asked the other mom why she would say that, and she said she doesn't like that people have to enter the country legally. This moment was a turning point. I had never been called a racist," says Lindsay. The double standard is that Democratic voters aren't asked to justify their choice—not by the school and not by the moms. It's special treatment only Republicans receive.

Lindsay was undeterred. Her platform was faith, family, and freedom. "Silence is no longer golden" was her motto. She couldn't ignore the stripping of parental rights and the indoctrination of children, no matter what names the initiatives were issued.

Lindsay went to an event to learn how to run a campaign. The District 27 state legislature seat was going to be open, as the current person would be termed out, and she stood a chance in the Republican-skewed district.

"I thought of my divorce and how the system is broken. The only way I can help fix it is to be part of the system. Running for state legislature seemed like the right move. But I learned quickly, running as a Republican means going up against the good old boys club. There's no change and no new ideas. The Republican party in Ohio is stagnant when it comes to women," says Lindsay.

Cincinnati is an old German Catholic town, home to Kroger and Procter & Gamble. It's stocked with ancestral family names and with that, old money and power brokers. Both Mark Twain and Will Rogers have been quoted as saying something along the lines of if the world were to come to an end, they'd want to be in Cincinnati because everything happens ten years later there.[208] Change is hard, slow, and uncomfortable there. For a divorced mom in her early forties, trying to break into the Republican Party is especially challenging. "I was immediately greeted with a slammed door by the Hamilton County establishment, but I kept moving forward," says Lindsay.

Calling contacts, networking, going to fundraisers and other events big and small, Lindsay persevered and looked to make inroads. All the while, she was working full-time, dealing with a divorce, and raising two young kids in school.

Lindsay was about to learn that it wasn't just the divorce system that has been totaled; it's pretty much anything that the government touches. "The state of Ohio can't get its shit together regarding gerrymandering. Sorting out the redistricting maps took so long, I missed my May 2, 2022, primary," she says.

Then on May 2, 2022, the likelihood that *Roe v. Wade* would be overturned was leaked, setting the country on fire. The timing was suspicious. The leak occurred just before midterm elections and amid calamity after calamity the Biden administration had exacerbated—inflation, crime, the open border, the supply-chain breakdown, the Ukraine–Russia war—and the mom army's going to the mat over parental rights, mask mandates, and CRT. Lindsay had a terrible premonition. Her friends, even the Republicans, were upset about the potential reversal of *Roe v. Wade* because of the mainstream media's intentional misrepresentation over what it would mean—in effect, that women's rights would be stripped. The reality is that nine Supreme Court judges ultimately decided that it was faulty law, and that the right to decide never should have left the jurisdiction of individual states. Moreover, the media implied that nine justices shouldn't be responsible for shouldering what is the right and duty of voters. If people want abortion, they must vote in pro-abortion representatives in their respective states.

Abortion became the focal point of Lindsay's election. The state of Ohio has the Heartbeat Bill; if a heartbeat is detected at six weeks, abortion is illegal. "I believe life is messy. I have a seven-year-old daughter and a ten-year-old son. After all I have been through, an abusive relationship, I can't imagine the trauma of a child being raped, and so I believe in exemptions and exceptions," says Lindsay. Her opponent didn't; she was staunchly pro-life and received the pro-life endorsement in Ohio.

There was a candidates' debate with 150 people in attendance. "My opponent's tagline was 'True Conservative.' I was painted as a liberal and Republican imposter," Lindsay says.

Lindsay lost in the late primary on August 2, 2022, but she hasn't given up. While disappointed with the results, she notes that she's part of an infinitesimal group that has had the courage to put it all on the line. According to Pew Research Center, only 2 percent of Americans have ever run for federal, local, or state elected office. There are 7,386 total legislative seats throughout the states, and currently 2,291 are held by women.[209]

While more mothers than ever before are running for office, the numbers leave room for improvement: 5.3 percent of state legislators across the nation are moms with children under the age of eighteen at home; 7 percent of Congress members are moms with children under the age of eighteen at home.

"I'm trying to figure out a different way to have a voice and represent the suburban mom. I'm trying to turn my loss into a win. I am analyzing the best way to move forward. There will be redistricting for the state legislature again in two years. Maybe a congressional race is in my future. I'm never giving up; I'm just not sure in what capacity I will serve," says Lindsay.

In October 2022, Lindsay quit her job as a sales representative in the pharmaceutical industry. She is still involved with FAIR and serves on the board of directors for both SHELeads and the Northeast Hamilton County Republican Club. She also hosts the podcast *High Heels and Politics*, which is a platform to interview politicians and women with influence. She started a 501(c)(3) nonprofit, This Precious Messy Life. She is hoping to help others avoid relationships like the one she had, which culminated in divorce; the organization is dedicated to helping abused women.

Lindsay is picking up the pieces of not only her professional life but her personal life, which was the impetus behind her run for office. "Within the last year, my kids stopped getting asked for playdates. It has affected my daughter more. Because I had gone to the board of education meetings, the moms fighting against me for masking on the other side have taken it out on my kids," says Lindsay. Being brave, going public, comes at a cost that goes beyond the individual in the spotlight and touches family and friends as well.

Lindsay's call to action is to "stand firm and keep the faith." She adds, "I can't stop because of detractors. Countervoices to the Left must be heard, even when it's hard and feels isolating. You know why moms are good candidates? Because we're CEOs of our homes. I was juggling two kids and their respective sports, dealing with school and lack thereof, taking care of the home, preparing meals, mowing my own lawn in the evening, working full-time during the day, divorcing, running a campaign, paying bills, budgeting, and socializing. I know how to do so much—all moms do. And we're born fighters. You know what will happen if you come for my kids? You know what will happen if you go for another mom's kids?"

This is only the beginning, says Lindsay. The Democrats took their time, like boiling a frog, with the catastrophic agenda to "reimagine" America. It was decades in the making, set in stages, and strategic. It will take time to reverse the damage as well as change the morale. Torchbearers like Lindsay, soldiers in the Mom Army, are coming to the rescue.

# CHAPTER 11:
# JULIE GUNLOCK

**ALEXANDRIA, VIRGINIA
DIRECTOR OF THE CENTER FOR PROGRESS
AND INNOVATION AT INDEPENDENT
WOMEN'S FORUM (IWF); LIVES IN VIRGINIA.
FIFTY-YEAR-OLD MARRIED MOTHER OF
THREE BOYS, AGES FIFTEEN, FOURTEEN, AND
TWELVE. HAS ALWAYS BEEN A REPUBLICAN.**

Since 2020, women—moms in particular—have been described by Monday-morning quarterbacks in the mainstream media as the voting-bloc sleeper cell that no one in politics saw coming. A force of this magnitude from this demographic hasn't previously been seen. Moms themselves were caught off guard; they never imagined their own government coming after them with a vengeance. When it did, many reacted quickly and furiously, like lifting an overturned vehicle pinning down their babes. The disruptors caught the campaign consultants pulling in the big bucks flat-footed. Sleepy candidates were forced to pivot from the run-of-the-mill topics beaten over the drum for decades, and adopt new platform commitments overnight. Suddenly, they had to address parental rights, mandates, education, and critical race theory. It was uncharted territory. Smart candidates bent over backward looking to get a new type of endorsement, one that didn't come with oodles of cash and D.C. connections. They went to the moms.

Why the change? Prior to 2020's COVID pandemic and BLM riots, things in America were humming under President Trump. Peaceful and prosperous times in the United States meant moms didn't have to be soldiers. They went from raising their kids to furthering their careers; they were busy. That busyness left a gaping hole for nefarious actors—including Democrats and globalists married to woke ideology—to infest. Politicians didn't have to incorporate the moms into the fold, and seldom did. The Democrats claimed ownership of them, specifically the younger ones, appealing to their maternal inclinations to help starving children and heal the environment; when that failed, abortion was unleashed like clockwork.

When March 2020 came around and brought with it COVID, mandates, BLM, defunding the police, CRT, open borders, and drugs, fighting paper dragons took a backseat. Moms had no other choice but to look behind the hood. What they discovered was shocking. When the Left went full frontal and came after the kids, the sleeping giant, moms, woke up and took to the battlefield.

Julie Gunlock was never in hibernation. She's been politically active for decades, assiduously working to advance issues concerning women and children. She has served as a staff member on the Senate Committee on Homeland Security and Governmental

Affairs and on the House Committee on Homeland Security. She's worked for Ohio senators Mike DeWine and George Voinovich and for Oklahoma senator Tom Coburn, and served on the leadership staff of U.S. representative Christopher Cox from California.

Presently, Julie directs the Independent Women's Network as well as the Independent Women's Forum's Center for Progress and Innovation. She is also the Monday and Tuesday cohost of WMAL-FM's radio show *O'Connor & Company*, the leading talk radio station in the D.C. area.[210] Julie is a published author and a contributor to the *Wall Street Journal*, the *New York Post*, the *Washington Post*, the New York *Daily News*, the *Los Angeles Times*, *USA Today*, *National Review*, and HuffPost. She has provided political commentary on Fox News, PBS, CNN, and Blaze TV. In other words, Julie has been in the fight for a while, even before many of the other mothers came to realize what Machiavellian machinations were afoot.

Julie joined IWF fourteen years ago when she got pregnant and wanted to work from home. "Previously, I worked on Capitol Hill, which is no place for a new mom," she says. As a committee staffer, she found the hours grueling, oftentimes necessitating sleeping on a couch in the office. Julie desired a flexible career with flexible hours. IWF was virtual before "virtual" became a household word, and she was able to carve out a schedule that suited her lifestyle.

At IWF, Julie runs the Center for Progress and Innovation. This is a pretty progressive niche for a Republican woman to commandeer; the party struggles to put forth an image of being modern and forward-thinking to the public. It's a strange thing because on one hand, the party *is* old-fashioned, feverishly guarding its Judeo-Christian principles and traditions created by our Founding Fathers. On the other hand, the Founding Fathers, who drafted the Constitution and the Declaration of Independence, were and are as modern as it gets; both documents have stood the test of time, providing the framework to deal with any issue from 1776 to the present day. Furthermore, the Founding Fathers were by and large Federalists—members of the conservative political party that was the first political party in the United States. Approximately seventy-five years after America's creation, it was the Republicans who were futuristic enough to fight the American Civil War to end slavery, which the Democrats wanted to keep.

"As an opinion writer and media spokeswoman, I talk about modernity and innovation in technology, farming, and manufacturing. I walk my audience through the transitions and explain how they're good for humankind. I try to take fear out of the evolution and reassure moms about what's available in the marketplace and the benefits," says Julie.

"I am extremely pro-vaccine and anti-mandates, a nuanced position," she continues. She believes the COVID vaccine reduces symptoms and makes it easier to survive if one has comorbidities, struggles with obesity, or is older. However, Julie is troubled by how the FDA has handled the rollout campaign.

The response of Democratic elected officials and unelected bureaucrats like those at the World Health Organization, the Centers for Disease Control and Prevention, and the teachers' unions to the COVID pandemic was earth-shattering for so many, but Julie, at least from a work perspective, was largely unscathed. While she already was accustomed to working virtually at IWF, there were some changes. In-person meetings and other events moved to Zoom. Julie felt the isolation of no longer being allowed to meet with colleagues and friends.

"Alexandria, Virginia, during the COVID pandemic, was akin to Berkeley and San Francisco. We have a radical school board; a liberal mayor, Justin Wilson; and an extreme city council. We're deep blue. The Democrats were happy to close schools for as long as possible and were deeply angry with the unmasking position [Virginia] governor [Glenn] Youngkin put forth," says Julie. The newly elected Youngkin kicked off his term by signing nine executive orders and two executive directives. One of those orders stated that parents with children in public schools "may elect for their children not to be subject to any mask mandate in effect at the child's school or educational program."[211]

The school district filed a lawsuit against Youngkin to remove the mask mandate–lifting executive order. "To demonstrate how misguided the school district is in Alexandria, Virginia, one need only to look at the demographic most in harm's way. Public schools are majority minority. A very strained socioeconomic group makes up the largest part of public school, qualifying for free lunch. Instead of spending the money on school services, they spent it on a lawsuit to uphold masks, which they could have worn at their discretion anyway," says Julie.

What happened in Alexandria is no mystery. As in most other places in America, specifically Democratic enclaves, no aspect of life was left untouched in Alexandria beginning in March 2020. The Colonial city was reimagined. Names of roads, buildings, and schools were changed to downplay Colonial history. CRT was implemented not just in schools but community-wide. However, the woke Democratic agenda hit the skids with respect to tourism, revenues from which pad the local government's coffers. "People come from all over the country and world to see the home of George Washington," says Julie.

George Washington is chief among the figures that the Left loves to hate. He's a Founding Father, white, and Anglican, and his name is synonymous with the creation of America. He also owned slaves, as was common during that period in history throughout the world and among whites, Asians, and blacks.[212] But revising history is paramount for CRT ideology and acolytes, so addressing the origins of slavery, its prevalence throughout the world, and the fact that it still goes on in over 150 countries, *all* of which are outside white Judeo-Christian America and white Christian Europe and inside Africa, Asia, and the Middle East (with the exclusion of Israel), is completely ignored.[213]

Under the auspices of CRT, everything that started in 1776 with the creation of America as we know it must be rejected and "reimagined" because white Christian men were the founders and everything is tainted with racism under that construct. The law, government, education, culture and entertainment, climate, housing, the nuclear family, academic and job standards, time, math, science, classic literature and music, academic grades— everything and anything must be repudiated in order to start to chip away at fictitious systemic racism. However, *just* doing this isn't enough; CRT demands that black people be given preferential treatment, whites be punished, and Asians be ignored. As an inherently racist system, it's failing. Americans, as is their history, reject racism. America's bedrock is a meritocracy.

The American experiment was successful for more than two hundred years. It was long understood that the success of that experiment was a break from aristocracy and the divine right to be placed at the top of society. The American experiment was to allow merit to succeed and eventually lead. That was long understood to be American exceptionalism—that is, it existed only in America and not in any other country.[214] The mantra of the Obama/Biden administration was that America wasn't exceptional and that fundamentally transforming it was key. That's the basis of removing merit in favor of so-called diversity, under the guise of rejecting white supremacy.

Even though "reimagining" America started long before Obama and Biden, it was brought to the public's attention with the pervasive Marxist policies and rhetoric of these two presidents. Right after COVID hit the United States in March 2020, the Left unleashed BLM, which mainstreamed CRT. During these times that were inhospitable to education, all three of Julie's kids were enrolled in public school—two in elementary school and one in middle school.

"Mid-March 2020, I was told schools will close just for a short amount of time, just a couple of weeks, and resume after recess. Obviously, this wasn't the case, and school buildings remained closed past spring break. I was allowed to go to classrooms to pick up our school items, and received a packet of paper worksheets. The kids had Chromebooks, and we did our best to assemble online classes. This went on through mid-June 2020. It was a disaster—a combination of being completely confused and frustrated, to being made to feel bad if I asked a question to the school administration," says Julie.

There were two phrases that the teachers would repeat when Julie inquired about the timeline for the resumption of in-person education, which irked her to no end: "This is uncharted territory" and "Give us grace."

"We knew something was happening in March 2020. We were all patient. We gave them grace. But that phrase, after a protracted period of time, when the school year was coming to an end and there was no word on what would be [happening] the following year, was wielded like a shut-up tactic. It was meant to silence the parents from asking questions, and it felt inhumane," says Julie. She was angered by the terrible communication. "On top of this, there was zero empathy given to the parents and students; it was all eaten up by the educators fawning over themselves. It became 'Teachers are heroes' and nothing else. I have a job and am the luckiest of most of the struggling parents, able to work from home and be present for my children, but it was so difficult, and we got no reciprocal empathy from school or mention of heroism. We got the opposite treatment—that of annoyances, rubes, and enemies," Julie says.

As accomplished, politically savvy, and financially and personally fortunate as Julie was, even she was starting to lose it. "I wrote the teachers with questions and received an automated email response saying that they were out of the office. This happened frequently enough for me to take my questions to the next level; I wrote to the school board. When I got the 'Give us grace' retort, that was it. Teachers are still supposed to be pretending they're teaching the kids. The canned, generated responses, as families are untethered, just waiting for anything—a word, something—was galling. It was like they convened with legal to figure out how to collectively blow people off. This even happened when I wrote to the superintendent," Julie recounts. For eighteen months, she was kept in the dark and at bay.

Julie was keeping tabs. She never received a call from the principal of the elementary school, which has fewer than four hundred kids. No one checked in on the families to see how they were coping. Parents like Julie recount how they felt acutely disconnected from the school community, members of which had hammered home the importance of the school community prior to March 2020, insisting that it was a second family. Now, that second family wanted a divorce in absentia. Julie felt like it was an "us against them" mentality that was created by the educational complex's abominable communication, lack of transparency, growing and visceral disdain for the parents, and genuine desire to not reopen schools.

"The teachers didn't give a crap about my kids. I can crank out three thousand calls in a couple of days. They had eighteen months. I checked in with other parents; they never got calls either," Julie says.

The situation was deteriorating rapidly between Julie and one of her sons' math teachers. It was so emotionally charged that Julie wept when she was finally able to get the principal on the phone and relay some of the issues. The math teacher was constantly late to the online classes, wouldn't participate in the chatroom questions, and created breakout rooms where other kids from the class would teach minus an educator's presence. Many of the parents complained, and all were summarily ignored. "The principal listened but said nothing constructive or of value," laments Julie.

As late as mid-June 2020, no one had a clue if school would be reopening after Memorial Day. "School wouldn't tell us, and the federal government failed to lead. Power was outsourced to the unelected bureaucrats in the CDC, which the public later found out was bullied into submission by the teachers' unions that didn't want to go back to in-person learning," says Julie. Her stress level was crescendoing, compounded by the fact that one of her sons had special needs.

"My eldest has an IEP [individual education plan, required by law. In late August, two weeks prior to the resumption of school, necessary material and prompts to help my son organize were supposed to be set in place for the academic year. I met with the seventh-grade principal and was horrified to find out that no plan to accommodate him [was in place]. This is on the heels of nearly six months of isolation, from March to August, which for children with special needs was calamitous," says Julie.

Many moms like Julie, who have children with special needs, faced especially cruel scenarios at the hands of the Biden administration and Democratic local leaders farming out leadership decisions to unelected globalist bureaucrats like the WHO (World Health Organization) and CDC (Centers for Disease Control and Prevention) during the COVID pandemic. The CDC's website says, "In 2020–21, the number of students ages 3–21 who received special education services under the Individuals with Disabilities Education Act (IDEA) was 7.2 million, or 15 percent of all public school students. Among students receiving special education services, the most common category of disability was specific learning disabilities, 33 percent." The CDC also states, "Early childhood programs and systems report that early identification of developmental delays and disabilities among children from birth to age 5 years have been greatly impacted by the COVID pandemic."

Despite the volume of children most at risk and its own admission as to the dangers of what shutting down in-person learning created for all children, the CDC forged ahead. Data corroborates what mothers knew and stated to deaf ears from the beginning: the learning loss would be profound and would never be recouped.[215]

Children born during the pandemic have "significantly reduced verbal, motor, and overall cognitive performance compared to children born pre-pandemic."[216] Prior to shutdowns, children averaged an IQ of one hundred. Scores plummeted to an average of seventy-eight for babies born during the pandemic.[217] The reasons why are obvious. Researchers at Brown University compared the verbal, motor, and overall cognitive skills of infants born in 2020 and 2021 with those born from 2011 to 2019 and found that "males and children with mothers with lower educational attainment, used as a proxy for socioeconomic status (SES), suffered greater losses. The researchers postulated that the environmental changes, especially less parental availability, contributed to the decline."[218]

As per the *New York Post*, "Student test scores plunged in the US as the COVID pandemic erased decades of academic progress—with math scores recording their largest decrease ever and reading scores at a 30-year low, alarming new data known as the 'nation's report card.[219] No state or big city notched any improvements on national math tests—while kids on the cusp of high school were particularly impacted, according to results from the National Assessment of Educational Progress."

We can never forget that the CDC as well as Democratic elected officials were cowed by the teachers' unions into keeping schools closed. Collectively, educators refused. Those in the most innocent subset of an already vulnerable group were grotesquely treated like political prisoners. The dramatic learning loss due to lack of consistent, Monday-through-Friday, morning-to-afternoon class time is criminal. And to date, no one has faced accountability, let alone issued an apology.

"We pulled my oldest son going into seventh grade due to lack of accommodations for a special needs child, which are required by law. They were so cold about it. How do you teach a kid to hold a pen virtually?" asks Julie. She feels the schools were intentionally vague about timelines and intentions for fear of being sued and having to mitigate an influx of parental concerns and critiques.

Julie was incensed when the Alexandria City Public Schools division allowed two city nonprofits to run babysitting services inside the very schools that were shut down. "Thousands of dollars were given so that parents could drop kids off with a mask and sit at desks six feet apart and do Zoom. It was completely hypocritical and another instance of illogical 'science' and amorphous rules. The CDC says no to school but yes to nonprofit organizations costing thousands so that rich parents can get a measure of help," says Julie.

In September 2021, Julie traveled the difficult road many moms with multiple kids journeyed during the pandemic: different schools, different schedules, and different academic programs.

She pulled her oldest son out of the educational complex due to the lack of educational support he needed, and decided to homeschool. Her middle child was slated to return to public school, but tone-deaf and unforgivable propaganda necessitated a game-plan change. "On August 10, 2021, there was an orientation for middle school on Zoom. The dean of students had for his screen background a poster that read, 'Black lives matter,' 'Womens [sic] lives matter,' 'Climate change exists,' and other political statements in an environment that isn't supposed to be political. After what moms and children have been put through due to politics, I said, 'I'm done with this school district,'" says Julie.

Her middle son was enrolled in an online Catholic school. "We would have done in-person but missed the deadline—all families did, because once again, communication was terrible," she says. Her youngest remained in public school.

"The comparison between the two virtual schools, private Catholic versus public, was startling. My middle son in Catholic school had worksheets, homework, no breakout rooms, and was constantly on the screen with a teacher. There was collaboration amongst the students and interaction with a present educator that took the job seriously. There was accountability and parental involvement. Classic literature was read, students wrote reports, and class discussions ensued. They memorized poems and plays, and the curriculum was rigorous. For my youngest in public school elementary, there were no printouts, no homework, no feedback, and a barely there teacher. The report cards were a canned sentence and not individualized. It was like *Lord of the Flies*, each kid for him- or herself. Why? Because a public school teacher's job is secure, and so accountability isn't a concern," says Julie. She ended up hiring math tutors for her youngest son, which cost a fortune.

Julie says her worst moment occurred when she requested worksheets and supplementary answers so she could check her son's competence. The teacher provided all the wrong answers. On top of this, her youngest son's grades improved, inexplicably. "He went from a two to a three. Why? My hypothesis is that grades were rounded up to shut up the parents," concludes Julie.

"We had a stabbing murder of a child. We also had a shootout between kids during a lunch break at a McDonald's close to school. Weapons, including guns, have been confiscated. There are regular massive brawls within the public school, whereby both teachers and students have been injured. We had a gang rape in middle school, which happened at school in the bathroom once schools reopened. We even closed down due to a fatal stabbing three weeks prior to graduation. SRO [school resource officers] were removed because of BLM and the defunding-police mentality; the radical city council did what BLM told them to do," says Julie.

It wasn't *just* the degraded class time that was so troubling; it was the curriculum. Julie notes the complete academic shift post–George Floyd. The superintendent introduced diversity training books for parents; one of the authors was Bettina Love. Unsurprisingly, she's a professor at Teachers College, Columbia University, home base of the teachers spouting CRT. Love has been credited with coining the term "abolitionist teaching" in schools."[220] Another author the superintendent encouraged parents to read was Ibram X. Kendi, who wrote *How to Be an Antiracist* and *How to Raise an Antiracist*. Rounding out the list of racist nonracist books was Robin DiAngelo's *White Fragility*, in which DiAngelo posits that all white people are racists, including fetuses. She says, "As a white person, you were born into a racialized hierarchy, the forces of which had been operating in your life before you even took that first breath and every breath." She is a *New York Times* bestselling author. If it weren't for schools forcing these loads to read, these authors would be out of a career.

"I was concerned by the books; they were current pieces with crude plots, lacking in character development and simply written. There were no classics. Everything was woke and supplementing the Democrat agenda to 'reimagine,'" Julie says.

Race-baiting has been one of the biggest financial grifts of all time. University and grade-school administrators and school boards and corporate human resources offices mandate or strongly encourage people to read the works of authors spouting racism. Unsurprisingly, tracking down the vast sums professional grievance collectors and racists charge, is difficult. Showing how rich they've become off of sowing discord doesn't jive with showing how terrible Capitalism is and how minorities are systemically oppressed. Bettina Love was paid $11,000 for a speaking event organized by the Deputy Education Secretary Cindy Marten, who headed the San Diego school system.[221] Ibram X. Kendi, one of the highest-paid activists, has an estimated $75 million in combined earnings. He charges $25,000 for a one-hour presentation.[222] Robin DiAngelo has amassed over $2 million. For a sixty- to ninety-minute keynote, she charges $30,000; for a two-hour workshop, she charges $35,000; and for a half-day event, she charges $40,000.[223]

Julie also opted her son out of sex education because the educators could no longer be trusted.

She says the path forward is to defund the teachers' unions. "Every single educational dollar provided by states should go to families," she maintains. This will introduce and spur competition and revolutionize education in America. Schools that have a classical model with religion and serious athletics churned out students that fared better during the COVID lockdowns. The students were held to higher standards and had structure, and as a result were more content than those in public schools.

"Taxpayers spend approximately eighteen thousand dollars per public school child annually in Alexandria, Virginia, for a child without special needs.[224] They spend thirty-six thousand dollars for a public school child with special needs. The needs of all these children are statistically not being met," says Julie. Moms shouldn't be the only ones disgusted. All taxpayers should take issue with the financial malfeasance; subpar education creates an economic calamity down the line for employers as well as for the government, which then has to provide assistance.

Parents are now grappling with a manmade situation that schools have normalized: children are now accustomed to being online all day. Smart devices and computers have replaced family. It was an easy substitution during lockdowns, as parents were working and were overextended emotionally, physically, and financially. Their defenses went down. Screens were not as prevalent among kids pre-COVID due to time spent away from home in school, sports, and after-school clubs and with friends. Then for two years screens were readily available, as kids were stuffed in a bedroom literally left to their own devices.

Julie maintains that there's a real issue with parental neglect, lack of discipline, and lack of instilling the importance of being an upstanding member of civil society. "Schools have become social welfare centers. You drop your kid off at seven a.m., which is called 'before care.' They get food because feeding kids is fundamental. Then there's actual school, lunch, and wellness centers so that teenagers who need condoms or STD assistance can be taken care of minus parental notification. This system really begs an answer to the question 'Why do we need parents?'" says Julie.

Julie wishes she had intervened at school sooner, pre-COVID. "But they lied; they told me things were great. Parents are okay with the lying because wrapping one's head around the alternative, the truth, is too much to bear," says Julie. "For thirty-six thousand dollars, my eldest son attended public school through seventh grade. It was terrible, but he got good grades. When he finished school in June 2020 and I got him assessed by a for-profit called Fusion, and spent thousands of dollars on math assessment just for his seventh-grade performance, I learned he was *just* proficient in fourth-grade math." She continues, "The summer prior to his first year of homeschooling in September 2021, we reviewed fourth- and fifth-grade math. Then he spent the first year homeschooling for eighth grade doing fifth- and sixth-grade math. I was lied to; he got good grades in public school! I was told, 'He's set, ready for pre-algebra.'" She encourages parents to face the truth before it's too late.

Julie stresses that her job, her time in politics, and her work writing about moms and parenting issues prepared her better than most for the reaction to COVID, and yet she too couldn't imagine how bad things really were. "Special education is a disaster. My work in policy for over thirty years, knowing about the teachers' union, the mess of public schools, and the bloated administrative monster afforded me the luxury of instantly making a decision to pull my son. Taxpayer money goes to diversity officers, building offices for the superintendent, directors of new and unnecessary positions like equity officers and SEL staff trained to tell white kids they're bad and Black kids are victims. Liberals can't admit that shit is screwed up; they can't admit it because then the entire house of cards falls. It's supported by the left-wing apparatus," says Julie. She maintains that BLM, climate change, and other politicized movements are weapons used to hold families hostage.

Julie is optimistic that a revolution by parents vis-à-vis kindergarten through twelfth-grade education is underway. Parents can no longer ignore what they see, from the below–grade-level proficiency to the violence to CRT. Massive changes have already begun.

Homeschooling increased from 5.4 percent in spring 2020 to 11.1 percent in fall 2021, according to the U.S. Census Bureau.[225] According to an Education Week analysis, since January 2021, forty-four states have introduced bills or taken other initiatives to restrict teaching CRT or limit how teachers can discuss racism and sexism.[226] Eighteen states have imposed bans and restrictions either through legislation or other means.[227] Also, approximately 270 school boards have been flipped to represent pro–parent rights members.[228] But the battle is *just* beginning. There are sixteen thousands eight hundred school districts in America, and until all of these are flipped, no family is safe from the poisonous CRT ideology that strips rights from parents and erases merit from the classroom.[229]

As to the cost for speaking out and being a torchbearer in the battle to save the nation's kids, Julie is unfazed. "I have a tight-knit family. When I go on outlets like Fox News, my kids pay the price for my political views," she says. But the stakes are too high to remain quiet or passive.

Julie is clear that she will not compromise. A growing number of moms that weren't previously politically active or even aware of what CRT is are paying attention now. "Education is a bridge connecting moms from all walks of life who reject the creation of an underclass," says Julie.

# CHAPTER 12:
# OLIVIA BARNARD

**TRUSTEE FOR THE DRIPPING SPRINGS INDEPENDENT SCHOOL DISTRICT IN TEXAS (NEAR AUSTIN). FORTY-FIVE-YEAR-OLD SINGLE MOM OF ONE SON, AGE NINE; LIVES IN AUSTIN. REPUBLICAN.**

Since the November 2022 midterm elections, only one issue in particular has shaken the Biden administration: school boards.[230] It's the canary in the coal mine for what is to come. The Democrats' proxies, the mainstream media and unelected bureaucrats, are tied to woke ideology that is inculcated in children starting in nursery school and going up through higher education; they've gone all-in against parents vying for the formerly little-known posts. So critical are these spots within the small boards, however, that they're now being hotly contested, with races getting nationwide attention.

While Republicans are smarting over the lack of the big red wave that was predicted for 2022, many within the party, still in the fetal position, have lost sight of the big issue that they *did* win on. Many pro–parental rights moms have been elected to school boards, and there are approximately thirteen thousand eight hundred public school districts in the United States.[231] Not only have seats been won, but in some cases, the majority of a given school board has been flipped to pro–parental rights members.

The Democrats saw the revolution coming and did everything possible to try and stop it. The mainstream media hosts tried to ward off conservative-leaning prospective candidates, calling them things like "crazy," "racist," and "conspiracy theorist." The Biden administration unleashed the United States attorney general, Merrick Garland, and concerned moms and dads were labeled "domestic terrorists."[232] The president of the 1.7-million-member-strong American Federation of Teachers, Randi Weingarten, even weighed in, echoing Garland's aspersion.[233]

It was a warning that basically was, "Don't you fucking dare. Parents, moms: shut up, sit down, and toe the line; we own your kids." Calling concerned parents "domestic terrorists" was meant to dissuade parents from going to school board meetings, voicing criticism, forming grassroots factions, and from running to become a member.

A single mom of one son, Olivia Barnard dared. Running as a first-time candidate for school board in Austin, Texas, she looked the behemoth in the face and repeated the refrain that has now become synonymous with the pro–parental rights movement and said, "I don't coparent with the government." In May 2022, she was elected to the school board and became a trustee for the nearby Dripping Springs Independent School District.

Olivia wasn't the only mom fighting back against tyrannical anti-parent Democrats. On November 8, 2022, the party was knocked down a peg. While it hasn't lost its monopoly on the school boards, its reign is coming to an end. It's hard to rule something that is supposed to be geared toward education and families when the message is anti-parent and the actions repudiate education and the nuclear family.

The Democrats, realizing they had lost the group they demonized, came up with a decision. It wasn't to do an about-face, offer an apology or an explanation, or attempt to recruit the moms back to team Democrat, where they'd happily been for decades.

These sick and twisted stunts and financial malfeasance are what has galvanized moms like Olivia. When she ran for school board, she didn't fully grasp all the military maneuvers, mudslinging, and budgetary obligations, or the lay of the land. However, she was in command of the issue at stake and the one the unions have squelched: the kids. She realized the Democrats' goal: a hostile takeover of ground zero; militarizing the Left's next foot soldiers, kids, where they spend the most time outside of the home: in school.

Olivia is proof that one doesn't have to be a seasoned political player to get involved. "I never attended a school board meeting. I thought those serving on the board are glorified school monitors," she says. But in 2020, Olivia perceptively saw the power these tiny boards wielded over the entire community and, when put together, the nation. She opted not to make her first foray into politics at the state or federal level; those are expensive and difficult races to run and win. Olivia understood that the school board is the inflection point.

Olivia grew up in Tulsa, Oklahoma, and was raised by her father. "My mother left when I was eight or nine years old," she says. The environment in her household was nonpolitical but centered around conservative values.

From the age of nine, Olivia started working, pounding the pavement with a little red wagon to sell ice cream around the neighborhood. By the time she was sixteen years old, she was working full-time. "A truancy officer called my dad. I was in retail, selling boots and jeans," she says.

Whether selling ice cream or clothing, Olivia was activated by forging relationships. She learned how to listen and pick up on social cues. She perfected the subtle art of filling a void, providing something that the customer wants or doesn't realize he or she wants yet. Olivia's confidence blossomed. She became resilient, okay with not closing a deal, learning from the rejection and figuring out how to close the next time. "Connecting with people and building relationships is addictive. I received 3 percent on sales commission, and knowing that I alone controlled how much money I'd reap was intoxicating. The harder I worked, the more money I made," says Olivia.

Economizing, budgeting, and contributing to her household were instructional. In her formative years, Olivia dealt with life lessons of abandonment from one parent, and developed an understanding of the values of family, hard work, and sharing household responsibilities. These life skills shape how one runs one's own household as well as a position on a school board.

Every mom knows the power of "no." Buying anything and everything results in bankruptcy and debt. When one works and makes money, spending that money is an exercise in judgment. People who don't live off others, who are self-sufficient, don't spend more than what they have in order to avoid financial ruin. School boards and government employees have lost sight of or never understood Economics 101. This is likely due to a combination of factors. First, the sorry educational system likely doesn't explain economics. Second, entering the political arena without ever having working experience or a family for which to provide makes grasping simple economics difficult. School boards and politicians play with and waste other people's money. For doing so, they receive a salary funded by taxpayers.

Despite the economy's being a top issue for voters in the November 2022 midterm elections, change is incremental.[234] The rot is deep and wide. Powerful and wealthy globalists have a vice grip on the media, elected officials, and unelected bureaucrats, and are unwilling to cede control. The moms have to wrestle to unseat them. Financial derelicts haven't been fired for their failure. In fact, too many have been rewarded.

The economy—along with education, as the two subjects are intertwined—has made moms more politically engaged than ever.

Olivia understood economics at an early age. After high school, she went to Oklahoma State; she followed her boyfriend. "However, I didn't graduate college; I was too busy working in the real world," says Olivia.

In 1998, Olivia's work transferred her to Austin, Texas. She had a seven-year track record of success and was valuable to her employer. "I was able to buy my first house at twenty-three years of age. I bought a brand-new cute home right from the builder. I have never relied on men or the government. *Nada*," remarks Olivia. "This just doesn't happen now," she adds.

Olivia is right; skyrocketing home prices and soaring interest rates have destroyed the American Dream. First-time homebuyers are at an all-time low, according to the National Association of Realtors (NAR). Moreover, those able to afford a home are older than ever before due to a burgeoning lack of affordability. The average age of first-time homebuyers has gone up in one year, from 2021 to 2022, from thirty-three to thirty-six. First-time buyers accounted for 26 percent of all homebuyers in June 2022, down from 34 percent the year, before according to NAR's 2022 report on homebuyers and sellers. That was the lowest in the survey's forty-one-year history.[235]

Olivia seemed to do everything early: enter the workforce, move to a different state, move forward on a major investment. A family member's death came early to her as well. In 1999, after she closed on her house, her father suddenly died. "The only parent that ever raised me was gone. It was a life-changing moment, and I reevaluated a lot. Death does that," she says.

Olivia changed her career and got into homebuilding. She experienced professional heartbreaks but ultimately did well and climbed the ladder. She created a life for herself. She got married in 2010 and had a son in 2014. However, her union didn't last, and when her son was still in diapers and not yet two years old, she filed for divorce. "I married a broken person. There was just no saving the relationship. Moms, we're survivors; we just know what to do when it comes time to save our children," says Olivia.

Divorce and a layoff came simultaneously. After seventeen years in homebuilding, Olivia was once again in the position of reevaluating her life and figuring out how to pay the bills. She was a newly single mom of a toddler and someone who had always been self-sufficient. At forty years old, she went into general real estate. "It felt like everything was conspiring to break me. But I couldn't give up or give in. I have a son," says Olivia.

In fact, it was the beginning of a realignment. Looking for a sign, she prayed, reflected, and meditated. A vision came to her when she was at her lowest point. Scared, without family or a support system, and the sole provider for her son, she surrendered to something she couldn't see but could feel: a vision. "An equation came to me: $\frac{1}{2} = 2X$. I went into my closet, took out a lipstick, and wrote it down. I didn't know what it meant. It was just a feeling, an inner calling telling me to remember this formula," Olivia recalls.

Inexplicably, blessing after blessing graced Olivia. "No one goes into general real estate and has success," she says. The work is grueling, sometimes necessitating up to one hundred hours per week. For all three types of real estate—vacant land, residential properties, and commercial properties—selling demands nonstop hustle. Olivia, having worked for almost her entire life, put all the skills she'd picked up along the way into her new endeavor. "I literally built a beautiful life for my son through sheer resilience, indefatigableness, and gratitude for all my blessings. I didn't come from money, a home with two parents, or a cushion. Nothing stopped me," she notes. By the end of her first year of business, when she looked at her 1099 tax document, she got chills. "I made two times what I was formerly making. It was the equation

I had written with my lipstick when I was searching for a sign," says Olivia.

Both at home and at work, Olivia was on an upward trajectory. She had no reason to complain, and if she did have a reason, kept it to herself. She epitomizes the traits that many successful people have in common: determination and the ability to readjust, self-evaluate, and come up with solutions. As a result, she kept attracting more abundance.

Then 2020 hit and put all of Olivia's hard work in jeopardy. The real estate market was impacted like everything else during the pandemic. As a single mom and sole provider, she had no other source on which to rely for financial or childcare help.

"The night of the election changed everything for me. I knew we were in trouble. This is where formerly esoteric situations, like the election of a president, generally don't impact individuals in acute ways. Americans have always been able to thrive during my lifetime, no matter who was in the White House. But this was entirely different," says Olivia. She knew Biden's assumption of the presidency was going to hit home and affect her community— and certainly affect her family.

Olivia lives in the closest suburb to Austin, Texas. Austin, the state's capital, has an estimated population of 961,855.[236] It's part of Travis, Hays, and Williamson counties. In a red state representing cowboys, the wild west, and freedom, Olivia lives in a city that is so blue it gives the most radical places in California a run for their money. What's interesting about Texas is that it highlights perfectly what different-party rule looks like within one state.

On March 6, 2020, Austin, Texas, mayor Steve Adler, a Democrat, declared a local state of disaster for the city, activating the city's Emergency Operations Plan.[237] Austin was determined to be at an orange level of danger, or Stage 4. Somehow it evaded the most serious Stage 5. During the time of orange, Adler recommended that everyone stay home, avoid gatherings of more than ten people, and skip nonessential travel. To show what a true believer in these recommendations he was, Adler hopped on a plane to celebrate his daughter's wedding in Mexico during this time.

Austin schools were shut down. So were businesses. "All of my relationships changed. So many of my friends were wholly accepting of situations that made zero sense, and were closed off to asking or receiving questions. I isolated and established like-minded relationships with people across the country and even the world. Instagram was my lifeline. I'm the most social loner you will ever meet," says Olivia.

Humans thirst for connection. So although experts have warned that screen time is hazardous, it became the lifeline for many. Trailblazers in technology such as Steve Jobs have talked about the strict boundaries on technology they enforced when raising their own kids. Google CEO Sundar Pichai also enforced strict limits on his children's time in front of the screen. But lockdowns caused experts citing experts to change the experts' positions.

For all the negative effects of screen time—zoned-out kids addicted to social media, the mainstreaming of different identity groups, the encouragement of gender transitioning, the showcasing of the sexual exploitation of children—it did do some good. People like Olivia, following friends in New York City or Los Angeles, were able to see how different and terrible things were as opposed to what was being reported. Via citizen journalists, photographers, and videographers, they saw the gruesome reality that journalists weren't reporting because it went against the Left's agenda, which mainstream media supports. "I was supposed to go to New York City in 2020, but I saw the never-ending lines of people being spaced six feet apart and checked over by security at grocery stores. I saw the city transformed, vandalized, dirtied, and menacing during BLM riots. Seeing these images on Instagram caused me to cancel my trip," says Olivia.

Olivia wasn't political prior to 2016. "My evolution really came in 2020," she says. "I was the biggest Trump supporter. I grew up in [the] '80s and '90s, and his life was aspirational. It was the American Dream personified—hard work and the possibility of the beautiful reward. This resonated with me; I've always worked my ass off and am proud about what I've accomplished as a single mother and sole provider. Everyone loved him before he ran. But after he announced, those that had curried his favor and used him for news ratings flipped. It was illogical and screamed of avarice. I watched the debates and was on board with his message. I liked how unlike other politicians, he welcomed everyone into the fold and correctly stated that the war against him is really a war against Americans and American principles."

The debates and the pundits' debate wrap-ups were eye-opening. Olivia couldn't believe how frequently Trump's words were taken out of context and how he was misquoted to foment negative public opinion. Once again, she reevaluated everything, questioning what else the media was lying about—COVID, mandates, BLM, CRT, "social justice," sexual exploitation of children, the climate, the economy, wars?

"Through Instagram, I had been connecting to people who shared similar values," Olivia says. "It was so hard as a conservative just to be [one] during this time. In addition, I started following CPAC [the Conservative Political Action Conference, the nation's original grassroots conservative organization] and bought a ticket to attend my first event of theirs in 2020, not knowing what to expect. It was amidst the world falling apart, media attacks on conservatives, the climate of the election. In retrospect, I was looking to reignite the connection that politicians had done their best to snuff out. CPAC was like coming home; it felt like church camp. I was reunited with my long-lost relatives who I had never met before but knew intimately. We had been speaking via social media, sharing our lives, feelings of despair, hope for the country, and disbelief in what was happening to it—authentic conversations about things that matter most." The relationships she built at this event were like medicine for the soul.

Olivia's life was put under immense strain because of the government, mainstream media, teachers' unions, and unelected bureaucrats. Her son's school, like those around the nation, remained closed after spring break of 2020. The beginning of the new academic year in September 2020 was challenging. "One morning while I was making coffee, my son, age seven at the time, who never cries, broke down. He thrives in structure and is social. He said, 'Mama, I just don't want to live like this.' He was regressing and depressed and couldn't focus online in school, and then once back in school, deal with the masks. I fell to my knees and hugged him. But my consolation didn't feel like enough; people didn't want to do playdates, and I could only arrange for him to play with a couple of his friends. For an only child with a single parent, it was heartbreaking and felt unbearably isolating," recalls Olivia.

In October 2021, Governor Greg Abbott signed an executive order stating that no entity in Texas could mandate a COVID "vaccine" for its employees. Mayor Adler said, "I'm still really confused by the governor's order…that gives directions to private businesses about what they can do in their establishments. I mean, it just seems to me to be really anti-business and a real limitation of the freedoms and liberties for someone [in private business]. I just don't understand it."

Adler doesn't understand—businesses not being able to mandate a questionable vaccine on employees isn't an erosion of freedom or anti-business—it's the opposite. By way of example, New York City hospitals are overrun and short on staff. As per a *New York Post* article, "half the facilities [are] reporting they slashed or eliminated services because of staffing shortages while two-thirds said they're operating in the red, a shocking new industry report reveals."[238] Why? Well, hospital staff was fired or suspended for refusing to comply with COVID vaccine mandates.[239]

Adler was equally flummoxed by the Republican governor's stance on mask mandates. In July 2021, Texas districts were bound by an executive order from Governor Abbott, which banned governmental entities from instituting mask mandates. In July 2021, Adler tweeted, "As the CDC prepares to recommend all K-12 students wear masks, a reminder that @GovAbbott has made it impossible for Texas schools to protect students and for cities to protect its citizens." Adler continued, "Parents, share your concerns with your schools. They need to hear from you."[240]

"Austin is following the San Francisco trajectory: increased crime, homelessness, declining schools. It's all at my doorstep," says Olivia. As of 2022, Austin has the highest homicide rate it has experienced in two decades.[241] Austin police chief Joseph Chacon has said that Austin also has been seeing more aggravated assaults than in previous years.[242] Crime experts have speculated that the increase in violence originates from stress brought on by the pandemic and economic uncertainty.[243] Maybe it has something to do with the Austin city council's 2020 decision to cut about a third of the Austin Police Department's $434 million budget.[244]

As of 2022, homelessness in Austin has ballooned by approximately 20 percent since 2021.[245] Why? According to Redfin data, rents have increased 40 percent in the past year, between 2021 to 2022.[246] This is more than any other metro area in the country and about three times the national average. Also, the population is exploding—not just because of venture capitalists, tech companies, and those gravitating to the vibrant musical scene but because of illegals. According to Pew Research Center, "Austin is among 20 U.S. cities with the largest share of undocumented immigrants."[247] Austin is considered a sanctuary city because it doesn't comply with all federal immigration-related requests.

Laredo, Texas, and other cities overwhelmed by illegals have been busing overflow to Austin. Amid lockdowns, some illegals that were tested came back positive with COVID, contributing to an already overwhelmed hospital system and fraught climate. However, others weren't tested by authorities, causing ire among Austin residents who experienced no such luck. One woman watching a bus pull into an Austin Greyhound station told FOX

7, "These people are not being forced to take a vaccine. They're not being forced to even take a test at all."[248]

Olivia sympathized. Her freedoms, finances, and child were being subjected to amorphous and illogical rules. "The 'Summer of Love' compounded the total insanity. As I watched CNN put forth propaganda that was entirely different from reality, I felt like I was in the Twilight Zone. There was a fork in the road. Those with discernment went one way. Dependents, those needing to be told how to think, went the other way," Olivia says.

The restriction of freedom, the closure of school, the change of school philosophy, and the Democrats' creating BLM to insert CRT led Olivia to activate. "I thought of the stolen election, cities burning to the ground, and the school boards taking in all these events and not improving education and strengthening the community, but weakening both. I thought, 'This is the atmosphere in which I'm sending my son back to school,'" says Olivia.

"I never attended a school board meeting. I thought the members are glorified school monitors," she recalls. And she had moved specifically to her district because of school. Suddenly, she no longer trusted the seven school board members tasked with making decisions that impacted the entire community. "Half the community was fighting to be masked; half was fighting for freedom to choose. Then, amidst this mayhem, some teachers flirted with CRT and politicizing events," she says.

A few educators brought their personal ideologies into their workspace, the school's classrooms. During Black History Month, a teacher hung a poster in pre-K acknowledging the accomplishments of blacks. Everyone pictured on the poster was progressive: there was a sex worker, a transgender LGBTQ activist, and Colin

Kaepernick, among others. "I wrote the principal and superintendent, saying that a sex worker and transgender person shouldn't be featured in a poster displayed in a pre-K classroom," Olivia says. "I suggested other transformative Black figures—Candace Owens, Ben Carson, etc. What happened was an education fail: the poster was just taken down rather than highlighting Black people that weren't only on one side of the political aisle. The educator put up something that was an indoctrination tool and clearly wasn't interested in highlighting Blacks, but instead highlighting a woke agenda."

As mentioned, prior to 2020, Olivia, like so many others, never thought about the school board. She had no clue about its responsibility, the roles of the members, and the power it wielded over an entire community and really the nation, as it is funded by taxpayers. The reason being that up until COVID and BLM, life for moms and their children wasn't under direct threat by the system the moms fund. Even underperforming public schools at least were open, giving the appearance that educators were teaching and students were learning. While the educational complex left much to be desired, it wasn't actively turning children into racists, victims, and furries (people who identify as animals). Teachers didn't encourage students to lop off private parts or take hormones to become something that is impossible—a member of the opposite sex. There were no mask mandates or FDA-unapproved "vaccines" being forced. There was no support for violent, lawless movements such as BLM; this would previously have been unacceptable in schools.

Because of these manufactured events to gin up division, distraction, and decay, Olivia decided to run for the school board. "It happened organically. Parents approached me," she says.

Olivia was now in the public eye—politically connected and with friends whose names were associated with the populist movement. "Kari [Lake] and I met at a dinner at a private residence right after she announced she was leaving her Fox correspondence [job] and running for governor of Arizona. The dinner was a kickoff to the CPAC Dallas event, so there were lots of people in the movement—donors, candidates, Republicans like me just looking to network. Kari didn't really know anyone, what to wear, and didn't pack accordingly for the three-day event; I didn't either. I introduced myself and told her I've been following her; she was floored, and we exchanged numbers. The next night, driving to my first CPAC event from Austin to Dallas, realizing I had forgotten makeup, I pulled into a CVS drugstore; I loaded up on lipsticks and mascaras. While getting ready, I get this frantic text from Kari saying that she too had forgotten to bring mascara, and asked if I had any extra. This is how we bonded and established a true friendship—moms saving each other with a tube of mascara. For both of us, what woke us up was the media, the censorship, propaganda, and suppression. The rest is history. I went to Mar-a-Lago twice and then to Arizona for her campaign events. I was there so many times, including for primary and election night."

The parents who asked Olivia to run likely regarded her as an outspoken and unafraid ally in the fight to confront the zeitgeist and polarizing issues, based on her social circle and public positions. Olivia champions parental rights and shows steely resolve against unscientific mandates and Marxist CRT. "I didn't consider myself brave, just rooted in common sense and steadfast in stating the obvious," she says. Being authentic, taking a risk, and being outspoken when so many who felt the same way stayed quiet caused a ripple effect. Olivia's network of like-minded people grew.

"The parents that had asked me to run and I shared an unwavering belief that school boards must keep school buildings open for operation and mask-free. Our rights don't end where someone else's rights begin," says Olivia.

Two seats on the Dripping Springs school board were up for election. Four candidates were vying for these two seats, two Democrats and two Conservatives. Four debates were held so the community could hear from the contenders.

The Conservative Party organized. Olivia took on this challenge like she had taken on everything else: she set a goal, familiarized herself with the role, and came up with a plan to win.

A quick learner, Olivia immediately began to build a brand. Initially, she did a lot of listening and little talking, making sure she understood what the moms cared about most. With that information, she made videos addressing the issues, her positions, and plans. She attended candidate forums held by the Republican Party as well as by the PTA (parent-teacher association); she networked and she learned. Technology-savvy, Olivia tagged the other conservatives in her community consistently on social media, making them part of the conversation and recruiting them to her side. She understood that the campaign was about the other moms and that she was just the vessel delivering their message.

"It was a true team effort. It's important to understand how many are on the board and what motivates the people. I was challenged; I didn't make my personal [social media] page private. I resisted ever doing that; choosing to be honest about what I do, what I stand for, and what my life represents was important. I support candidates like Kari. I am who I am, and I stayed public," states Olivia. She returned every message and email.

For staying public, Olivia paid a price. "There's a group of white liberal women that attack me to this day. I was called a racist, fascist, and book banner. However, they did leave my son and business alone, for which I was grateful," she notes.

The Dripping Springs school board is made up of a team of eight—seven board members plus a superintendent. They decide how to allocate the budget and adopt and implement the curriculum for eight thousand people.

Olivia is now one of the board members. She won the race in May 2022. Her post is for three years and is an unpaid position. "First and foremost, the board was welcoming and the community is wonderful. Campaigning was brutal. I was smeared by detractors. But after I won, we all carried on with the business at hand," she says.

"There are two board meetings per month; nothing keeps me from them. Outside of my son, it's my priority. I also keep everyone in the loop, am diligent with correspondence and transparent. I'm hell-bent on keeping the other members accountable so that we stay open, mask-free, and focus on strong academics. I follow the chain of command; conversations start with the teacher and then the principal. I always keep communication respectful; this is a basic life skill and how you recruit people," says Olivia.

After Olivia's win, she did an interview with Mercedes Schlapp, who served as director of strategic communications for President Trump and is the wife of Matt Schlapp, the chairman of CPAC. Mercedes opened the interview by referencing a statement that a spokesperson from the Department of Education (DOE) told Fox News, citing "global warming" as a reason to revert back to online "education." A spokesman for the DOE said, "No one is immune from the impacts of climate change."[249]

Olivia is clear on the problem. She says, "That government can decide to shut down schools is terrifying. It's not good for families or communities. Parents need to go to work. Going to school is a safe haven for kids. Based on the evidence—tanking test scores; regression in social, emotional, and behavioral development, it's a travesty that the Democrats have weaponized school and held families hostage."

Indeed, schools are supposed to be under the individual state's auspices, not the auspices of the federal government. Since Democratic leaders closed schools and went remote, American children have had the largest decrease in reading scores in over thirty years.[250] The real issue is that the Democrats, their affiliates, the teachers' unions, and unelected bureaucrats have figured out a sinister way to destroy America, and it's by destroying the children. Not only have children taken a hit from school closures and the CRT ideology, but many parents—and usually the moms, according to Pew Research Center—have left the workforce to become de facto teachers.[251] So Democratic policies have screwed not only education but economics.

Olivia says, "We need to keep politics and social justice out of schools. Governor DeSantis did a phenomenal job. It is not the place of an educator to talk to our children with undeveloped minds about sexual orientation or identity. We need parental involvement more than ever. [Parents] are the key that picks the lock."

This is the path forward. Olivia believes that parents can't complain from the sidelines; they need to speak up and get involved—even when times are good. "We can never be complacent again," she says. "We saw what happened when we were. When we take our foot off the pedal, this is an opportunity for bad actors to seed bad ideas, which take years to undo—maybe decades."

These are her marching orders: "Organize a group of one hundred parents, check in with each other, let them know what's going on in the community; not everyone is up on the current situation, and different teachers and different classes do things differently. Alert your group of one hundred before a school board meeting is scheduled. Maybe only ten will show up, but they'll act as messengers and expand the network. They, too, should look to form a group."

Olivia is focused on the task at hand: being responsible with the budget and catching up children who have lost so much precious education time. She believes the way to bring people together is to start with the truth. The schools' keeping parents in the dark and then lying to them about what was happening vis-à-vis test scores, along with social regression and the implementation of CRT, are what ignited the mom army. To keep the fire burning and the Mom Army engaged, the foundation must be absolute truth. "We can all work together *only* if we agree that kids' physical and mental health is the priority. We can never accommodate a lie. For example, there are only two genders; the sexes *are* different.

Our school district is rooted in the truth with regards to biology, and if it wasn't, I'd find another school district," says Olivia.

This supermom encapsulates the position perfectly. Moms understand how to be soft—but don't mistake that for weakness. They are flexible and will come to the negotiation table, but only if the other seats are occupied by people willing to stick to the truth. There will be no compromise on facts and no compromise on the children.

# ENDNOTES

1   Amin, Reema. "As NYC Is Expected to Spend $38k per Student, Budget Watchdog Calls for Prioritizing 'Critical Services.'" *Chalkbeat New York*, 11 Apr. 2023, ny.chalkbeat. org/2023/4/11/23677827/budget-report-nyc-schools-funding-pupil-spending#:~:text=As%20NYC%20is%20expected%20to,calls%20 for%20prioritizing%20'critical%20services'&text=Students%20 at%20P.S.%2089%20in,the%202023%2D24%20school%20year.

2   Katherine Schaeffer and Ted Van Green, "Key Facts About U.S. Voter Priorities Ahead of the 2022 Midterm Elections," Pew Research Center, November 3, 2022, https://www. pewresearch.org/short-reads/2022/11/03/key-facts-about-u-s-voter-priorities-ahead-of-the-2022-midterm-elections/.

3   Hogan, Bernadette, and Emily Crane. "Mayor Eric Adams Says Biden's Migrant Crisis Has 'destroyed' NYC." *New York Post*, 21 Apr. 2023, nypost.com/2023/04/21/ mayor-eric-adams-says-bidens-migrant-crisis-has-destroyed-nyc/.

4   Christenson, Josh. "Illegal Immigration to Cost New Yorkers $10 Billion in 2023, US $150B: Report." *New York Post*, 21 Mar. 2023, nypost.com/2023/03/20/ illegal-immigration-to-cost-new-yorkers-10-billion-in-2023/.

5   Post Editorial Board, "The Price Tag for COVID School Closures That Led to Historic Learning Losses for Kids Could Top $28 Trillion," *New York Post*, January 1, 2023, https://nypost.

com/2023/01/01/the-price-tag-for-covid-school-closures-could-top-28t/?utm_campaign=iphone_nyp&utm_source=mail_app.

[6] Post Editorial Board, "The Price Tag for COVID School Closures."

[7] "Compton, California," Sperling's Best Places, last accessed May 1, 2023, https://www.bestplaces.net/crime/city/california/compton.

[8] "PTSD Affects Majority of Sexual Violence Survivors," Harvard T. H. Chan School of Public Health, 2020, https://www.hsph.harvard.edu/news/hsph-in-the-news/ptsd-affects-majority-of-sexual-violence-survivors/.

[9] Stephanie Marken and Sangeeta Agrawal, "K-12 Workers Have Highest Burnout Rate in U.S.," Gallup, June 13, 2022, https://news.gallup.com/poll/393500/workers-highest-burnout-rate.aspx.

[10] "Santa Cruz County Community High School," Public School Review, last accessed May 1, 2023, https://www.publicschoolreview.com/santa-cruz-county-community-high-school-profile.

[11] Johnny Magdaleno, "Welcome to the Youth Murder Capital of California," *Vice*, July 27, 2016, https://www.vice.com/en/article/qv55pp/salinas-the-youth-murder-capital-of-california.

[12] Magdaleno, "Welcome to the Youth Murder Capital."

[13] National Center for Education Statistics, "Public High School Graduation Rates," 2022, U.S. Department of Education, Institute of Education Sciences, last accessed May 1, 2023, https://nces.ed.gov/programs/coe/indicator/coi/high-school-graduation-rates#:~:text=Asian%2FPacific%20Islander%20students%20had,Native%20(74%20percent)%20students

[14] Carolyn Jones and John Fensterwald, "Why Some California School Districts Are Changing How Students Earn Grades," *EdSource*, December 3, 2021, updated December 14, 2021, https://edsource.org/2021/why-some-california-school-districts-are-changing-how-students-earn-grades.

[15] Fensterwald and Thomas Peele, "State Delays Public Release of English, Math and Science Test Score Results to Later This Year," *EdSource*, September 22, 2022, https://edsource.org/2022/state-delays-public-release-of-english-math-and-science-test-score-results-to-later-this-year/678462.

16  Peetz, Caitlynn. "Aft Head Weingarten Says Her Union Didn't Conspire with CDC on School Reopening Guidance." *Education Week*, 27 Apr. 2023, www.edweek.org/policy-politics/ aft-head-weingarten-says-her-union-didnt-conspire-with-cdc-on-school-reopening-guidance/2023/04#:~:text=The%20 leader%20of%20one%20of,pandemic%20are%20 %E2%80%9Cpatently%20false.%E2%80%9D.

17  Peetz, Caitlynn. "Aft Head Weingarten Says Her Union Didn't Conspire with CDC on School Reopening Guidance." *Education Week*, 27 Apr. 2023, www.edweek.org/policy-politics/ aft-head-weingarten-says-her-union-didnt-conspire-with-cdc-on-school-reopening-guidance/2023/04#:~:text=The%20 leader%20of%20one%20of,pandemic%20are%20 %E2%80%9Cpatently%20false.%E2%80%9D.

18  Diana Glebova, "Connecticut Private School Excludes White Families from Back-to-School Event," *National Review*, August 3, 2022, https://www.nationalreview.com/news/connecticut-private-school-excludes-white-families-from-back-to-school-event/.

19  Emo Desperado (@JoyAnnReid), "Maybe y'all should choose a different fake analogy for this apparently terrifying graduate level / law school theoretical school of thought that's not being taught in a single K-12 school? Or maybe just have the balls to come at the #1619Project and antiracist education by name…" Tweet, 9:16 PM, June 18, 2021, https://twitter. com/JoyAnnReid/status/1406073254452858884.

20  Caitlin O'Kane, "Head of Teachers Union Says Critical Race Theory Isn't Taught in Schools, Vows to Defend 'Honest History,'" CBS News, July 8, 2021, https://www.cbsnews.com/ news/critical-race-theory-teachers-union-honest-history/.

21  "Study: 1 in 20 Americans Under 30 Identifies as Transgender or Nonbinary," Morning Briefing, KFF Health News, June 9, 2022, https://khn.org/morning-breakout/study-1-in-20-americans-under-30-identifies-as-transgender-or-nonbinary/.

22  Tim Walker, "Survey: Alarming Number of Educators May Soon Leave the Profession," NEA, February 1, 2022,

https://www.nea.org/advocating-for-change/new-from-nea/
survey-alarming-number-educators-may-soon-leave-profession.

23 Casey Eggleston and Jason Fields, "Homeschooling on the Rise
During COVID-19 Pandemic," United States Census Bureau,
March 22, 2021, https://www.census.gov/library/stories/2021/03/
homeschooling-on-the-rise-during-covid-19-pandemic.html.

24 Brian D. Ray, "Research Facts on Homeschooling," National
Home Education Research Institute, March 11, 2023, https://
www.nheri.org/research-facts-on-homeschooling/.

25 Bethany Blankley, "Policy Center: California Spending on K-12
Schools Exceeds $20,000 per Student," *The Center Square*,
March 13, 2020, https://www.thecentersquare.com/california/
policy-center-california-spending-on-k-12-students-exceeds-20-
000-per-student/article_8e68f1be-67aa-11ea-bfde-53c18f4f152e.
html#:~:text=Currently%20California%20taxpayers%20
spend%20roughly,Something%20needs%20to%20change.

26 "Immigration," JoeBiden.com, https://joebiden.com/immigration/.

27 House of Representatives Judiciary Committee, "Jim Jordan:
Joe Biden 'Excited' About 'Going After Parents' with 'Domestic
Terrorism' Letter, 'All About Intimidation,'" press release, June 14,
2022, https://judiciary.house.gov/media/press-releases/jim-jordan-
joe-biden-excited-about-going-after-parents-with-domestic-terrorism.

28 News 19 WLTX, "'The Monster You've Become': Judge criticizes
Alex Murdaugh During Sentencing," YouTube video, 19:55, March
3, 2023, https://www.youtube.com/watch?v=V6o6peFHS-Y.

29 Moms for Liberty, "CNN Calls Moms for Liberty 'a DANGER
to DEMOCRACY,'" YouTube video, 7:17, December 20,
2021, https://www.youtube.com/watch?v=6mdj2HvrrDE.

30 Toboroff, Jacqueline. "Toboroff: No, Joe Biden,
America's Kids Do Not Belong to the to State." *Human
Events*, 26 Apr. 2023, humanevents.com/2023/04/26/
toboroff-no-joe-biden-americas-kids-do-not-belong-the-to-state.

31 Liberty, Moms for. "Moms for Liberty Is Empowering Parents
to Defend Their Parental Rights. Now @IlhanMN Calls @
moms4liberty 'Moms for Dictatorship.' and on Mother's
Day @msnbc Published on Op-Ed Titled 'Happy Mother's

Day to Everyone except Moms For Liberty.' @4tiffanyjustice Weighs in. PIC.TWITTER.COM/SKILUFC8EN." *Twitter*, 17 May 2023, twitter.com/moms4liberty/status/165862663 4583351297?s=43&t=4m81ZAqiS3wTft0NVuSR9w.

[32] Bailey Gallion, "Brevard County School Board Passes Roughly $1.5 Billion Budget; Property Tax Rate Drops," *Florida Today*, September 13, 2022, https://www.floridatoday.com/story/ news/education/2022/09/13/brevard-public-schools-final- 2023-budget-millage-rate-property-tax/8062232001/.

[33] Grace Chen, "An Overview of the Funding of Public Schools," Public School Review, June 22, 2022, https://www.publicschoolreview. com/blog/an-overview-of-the-funding-of-public-schools - :~:text=The last eight percent of,for students that need them.

[34] "Brevard Public Schools," U.S. News, last accessed May 2, 2023, https://www.usnews.com/education/ k12/florida/districts/brevard-112126.

[35] Undercover Mothers, "SEL - The Gateway Drug to CRT and Worse," Substack newsletter, October 17, 2021, https://undercovermother.substack.com/p/ sel-the-gateway-drug-to-crt-and-worse.

[36] Hannah Grossman, "K-12 Curriculum 'Socially Engineering' Millions into Enraged Young 'Social Justice Warriors,' Parents Warn," Fox News, March 21, 2023, https://www.foxnews. com/media/k-12-curriculum-socially-engineering-millions- enraged-young-social-justice-warriors-parents-warn.

[37] Brandon Gillespie, "CNN Reporter Repeats Questionable Claim that Critical Race Theory Is Not Being Taught in Virginia Schools," Fox News, November 3, 2021, https://www.foxnews.com/media/cnn- eva-mckend-claims-critical-race-theory-not-taught-virginia-schools.

[38] John Nichols, "Randi Weingarten Rips CRT Critics for 'Trying to Stop Us from Teaching Students Accurate History,'" *The Nation*, July 9, 2021, https://www.thenation. com/article/society/critical-race-theory-teachers/.

[39] Zara Woodcock, "Sean Penn Compares Being Unvaccinated to 'Pointing Gun in Somebody's Face,'" *Mirror*, August

22, 2021, https://www.mirror.co.uk/3am/celebrity-news/
sean-penn-reiterates-stance-everybody-24814721.

40  "Totals," American Federation of Teachers, Open Secrets,
last accessed May 2, 2023, https://www.opensecrets.org/orgs/
american-federation-of-teachers/totals?id=D000000083.

41  Staff of Ron DeSantis, "Governor DeSantis Emphasizes
Importance of Keeping Critical Race Theory Out of Schools
at State Board of Education Meeting," press release, June 10,
2021, https://www.flgov.com/2021/06/10/governor-desantis-
emphasizes-importance-of-keeping-critical-race-theory-
out-of-schools-at-state-board-of-education-meeting/.

42  National Assessment Governing Board, "Nation's Report
Card Shows National Score Declines in 4th and 8th Grade
Math and Reading," press release, October 24, 2022, https://
www.nagb.gov/news-and-events/news-releases/2022/report-
card-score-decline-4th-8th-grade-math-reading.html.

43  U.S. Department of Education, "Statement by U.S. Secretary of
Education Miguel Cardona on Nation's Report Card," October
24, 2022, https://www.ed.gov/news/press-releases/statement-
us-secretary-education-miguel-cardona-nations-report-card -
:~:text=Since Day One, the Biden, impact on our nation's students.

44  U.S. Department of Education, "Statement by U.S.
Secretary of Education Miguel Cardona."

45  "Endorsements," Moms for Liberty, last accessed May 2,
2023, https://www.momsforliberty.org/endorsements/.

46  Michael Scherer, "Ron DeSantis Leads Charge for More
Coercive Conservative Government," *Washington Post*,
March 10, 2023, https://www.washingtonpost.com/
elections/2023/03/08/ron-desantis-conservatism-government/.

47  Jemima McEnvoy, "14 Days of Protests, 19 Dead," *Forbes*, June 8,
2020, https://www.forbes.com/sites/jemimamcevoy/2020/06/08/14-
days-of-protests-19-dead/?sh=401723ac4de4.

48  LA to Make All Black Lives Matter Mural on Hollywood
Boulevard Permanent," ABC7, August 24, 2020, https://abc7.com/
hollywood-boulevard-blvd-all-black-lives-matter-pride/6386289/.

49  Danielle Wallace, "Santa Monica Police Chief Faces Calls to Resign after Officers Watch Businesses Being Looted, Do Nothing," Fox News, June 2, 2020, https://www.foxnews.com/us/santa-monica-police-chief-petition-resign-looting.

50  Wokeness, End. "'the Numbers Presented Are Accurate'but It's Still Misinformation Because a Graph about Interracial Crime Doesn't Include Non-Interracial Crime PIC.TWITTER.COM/MSDNS3SJ5F." *Twitter*, 10 May 2023, twitter.com/EndWokeness/status/1656371781568176129?cxt=HHwWgoDRhYHXzvwtAAAA.

51  *U.S. Census Bureau Quickfacts: United States*, www.census.gov/quickfacts/fact/table/US/PST045221. Accessed 18 May 2023.

52  "Biden Calls White Supremacy 'most Dangerous Terrorist Threat' in Speech at Howard." *POLITICO*, www.politico.com/news/2023/05/13/biden-howard-university-white-supremacy-terrorism-00096811. Accessed 18 May 2023.

53  News, Fox. "'view' Host Says Being Black or Hispanic 'Does Not Make You Immune' from Being a White Supremacist." *New York Post*, 9 May 2023, nypost.com/2023/05/09/view-host-ana-navarros-racial-comments-surprises-cohosts/.

54  Ayo (fka Opal) Tometi (@ayotometi), "Great day observing 6 polling sites in Venezuela. calm & seamless process. it was beautiful 2 see everyday ppl engaged throughout the day," Tweet, 3:21 PM, December 6, 2015, https://twitter.com/ayotometi/status/673613140697960453.

55  "Hollywood Demographics," Point2 Homes, last accessed May 2, 2023, https://www.point2homes.com/US/Neighborhood/CA/Los-Angeles/Hollywood-Demographics.html.

56  Kevin Rector, "LAPD after George Floyd: Fewer Officers, Fewer Arrests but Hardly Defunded," *Los Angeles Times*, May 30, 2021, https://www.latimes.com/california/story/2021-05-30/george-floyd-protests-altered-landscape-for-lapd.

57  Nation, "2 California Deputies Shot in Apparent Ambush in Patrol Car," PBS, September 13, 2020, https://www.pbs.org/newshour/nation/2-california-deputies-shot-in-apparent-ambush-in-patrol-car.

58  Jessica Corbett, "Protests Over George Floyd's Killing Met with Curfews, Police Crackdowns, and National Guard Troops

Across US," Common Dreams, https://www.commondreams. org/news/2020/06/01/protests-over-george-floyds-killing-met-curfews-police-crackdowns-and-national-guard.

59 Spectrum News Staff, "Vandalism, Looting Mark Fourth Day of Protests in SoCal," Spectrum News 1, May 31, 2020, https:// spectrumnews1.com/ca/la-west/public-safety/2020/05/30/ mayor-garcetti-issues-downtown-curfew-due-to-mass-demonstrations.

60 Jennifer A. Kingston, "Exclusive: $1 Billion-Plus Riot Damage Is Most Expensive in Insurance History," Axios, September 16, 2020, https://www.axios.com/2020/09/16/riots-cost-property-damage.

61 Nicholas Greitzer, "Rising Up: Property Damage vs the Loss of Life — The Debate over Looting," Fox 11 Los Angeles, May 25, 2021, https://www.foxla.com/rising-up/ rising-up-property-damage-vs-the-loss-of-life-the-debate-over-looting.

62 "Our Community," Sedona Chamber of Commerce & Tourism Bureau, last accessed May 2, 2023, https:// sedonachamber.com/our-community/ - :~:text=But once its unsurpassed natural,3 million tourists each year.

63 Juliana Walter, "Population Drop Nullifies Public Vote on Sedona Community Plan," Sedona Red Rock News, December 18, 2021, https://www.redrocknews.com/2021/12/18/ population-drop-nullifies-public-vote-on-sedona-community-plan/.

64 Robert Bryce, "Blackouts Loom in California as Electricity Prices Are 'Absolutely Exploding,'" The Daily Signal, June 25, 2021, https://www.dailysignal.com/2021/06/25/blackouts-loom-in-california-as-electricity-prices-are-absolutely-exploding/.

65 Bryce, "Blackouts Loom."

66 Julia Manchester, "Inflation, Crime, Immigration Top Voter Concerns Ahead of Midterms: Poll," The Hill, October 18, 2022, https://thehill.com/homenews/campaign/3693810-inflation-crime-immigration-top-voter-concerns-ahead-of-midterms-poll/.

67 Gwen Aviles, "Ocasio-Cortez: Detained Migrants Being Told to "Drink out of Toilets,'" NBC News, July 1, 2019, https:// www.nbcnews.com/news/latino/ocasio-cortez-detained-migrants-being-told-drink-out-toilets-n1025431.

68  Alexandria Ocasio-Cortez (@AOC), "I go back and forth on whether to go on Fox News. The main reason I haven't is squaring the fact that the ad revenue from it bankrolls a white supremacist sympathizer to broadcast an hour-long production of unmitigated racism, without any accountability whatsoever," Tweet, 12:37 PM, December 11, 2019, https://twitter.com/AOC/status/1204832541301248007?ref_src=twsrc%5Etfw|twcamp%5Etweetembed|twterm%5E12048336 76376326144|twgr%5Ebdd17f61f09f9228aa29109c1929a939348 97ae5|twcon%5Es2_&ref_url=https%3A%2F%2Fapnews.com%-2Farticle%2Fus-news-new-york-city-environment-alexandria-oca-sio-cortez-entertainment-5230165073281a3a2b1e7429b6af6d80.

69  Priscilla Alvarez, "Lawmakers, Including Ocasio-Cortez, Lash Out over Conditions Following Border Facility Tours," CNN, July 2, 2019, https://www.cnn.com/2019/07/01/politics/alexandria-ocasio-cortez-clint-texas-facility/index.html.

70  Ocasio-Cortez (@AOC), "The entire PREMISE of a wall is not based in fact. It's based in a racist + non-evidence based trope that immigrants are dangerous. Yet some Dems are willing to 'compromise' & spend BILLIONS on a trope because we've accepted some kinds of racism as realpolitik in America," Tweet, 11:05 PM, March 5, 2019, https://twitter.com/AOC/status/1103159551384305664?lang=en.

71  David Cortez, "I Asked Latinos Why They Joined Immigration Law Enforcement. Now I'm Urging Them to Leave," *USA Today*, July 3, 2019, https://www.usatoday.com/story/opinion/voices/2019/07/03/latino-border-patrol-ice-agents-immigration-column/1619511001/.

72  Tucker Carlson, "Tucker Carlson: AOC, Other Politicians Want to 'Reimagine' Your Public Safety but Not Their Own," Fox News, July 14, 2020, https://www.foxnews.com/opinion/tucker-carlson-aoc-politicians-reimagine-public-saftety.

73  Stephen A. Camarota and Karen Zeigler, "Estimating the Illegal Immigrant Population Using the Current Population Survey," Center for Immigration Studies, March 29, 2022, https://cis.org/Report/Estimating-Illegal-Immigrant-Population-Using-Current-Population-Survey.

74  Jo Kim, "With Support for 'Black Lives Matter' China Crosses a Thin Line," *The Diplomat*, June 30, 2020, https://thediplomat.com/2020/06/with-support-for-black-lives-matter-china-crosses-a-thin-line/.

75  Bob Goldberg, "The Woke Army Organized Against Israel," *Jewish Journal*, March 22, 2023, https://jewishjournal.com/culture/arts/books/357316/the-woke-army-organized-against-israel/.

76  Wikipedia, s.v. "Africans in Guangzhou," last modified 04:35, April 20, 2023, https://en.wikipedia.org/wiki/Africans_in_Guangzhou -:~:text=By 2020, there are an,the majority residing in Guangzhou.

77  Committee on Oversight and Accountability, "Comer Reveals Biden Family Members Receiving Payments from Chinese Energy Company," press release, March 16, 2023, https://oversight.house.gov/release/comer-reveals-biden-family-members-receiving-payments-from-chinese-energy-company    /.

78  "Civil War Casualties," American Battlefield Trust, November 16, 2012, updated January 26, 2023, https://www.battlefields.org/learn/articles/civil-war-casualties -:~:text=Roughly 2%25 of the population,high as 6 million souls.&text=The human cost of the Civil War was beyond anybody's expectations.

79  David Paul Kuhn, "Exit Polls: How Obama Won," Politico, November 5, 2008, https://www.politico.com/story/2008/11/exit-polls-how-obama-won-015297.

80  "Country of Birth: 2016," Pew Research Center, infographic, last accessed May 7, 2023, https://assets.pewresearch.org/wp-content/uploads/sites/7/2018/09/06132756/PH_2016-Foreign-Born-Statistical-Portraits_Current-Data_5_Country-of-birth.png.

81  Abby Budiman, "Key Findings About U.S. Immigrants," Pew Research Center, August 20, 2020, https://www.pewresearch.org/fact-tank/2020/08/20/key-findings-about-u-s-immigrants/.

82  David J. Bier, "Fentanyl Is Smuggled for U.S. Citizens by U.S. Citizens, Not Asylum Seekers," Cato Institute, September 14, 2022, https://www.cato.org/blog/fentanyl-smuggled-us-citizens-us-citizens-not-asylum-seekers.

83  Aria Bendix, "Fentanyl Drives Spike in Teen Overdose Deaths, Even as Drug Use Falls to New Low," NBC News, April

12, 2022, https://www.nbcnews.com/health/health-news/
teen-overdose-deaths-spiked-low-drug-use-rcna23103.

[84] "International Trade," Laredo Economic Development
Corporation, last accessed May 2, 2023, https://www.
laredoedc.org/site-selection/international-trade/ - :~:text=The
Port of Laredo is,Bureau data analyzed by WorldCity.

[85] Arelis R. Hernandez, Nick Mirnoff, and Maria Sacchetti, "46
Migrants Found Dead in Texas inside Sweltering Tractor-
Trailer," *Washington Post*, June 27, 2022, https://www.
washingtonpost.com/nation/2022/06/27/migrants-dead-texas/.

[86] "Wage War on the Cartels Killing Americans," Tom Cotton,
September 22, 2022, https://www.cotton.senate.gov/news/
op-eds/wage-war-on-the-cartels-killing-americans.

[87] "About CBP," U.S. Customs and Border Patrol, last accessed
May 2, 2023, https://www.cbp.gov/about - :~:text=With more
than 60,000 employees,lawful international travel and trade.

[88] "Does Your Member of Congress Vote with or Against
Biden?" FiveThirtyEight, January 3, 2023, https://projects.
fivethirtyeight.com/biden-congress-votes/henry-cuellar/.

[89] "Human Trafficking," Border Security, U.S. Customs and
Border Protection, last accessed May 2, 2023, https://
www.cbp.gov/border-security/human-trafficking.

[90] Carissa Lehmkuhl, "Overwhelmed Texas Border Community
Begins Busing Migrants to Austin," Fox 26 Houston, August 12,
2021, https://www.fox26houston.com/news/overwhelmed-texas-
border-community-begins-busing-migrants-to-austin?taid=611
804afced6e00001762433&utm_campaign=trueanthem&utm_
medium=trueanthem&utm_source=twitter.

[91] Lehmkuhl, "Overwhelmed Texas Border Community."

[92] Office of the Texas Governor, "Governor Abbott Calls
On NYC Mayor to Turn Attacks on President Biden's
Border Crisis," press release, July 22, 2022, https://gov.
texas.gov/news/post/governor-abbott-calls-on-nyc-mayor-
to-turn-attacks-on-president-bidens-border-crisis.

[93] Hogan, Bernadette, et al. "Adams Plays Race Card, Accuses
Abbott of Hurting 'black-Run Cities' with Migrant Buses."

*New York Post*, 1 May 2023, nypost.com/2023/05/01/
eric-adams-accuses-greg-abbott-of-racism-over-migrant-busing/.

94  "Why Is Critical Race Theory Dangerous for Our Kids?"
Marsha Blackburn, July 12, 2021, https://www.blackburn.senate.
gov/2021/7/why-is-critical-race-theory-dangerous-for-our-kids.

95  Texas Open Meetings Act, Texas Government Code, Chapter 551,
2006, https://www.austintexas.gov/edims/document.cfm?id=114914
- :~:text=Unauthorized Executive Sessions.&text=Intent
to Circumvent-,the Act.,months in jail, or both.

96  Cayla Harris and Edward McKinley, "As Hispanics Become
Texas' Largest Demographic Group, Their Political Clout
Lags," *Houston Chronicle*, September 20, 2022, https://www.
houstonchronicle.com/politics/texas/article/As-Hispanics-become-
Texas-largest-demographic-17445096.php - :~:text=There are
an estimated 11.86,annual and unofficial population figures.

97  Matthew Choi, "Visiting Texas Border, Kevin McCarthy
Calls on DHS Secretary Alejandro Mayorkas to Resign,"
*The Texas Tribune*, November 22, 2022, https://www.
texastribune.org/2022/11/22/kevin-mccarthy-border-visit/.

98  Thomas Jefferson High School for Science and Technology
2022 Rankings, U.S. News, last accessed May 2, 2023,
https://www.usnews.com/education/best-high-schools/
virginia/districts/fairfax-county-public-schools/thomas-
jefferson-high-school-for-science-and-technology-20461
- :~:text=Thomas Jefferson High School for Science and
Technology 2022 Rankings,they prepare students for college.

99  Rebecca T., "The 11 Most Expensive Counties in the
U.S.," California, February 1, 2022, https://www.california.
com/the-most-expensive-counties-in-the-us/.

100  Benjamin Elisha Sawe, "Richest Counties in the United
States," World Atlas, April 25, 2017, https://www.worldatlas.
com/articles/richest-counties-in-the-united-states.html.

101  Coalition for TJ v. Fairfax County School Board, "Fighting
Race-Based Discrimination at Nation's Top-Ranked High
School," https://pacificlegal.org/case/coalition_for_tj/.

102   Vernon Miles, "FCPS Proposed Budget to Add Middle School Athletics to Fairfax County," FFX Now, January 18, 2023, https://www.ffxnow.com/2023/01/18/fcps-proposed-budget-to-add-middle-school-athletics-to-fairfax-county/ - :~:text=Michelle C.,2022 and ends June 30.

103   "Harvard Admissions Lawsuit," Harvard, last accessed May 2, 2023, https://www.harvard.edu/admissionscase/lawsuit/.

104   "Students for Fair Admissions v. President and Fellows of Harvard College," The Federalist Society, last accessed May 2, 2023, https://fedsoc.org/case/students-for-fair-admissions-v-president-and-fellows-of-harvard-college?gclid=CjwKCAjwoIqhBhAGEiwArXT7K4Vie-sgL3kPX54zCso2kcK_g3veQfs_Pw5I_epnVtbP-OWkCdDV2BoCYZQQAvD_BwE.

105   Nick Anderson, "UC-Berkeley Can't Use Race in Admissions. Is it a Model for the Country?" *Washington Post*, November 27, 2022, https://www.washingtonpost.com/education/2022/11/27/uc-berkeley-admissions-race-diversity/.

106   Samuel Dorman, "Parents' Group Launches Database for Tracking Equity Consultants, 'Woke-Industrial Complex,'" Fox Business, October 21, 2021, https://www.foxbusiness.com/politics/parents-group-database-tracking-equity-consultants.

107   Eric Kaufmann, "Is This the End of White America?" Manhattan Institute, August 24, 2021, https://www.manhattan-institute.org/is-this-the-end-of-white-america.

108   97 "Back-to-School Statistics," Fast Facts, National Center for Education Statistics, last accessed May 6, 2023, https://nces.ed.gov/fastfacts/display.asp?id=372.

109   98 "Private School Enrollment," National Center for Education Statistics, May 2022, last accessed May 6, 2023, https://nces.ed.gov/programs/coe/indicator/cgc/private-school-enrollment.

110   Chuck Grassley, "Judiciary Republicans to Garland: Are Concerned Parents Domestic Terrorists or Not?" letter responding to Merrick Garland memorandum, December 6, 2021, https://www.grassley.senate.gov/news/news-releases/judiciary-republicans-to-garland-are-concerned-parents-domestic-terrorists-or-not.

111   100 "Public School," FindLaw, June 20, 2016, last accessed May 6, 2023, https://www.findlaw.com/education/education-options/public-school.html - :~:text=Every state has a public,their children to public schools.

112   Vince Watchorn, *Manual for Evaluation and Accreditation*, (New York: New York State Association of Independent Schools, 2022), https://www.nysais.org/wp-content/uploads/2022/07/NYSAIS-Manual-for-Accreditation-4.3.pdf.

113   "Substantial Equivalency," New York State Education Department, last updated September 2022, last accessed May 6, 2023, http://www.nysed.gov/nonpublic-schools/substantial-equivalency.

114   Undercover Mothers, "SYSTEMIC: OUR SCHOOLS ARE HELD ACCOUNTABLE TO NAIS," Substack newsletter, September 12, 2022, https://undercovermother.substack.com/p/systemic-our-schools-are-held-accountable.

115   Moore, Kathleen. "NYSUT's New Focus: Unionizing Private Schools and Libraries." *Times Union*, 1 May 2023, www.timesunion.com/education/article/nysut-s-new-focus-unionizing-private-schools-17920405.php.

116   "College Accreditation in the United States-- Pg 1." *Home*, 9 May 2023, www2.ed.gov/admins/finaid/accred/accreditation.html#:~:text=The%20goal%20of%20accreditation%20is,formally%20known%20as%20the%20Triad).

117   "Home Instruction." *New York State Education Department*, www.nysed.gov/nonpublic-schools/home-instruction#:~:text=Parents%20of%2C%20or%20persons%20in,in%20certain%20required%20courses%2Fsubjects. Accessed 18 May 2023.

118   Tung, Mao Tse. *Quotations from Mao Tse Tung - Chapter 30*, www.marxists.org/reference/archive/mao/works/red-book/ch30.htm. Accessed 18 May 2023.

119   Daphne Kenyon, Bethany Paquin, and Semida Munteanu, "Public Schools and the Property Tax: A Comparison of Education Funding Models in Three U.S. States," *Land Lines* (April 2022) https://www.lincolninst.edu/publications/articles/2022-04-public-schools-property-tax-comparison-education-models - :~:text=But in the three decades,much from that 35 percent.

[120] Leana Garfield and Melia Robinson, "Thousands of Women Wore Pink 'Pussy Hats' the Day after Trump's Inauguration," *Business Insider*, January 21, 2017, https://www.businessinsider.com/pussy-hats-womens-march-washington-trump-inauguration-2017-2.

[121] Sarah Aswell, "Some Schools Are Ditching Mother's Day and Father's Day for More Inclusive Options," Scary Mommy, May 13, 2022, https://www.scarymommy.com/parenting/mothers-day-fathers-day-important-grownup-day.

[122] Joseph Wulfsohn, "CNN Panned for On-Air Graphic Reading 'Fiery but Mostly Peaceful Protest' in Front of Kenosha Fire," Fox News, August 27, 2020, https://www.foxnews.com/media/cnn-panned-for-on-air-graphic-reading-fiery-but-mostly-peaceful-protest-in-front-of-kenosha-fire.

[123] Dennis Green, "It Turns Out that Dressing Well Can Actually Make You More Successful," *Business Insider*, February 26, 2016, https://www.businessinsider.com/dressing-for-success-actually-works-2016-2.

[124] Paola Belloso, "Technical Schools See Increased Enrollment, Businesses Struggle to Hire Skilled Workers," Fox 43 News, January 9, 2023, https://www.fox43.com/article/news/local/technical-schools-seeing-an-increase-in-enrollment-while-businesses-struggle-to-hire-skilled-workers-contractors-electricians-plumbers-heating/521-aca445bc-4097-450d-a157-2eeac0da8135.

[125] Ihmed Bouchrika, "101 American School Statistics: 2023 Data, Trends & Predictions," Research.com, April 4, 2023, last accessed May 6, 2023, https://research.com/education/american-school-statistics - :~:text=The U.S. is currently home,school districts in the U.S.

[126] Erica Pandey, "America the Generous: U.S. Leads Globe in Giving," Axios, March 12, 2022, https://www.axios.com/2022/03/09/america-charitable-giving-stats-ukraine.

[127] Alec Schemmel, "HOP Favored by Married People, Dems Strongly Supported by Unmarried Women, Exit Polls Show," ABC 7, November 9, 2022, https://katv.com/news/nation-world/gop-favored-by-married-people-while-dems-strongly-supported-by-unmarried-women-exit-polls.

128   [113] "United States of America – Economic sectors" in Nations Encyclopedia, last accessed May 6, 2023, https://www. nationsencyclopedia.com/economies/Americas/United-States-of-America-ECONOMIC-SECTORS.html.

129   Alexandra Steigrad, "CNN's Profits Seen Dipping Below $1B for First Time Since 2016: Report," *New York Post*, August 2, 2022, https://nypost.com/2022/08/02/cnns-profits-to-dip-below-1b-for-first-time-since-2016-report/.

130   Michael M. Grynbaum and John Koblin, "CNN's Prime-Time Experiment Is Off to a Slow Start," *New York Times*, March 17, 2023, https://www.nytimes.com/2023/03/17/business/media/cnn-ratings-primetime.html.

131   Natasha Anderson, "Tuning Out! Viewership at Scandal-Plagued CNN Plummets by as Much as 80% from Last Year in Both Overall Audience and in Adviser-Coveted 25-to-54 Demographic," *Daily Mail*, January 12, 2022, https://www.dailymail.co.uk/news/article-10394997/CNN-loses-nearly-90-advertiser-coveted-demographics-overall-total-audience.html.

132   Mark Joyella, "Fox News Gains as CNN, MSNBC Drop Significantly in February Cable News Ratings," *Forbes*, March 1, 2022, https://www.forbes.com/sites/markjoyella/2022/03/01/fox-news-gains-as-cnn-msnbc-drop-significantly-in-february-cable-news-ratings/?sh=e6345371fd9f.

133   Joyella, "Fox News Gains."

134   Joyella, "Fox News Dominates Q3 Cable News Ratings as All Networks See Declines in Prime Time," *Forbes*, September 27, 2022, https://www.forbes.com/sites/markjoyella/2022/09/27/fox-news-dominates-3q-cable-news-ratings-as-all-networks-see-declines-in-prime-time/?sh=30a6f5ba43f5.

135   Megan Brenan, "Americans' Trust in Media Remains Near Record Low," Gallup, October 18, 2022, https://news.gallup.com/poll/403166/americans-trust-media-remains-near-record-low.aspx.

136   Chris Ariens, "Here's How Much Ad Revenue the Cable Networks Bring in from Their Biggest Advertisers," TVNewser, April 4, 2018, https://www.adweek.com/tvnewser/heres-how-much-ad-revenue-the-cable-networks-bring-in-from-their-biggest-advertisers/361164/.

137  Yaron Steinbuch, "Prof Placed on Leave after Saying Sexual
     Attraction to Kids Not Always Immoral," *New York Post*, November
     17, 2021, https://nypost.com/2021/11/17/prof-placed-on-leave-
     after-saying-sexual-attraction-to-kids-not-always-immoral/.

138  Dana Kennedy, "Sex-Ed Teacher out at Dalton after
     'Masturbation' Lesson for First Graders," *New York Post*, June
     12, 2021, https://nypost.com/2021/06/12/sex-ed-teacher-
     out-at-dalton-after-masturbation-lesson-for-first-graders/.

139  Kennedy, "Sex-Ed Teacher."

140  Yasmin Tinwala, "Minnesota Public School Accused of Asking
     Senior Students to Role-Play Sex Scenarios," Meaww, September
     24, 2021, https://meaww.com/minnesota-school-richfield-
     parents-complained-sexually-explicit-sex-ed-curriculum.

141  Tinwala, "Minnesota Public School."

142  James Gordon, "New Jersey Public School Students as Young
     as 10 Could Be Taught that Puberty Blockers Are an Acceptable
     Way to 'Manage' Adolescence and that Masturbating 'A Few
     Times a Day' Is a Healthy Way to Relieve Stress, Sample Lesson
     Plan Reveals," *Daily Mail*, April 11, 2022, https://www.dailymail.
     co.uk/news/article-10709217/New-Jersey-public-school-
     students-young-10-taught-explicit-sexual-acts-lessons.html.

143  Jessica Chasmar, "NJ Sample Lesson Plans Push Videos
     for 5th Graders on Graphic Sex-Related Content," Fox
     News, April 11, 2022, https://www.foxnews.com/politics/
     nj-sample-lesson-plans-push-videos-5th-graders.

144  Kimmy Yam, "Anti-Asian Hate Crimes Increased 339 Percent
     Nationwide Last Year, Report Says," NBC News, January 31, 2022,
     https://www.nbcnews.com/news/asian-america/anti-asian-hate-
     crimes-increased-339-percent-nationwide-last-year-repo-rcna14282.

145  Yam, "Anti-Asian Hate Crimes."

146  Caroline Downey, "Judge Jackson Refuses to Define
     'Woman' During Confirmation Hearing: 'I'm Not a
     Biologist,'" *National Review*, March 23, 2022, https://www.
     nationalreview.com/news/judge-jackson-refuses-to-define-
     woman-during-confirmation-hearing-im-not-a-biologist/.

147   Zoe Aldridge, Shireen Patel, Boliang Guo, et al., "Long-Term Effect of Gender-Affirming Hormone Treatment on Depression and Anxiety Symptoms in Transgender People: A Prospective Cohort Study," *Andrology* 9, no. 6 (August 2020), https://onlinelibrary.wiley.com/doi/full/10.1111/andr.12884 - :~:text=Cross-sectional studies show that,affirming hormone treatment (GAHT).

148   Ryan Chatelain, "Study Estimates Trans Youth Population Has Doubled in 5 Years," Spectrum News NY 1, June 10, 2022, https://www.ny1.com/nyc/all-boroughs/news/2022/06/10/study-estimates-transgender-youth-population-has-doubled-in-5-years.

149   William A. Haseltine, "Study Finds Children to be Vectors of COVID-19 and Emerging Variants," *Forbes*, October 21, 2021, https://www.forbes.com/sites/williamhaseltine/2021/10/21/study-finds-children-to-be-vectors-of-covid-19-and-emerging-variants/?sh=451efd351819.

150   Emily Rochotte, "Maybe He's Born with It: Makeup Companies Choose Male Models," Equally Wed, 2017, https://equallywed.com/maybe-hes-born-male-models/.

151   "More Beauty Brands Are Featuring Men in Makeup," Beauty Packaging, July 20, 2016, https://www.beautypackaging.com/contents/view_breaking-news/2016-07-20/more-beauty-brands-are-featuring-men-in-makeup/ - :~:text=Anastasia Beverly Hills, Make and,enlisted beauty vlogger Patrick Starr.

152   "Recidivism Rates: What You Need to Know," Council on Criminal Justice, September 1, 2021, last accessed May 6, 2023, https://counciloncj.org/recidivism_report/ - :~:text=Historically, the most common measure,within three years of release.

153   Marcel Gemme, "Mass Incarceration and the Revolving Door of the Drug Addicted Prison Population," Drug Rehab Services, February 21, 2023, https://www.addicted.org/news/mass-incarceration-and-the-revolving-door-of-the-drug-addicted-prison-population/.

154   "Alternative to Incarceration (ATI) Programs," New York State Division of Criminal Justice Services, last accessed May 6, 2023, https://www.criminaljustice.ny.gov/opca/ati_description.htm.

155   Amanda Woods, Craig McCarthy, and Aaron Fels, "NYPD Reached 25-Year High in NYC Gun Busts Last Week," *New*

*York Post*, September 8, 2020, https://nypost.com/2020/09/08/nypd-reached-25-year-high-in-nyc-gun-busts-last-week/.

156 Rafael A. Mangual, "By Fostering Crime, de Blasio Has Deepened the 'Two New Yorks' Divide," Manhattan Institute, September 10, 2020, last accessed May 6, 2023, https://www.manhattan-institute.org/by-fostering-crime-de-blasio-has-deepened-the-two-new-yorks-divide.

157 Samuel Stebbins, "How the Violent Crime Rate in New York Compares to Other States," 24/7 Wall Street, last accessed May 6, 2023, https://247wallst.com/state/how-the-violent-crime-rate-in-new-york-compares-to-other-states/ - :~:text=The Northeastern U.S. tends to,lower than the national rate.

158 "U.S. Prison Population vs. the World," BackgroundChecks.org, last accessed May 6, 2023, https://backgroundchecks.org/us-prison-population-vs-the-world.html - :~:text=Recidivism rates in the United States,-One basic way&text=The rate of recidivism in,just 20%25 within 5 years.

159 U.S. Department of Justice, "U.S. Jail Population Increased while Prison Population Decreased in 2021," press release, December 20, 2022, https://www.ojp.gov/files/archives/pressreleases/2022/us-jail-population-increased-while-prison-population-decreased-2021.

160 Melissa Klein, "NYC Convictions Plummet, Downgraded Charges Surge under Manhattan DA Bragg," *New York Post*, November 26, 2022, https://nypost.com/2022/11/26/convictions-plummet-downgraded-charges-surge-under-manhattan-da-bragg/.

161 Klein and Larry Celona, "Hundreds of NYC Prosecutors Quitting Woke Bosses and Onerous Reforms," *New York Post*, June 25, 2022, https://nypost.com/2022/06/25/more-nyc-prosecutors-quit-because-of-reform-laws/.

162 "Black Abortions by the Numbers," Right to Life of Michigan, last accessed May 6, 2023, https://rtl.org/multicultural-outreach/black-abortion-statistics/.

163 Ari Ephraim Feldman, "Economic Issues Motivated Voters across Party Lines in Race Where Public Safety Dominated," Spectrum News NY 1, November 9, 2022, https://www.ny1.com/nyc/all-boroughs/news/2022/11/09/economic-issues-motivated-voters-across-party-lines-in-race-where-public-safety-dominated.

164  Steve Peoples, "More than 1 Million Voters Switch to GOP, Raising Alarm for Democrats," PBS News, June 27, 2022, https://www.pbs.org/newshour/politics/more-than-1-million-voters-switch-to-gop-raising-alarm-for-democrats.

165  Nick Reisman, "Siena Poll: New Yorkers Call Crime Serious Problem," Spectrum News 1, June 16, 2022, https://spectrumlocalnews.com/nys/central-ny/ny-state-of-politics/2022/06/15/siena-poll--new-yorkers-call-crime-serious-problem-.

166  Carl Campanile, "74 Percent of NYC Voters Say Crime Is Very Serious Problem in Big Apple: Poll," *New York Post*, February 9, 2022, https://nypost.com/2022/02/09/74-percent-of-nyc-voters-say-crime-is-a-very-serious-problem/.

167  Nolan Hicks, Bernadette Hogan, Jesse O'Neill et al., "Democrat Kathy Hochul Edges Out Republican Lee Zeldin in NY Gov Race," *New York Post*, November 8, 2022, https://nypost.com/2022/11/08/kathy-hochul-beats-lee-zeldin-in-ny-gov-race/.

168  Hicks, Hogan, O'Neill et al., "Democrat Kathy Hochul."

169  Yam, "NYPD Reports 361 Percent Increase in Anti-Asian Hate Crimes Since Last Year," NBC News, December 10, 2021, https://www.nbcnews.com/news/asian-america/nypd-reports-361-percent-increase-anti-asian-hate-crimes-last-year-rcna8427.

170  "Bronx High School of Science," U.S. News, last accessed May 6, 2023, https://www.usnews.com/education/best-high-schools/new-york/districts/new-york-city-public-schools/bronx-high-school-of-science-13207.

171  Mary Kay Linge, "High School Guide: The Specialized Elite 8," *New York Post*, December 9, 2021, https://nypost.com/2021/12/09/high-school-guide-the-specialized-elite-8/.

172  "How to Get into the Bronx High School of Science," Ivy Tutors Network, February 3, 2022, https://ivytutorsnetwork.com/blog/bronx-high-school-of-science.

173  "The Anderson School," U.S. News, last accessed May 6, 2023, https://www.usnews.com/education/k12/new-york/the-anderson-school-231287 - :~:text=The Anderson School 2021 Rankings,their students for high school.

174 "Stuyvesant Hugh School Admissions," Caddell Prep,
     last accessed May 6, 2023, https://caddellprep.com/
     stuyvesant-high-school-admissions/ - :~:text=During
     the month of March,are accepted by the school.

175 "Stuyvesant High School," U.S. News, last accessed May 6, 2023
     https://www.usnews.com/education/best-high-schools/new-york/
     districts/new-york-city-public-schools/stuyvesant-high-school-13092.

176 Diane Ravitch, "Gary Rubinstein: Is Stuyvesant High School—
     One of the Most Selective in the Nation—a 'Good School'?"
     *Diane Ravitch's Blog* (blog), June 30, 2021, https://dianeravitch.
     net/2021/06/30/gary-rubinstein-is-stuyvesant-high-school-
     one-of-the-most-selective-in-the-nation-a-good-school/.

177 Wikipedia, s.v. "Shuang Wen School," last modified April 19, 2023,
     22:17, https://en.wikipedia.org/wiki/Shuang_Wen_School.

178 Paul G. Kengor, "Birthday of a Bloodbath," Mises Institute,
     November 24, 2017, https://mises.org/wire/birthday-bloodbath.

179 Hegel, "The Embodiment Spirit Assumes — The State,"
     Marxists.org, last accessed May 6, 2023, https://www.marxists.
     org/reference/archive/hegel/works/hi/history4.htm.

180 Susan Edelman, "'Educational Genocide': NYC Schools Are
     Leaving Black and Hispanic Students Behind," *New York Post*, April
     6, 2019, https://nypost.com/2019/04/06/educational-genocide-
     nyc-schools-are-leaving-black-and-hispanic-students-behind/.

181 *The Negative Effects of Instability on Child Development: A*
     *Research...*, www.urban.org/sites/default/files/publication/32706/
     412899-The-Negative-Effects-of-Instability-on-Child-Deve-
     lopment-A-Research-Synthesis.PDF. Accessed 18 May 2023.

182 "De Blasio Calls For an End to Admissions Test for the
     NYC Specialized High Schools," Spectrum News NY 1,
     June 2, 2018, https://www.ny1.com/nyc/all-boroughs/
     news/2018/06/02/nyc-mayor-bill-de-blasio-calls-for-an-
     end-to-specialized-high-school-admissions-test.

183 Ray Domanico, "A Statistical Profile of New York's K-12
     Educational Sector: Race, Income and Religion," Manhattan
     Institute, February 19, 2020, https://www.manhattan-institute.

org/complex-demographics-new-york-public-private-schools -
:~:text=New York City is more,the city, attend private schools.

184  Bruce Sacardote, "Tracking Students by Ability Produces
Academic Results," *New York Times*, June 4, 2014,
https://www.nytimes.com/roomfordebate/2014/06/03/
are-new-york-citys-gifted-classrooms-useful-or-harmful/
tracking-students-by-ability-produces-academic-results.

185  Amanda Luz Henning Santiago and Sara Dorn,
"Understanding Mayoral Control," City & State New
York, April 24, 2022, https://www.cityandstateny.com/
politics/2022/04/understanding-mayoral-control/366018/.

186  Benjamin Elisha Saw, "Largest School Districts in the United
States," WorldAtlas, April 25, 2017, https://www.worldatlas.
com/articles/largest-school-districts-in-the-united-states.html
- :~:text=New York City department of Education&text=New
York City's school district,more than 1,800 different schools.

187  Cayla Bamberger, "NYC Projects Enrollment Losses
of Another 30,000 Students This Fall," *New York
Post*, July 15, 2022, https://nypost.com/2022/07/15/
nyc-projects-enrollment-loss-of-another-30000-students-in-fall/.

188  Campanile, "Startling Data Reveals How Many People
Have Fled NYC During COVID Pandemic," *New York
Post*, March 24, 2022, https://nypost.com/2022/03/24/
manhattan-led-us-in-population-loss-during-year-of-pandemic/.

189  James Brasuell, "Where New Asian Residents Are Transforming
New York City," Planetizen, October 20, 2021, https://
www.planetizen.com/news/2021/10/115031-where-new-
asian-residents-are-transforming-new-york-city.

190  Yam, "Number of Poor Asian Americans in N.Y.C. Area up 15
Percent in 10 Years, Study Says," NBC News, October 21, 2021,
https://www.nbcnews.com/news/asian-america/number-poor-asian-
americans-nyc-area-15-percent-10-years-study-says-rcna3534.

191  Wikipedia, s.v. "Shuang Wen School."

192  James FitzGerald and Sophie Williams, "China Xinjiang:
Urumqi Rocked by Covid Lockdown Protests after

Deadly Fire," BBC News, November 26, 2022, https://www.bbc.com/news/world-asia-china-63766125.

[193] Greg Wehner, "NYC Mayor Says COVID Mandates May Need to Return, Blasts People Who Say 'I want to Do Whatever I Want,'" Fox News, February 12, 2023, https://www.foxnews.com/politics/nyc-mayor-covid-mandates-return-blasts-people-i-want-do-whatever-i-want.

[194] Sara Boboltz, "This Is Why It's So Great to Be a Midwesterner, According to Science," HuffPost, June 18, 2014, https://www.huffpost.com/entry/midwest-is-the-best-studies_n_5500725 - :~:text=The stereotype, it turns out,don't know, guys.

[195] Olafimihan Oshin, "Twitter Bans Conservative Author Alex Berenson," The Hill, August 29, 2021, https://thehill.com/homenews/media/569908-twitter-bans-conservative-author-Alex-Berenson/.

[196] Arthur Allen, "How Pfizer Won the Pandemic, Reaping Outsize Profit and Influence," KFF Health News, July 5, 2022, https://khn.org/news/article/pfizer-pandemic-vaccine-market-paxlovid-outsize-profit-influence/ - :~:text=Pfizer recorded %247.8 billion in,be donated to poor countries.

[197] Amanda Barroso and Juliana Menasce Horowitz, "The Pandemic Has Highlighted Many Challengers for Mothers, but They Aren't Necessarily New," Pew Research Center, March 17, 2021, https://www.pewresearch.org/fact-tank/2021/03/17/the-pandemic-has-highlighted-many-challenges-for-mothers-but-they-arent-necessarily-new/.

[198] "Terrace Park, Ohio Population 2023," World Population review, last accessed May 6, 2023, https://worldpopulationreview.com/us-cities/terrace-park-oh-population.

[199] "Sample Position Description and Tips," University of Washington Human Resources, last accessed May 6, 2023, https://hr.uw.edu/diversity/hiring/sample-position-description-and-tips/.

[200] Samantha Aschieris, "27 of Top 30 Crime-Ridden Cities Run by Democrats," The Daily Signal, November 4, 2022, https://www.dailysignal.com/2022/11/04/democrat-run-cities-counties-have-a-murder-problem-report-shows/.

201 Amy B. Wang, "The World Happiness Report Is Out and the U.S. Has Fallen. Sad!" *The Washington Post*, March 20, 2017, https://www.washingtonpost.com/news/worldviews/wp/2017/03/20/the-world-happiness-report-is-out-and-the-u-s-has-fallen-sad/.

202 Enten, Harry. "American Happiness Hits Record Lows | CNN Politics." *CNN*, 2 Feb. 2022, www.cnn.com/2022/02/02/politics/unhappiness-americans-gallup-analysis/index.html.

203 "Major Depression," National Institute of Mental Health, last accessed May 6, 2023, https://www.nimh.nih.gov/health/statistics/major-depression - :~:text=An estimated 21.0 million adults,compared to males (6.2%25).

204 "Mariemont High School," Public School Review, last accessed May 6, 2023, https://www.publicschoolreview.com/mariemont-high-school-profile - :~:text=Mariemont High School serves 502,the 2020-21 school year.

205 Positive Action Staff, "The Five Social Emotional Learning (SEL) Core Competencies [+ Teaching Lessons]," Positive Action (blog), September 4, 2020, https://www.positiveaction.net/blog/sel-competencies.

206 Kristin M. Gagnier, Akaya Okawa, and Sonji Jones-Manson, "Designing and Implementing Social Emotional Learning Programs to Promote Equity," white paper, February 4, 2022, https://oese.ed.gov/files/2022/03/FINAL-EIR_SEL-Programs-White-Paper.pdf.

207 Kelly Field, "Social and Emotional Learning Is the Latest Flashpoint in the Education Wars," Hechinger Report, February 21, 2022, https://hechingerreport.org/social-and-emotional-learning-is-the-latest-flashpoint-in-the-education-wars/.

208 "When the End of the World Comes, I Want to be in Cincinnati. It Is Always Ten Years Behind the Times," Quote Investigator (blog), March 20, 2012, https://quoteinvestigator.com/2012/03/20/end-of-world-time-lag/.

209 Seth Motel, "Who Runs for Office? A Profile of the 2%," Pew Research Center, September 3, 2014, https://www.pewresearch.org/fact-tank/2014/09/03/who-runs-for-office-a-profile-of-the-2/.

210 "Julie Gunlock," Independent Women's Forum, last accessed May 6, 2023, https://www.iwf.org/people/julie-gunlock/.

211  Executive Order Number Two (2022) ad Order of Public Health Emergency One, Virginia Governor's Office, January 15, 2022, https://www.governor.virginia.gov/media/governorvirginiagov/governor-of-virginia/pdf/74---eo/74---eo/EO-2---School-Mask-Mandate-Executive-Order-Exception.pdf.

212  Adaobi Tricia Nwaubani, "When the Slave Traders Were African," *Wall Street Journal*, September 20, 2019, https://www.wsj.com/articles/when-the-slave-traders-were-african-11568991595.

213  "Countries that Still Have Slavery 2023," World Population Review, last accessed May 6, 2023, https://worldpopulationreview.com/country-rankings/countries-that-still-have-slavery.

214  Helle C. Dale, "The American Experiment," Heritage Foundation, July 5, 2007, https://www.heritage.org/political-process/commentary/the-american-experiment - :~:text=The American experiment was unique,on earth at the time.

215  Megan Kuhfeld, Jim Soland, Karyn Lewis, and Emily Morton, "The Pandemic Has Had Devastating Impacts on Learning. What Will It Take to Help Students Catch Up?" Brookings, March 3, 2022, https://www.brookings.edu/blog/brown-center-chalkboard/2022/03/03/the-pandemic-has-had-devastating-impacts-on-learning-what-will-it-take-to-help-students-catch-up/.

216  Sean CI Deoni, Jennifer Beauchemin, Alexandra Volpe, and Viren Dâ Sa, "The COVID-19 Pandemic and Early Child Cognitive Development: A Comparison of Development in Children Born During the Pandemic and Historical References," *medRxiv* (August 2022), https://pubmed.ncbi.nlm.nih.gov/34401887/ - :~:text=Infants born during the pandemic,was found to be protective.

217  Natalie Grover, "Children Born During Pandemic Have Lower Iqs, US Study Finds," *The Guardian*, August 12, 2021, https://www.theguardian.com/world/2021/aug/12/children-born-during-pandemic-have-lower-iqs-us-study-finds.

218  "Children Born During Pandemic Have Reduced Cognitive Skills, Finds New Study Led by Brown Professor," GoLocalProv News, August 15, 2021, https://www.golocalprov.com/news/children-born-during-pandemic-have-reduced-cognitive-skills-says-new-study.

219 Bamberger, "COVID Pandemic Undid Decades of Math, Reading Progress: Federal Data," *New York Post*, September 1, 2022, https://nypost.com/2022/09/01/covid-undid-decades-of-math-reading-progress-federal-data/.

220 Julie Deardorff, "Abolitionist Teaching: A Conversation with Bettina L. Love," Northwestern School of Education and Social Policy, October 6, 2022, https://www.sesp.northwestern.edu/news-center/news/2021/01/abolitionist-teaching-a-conversation-with-bettina-l-love.html.

221 Barton, Ethan. "CRT Group Promoted by Biden Admin Has Ties to Top Education Department Officials." *Fox News*, 22 July 2021, www.foxnews.com/us/critical-race-theory-activist-education-department-connections.

222 Carol Kearney, "Ibram X. Kendi Highest-Paid Activist in the World," MediaMass, last updated May 7, 2023, https://en.mediamass.net/people/ibram-x-kendi/highest-paid.html.

223 Christopher Eberhart, "Anti-Racist Author Doubles Speaking Fees as America Goes Woke: 'White Fragility' Writer Robin DiAngelo Charges an Average of $14,000 per Speech and Makes '$728K a Year,'" Daily Mail, July 2, 2021, https://www.dailymail.co.uk/news/article-9749517/An-anti-racist-author-Robin-DiAngelo-makes-728K-year-speaking-engagements.html.

224 "Alexandria City Public Schools," U.S. News, last accessed May 6, 2023, https://www.usnews.com/education/k12/virginia/districts/alexandria-city-pblc-schs-102152.

225 Laura Wamsley, "Homeschooling Doubled During the Pandemic, U.S. Census Survey Finds," NPR, March 23, 2021, https://www.npr.org/2021/03/22/980149971/homeschooling-doubled-during-the-pandemic-u-s-census-survey-finds.

226 Sarah Schwartz, "Map: Where Critical Race Theory Is Under Attack," *Education Week*, June 11, 2021, https://www.edweek.org/policy-politics/map-where-critical-race-theory-is-under-attack/2021/06.

227 Schwartz, "Map: Where Critical Race Theory Is Under Attack."

228 Moms For Liberty, last accessed May 6, 2023, https://www.momsforliberty.org/.

229 Bouchrika, "101 American School Statistics."

230 Collin Binkley and Julie Carr Smyth, "Conservative PACs Inject Millions into Local School Races," AP News, October 11, 2022, https://apnews.com/article/entertainment-elections-education-school-boards-teaching-059f24 65829ab009394469b95c8cc94a.

231 Ballotpedia, s.v. "Public school district (United States)," last accessed May 6, 2023, https://ballotpedia.org/Public_school_district_(United_States) - :~:text=There are approximately 13,800 public,educate approximately 55.2 million students.

232 Shannon Thaler and Jennifer Smith, "Republican Politicians and Parents Rage over Biden 'Weaponizing' DOJ to Target Those Who Dissent with Woke School Boards over COVID Restrictions and CRT Curriculum," Daily Mail, October 5, 2021, https://www.dailymail.co.uk/news/article-10062971/Republicans-rage-Biden-weaponizing-DOJ-label-parents-domestic-terrorists.html.

233 GOP War Room, "Union Boss Randi Weingarten Aggres with Letter That Calls Protesting Parents 'Domestic Terrorists,'" YouTube video, 0:34, October 15, 2021, https://www.youtube.com/watch?v=7n7BdSujP6w.

234 Ariel Edwards-Levy, "Polling Shows That Most Voters Say Economic Concerns Are Top of Mind," CNN, November 5, 2022, https://www.cnn.com/2022/11/05/politics/voters-issues-economy-midterms-2022/index.html.

235 Troy Green, "NAR Finds Share of First-Time Home Buyers Smaller, Older than Ever Before," National Association of Realtors, November 3, 2022, https://www.nar.realtor/newsroom/nar-finds-share-of-first-time-home-buyers-smaller-older-than-ever-before.

236 "About the City of Austin," City of Austin, last accessed May 6, 2023, https://www.austintexas.gov/resident/about-city-austin.

237 Steve Adler, "Order by the Mayor of the City of Austin," March 14, 2020, last accessed May 6, 2023, https://www.austintexas.gov/edims/document.cfm?id=337524.

238 Campanile, "New York Hospitals on Brink with Staffing Shortages, Financial Woes: Report," New York Post, December 14, 2022, https://nypost.com/2022/12/14/

new-york-hospitals-on-brink-with-staffing-shortages-financial-woes-report/.

239    Maria Caspani, "New York Hospitals Fire, Suspend Staff Who Refuse COVID Vaccine," Reuters, September 28, 2021, https://www.reuters.com/world/us/new-york-hospitals-face-staff-shortages-vaccine-mandate-kicks-2021-09-27/.

240    Mary Ellen Cagnassola, "Austin Mayor Says Greg Abbott 'Made It Impossible' for Texas Schools to Protect Students," *Newsweek*, July 27, 2021, https://www.newsweek.com/austin-mayor-says-greg-abbott-made-it-impossible-texas-schools-protect-students-1613728.

241    Dalton Huey, "Homicides on the Rise: How Austin Compares to Other Big Cities," kxan, October 29, 2021, https://www.kxan.com/investigations/homicides-on-the-rise-how-austin-compares-to-other-big-cities/.

242    Joshua Fechter, "Austin Police Chief Weighs In on City's Deadliest Year in Decades, Police Reform and 'Defunding' the Department," *The Texas Tribune*, December 10, 2021, https://www.texastribune.org/2021/12/10/austin-police-homicides-spending/.

243    Fechter, "Austin Police Chief Weighs In."

244    "Austin City Council Moves to Cut Police Budget by 1/3, Directs Money to Social Services," CBS Texas, August 14, 2020, https://www.cbsnews.com/texas/news/austin-cut-police-budget-by-third-money-social-services-defund/.

245    Lucy Tompkins, "Austin Voters Banned Homeless People from Camping in Public Spaces. The City Is Creating Housing for Them but Not Fast Enough," *The Texas Tribune*, August 31, 2022, https://www.texastribune.org/2022/08/31/texas-austin-homeless-camping-ban/.

246    Angela Cherry, "Redfin Reports Asking Rents Increased 40% Year over Year in Austin," Business Wire, March 21, 2022, https://www.businesswire.com/news/home/20220321005298/en/Redfin-Reports-Asking-Rents-Increased-40-Year-Over-Year-in-Austin.

247    Jeffrey S. Passel and D'Vera Cohn, "20 Metro Areas Are Home to Six-in-Ten Unauthorized Immigrants in U.S.," Pew Research Center, March 11, 2019, https://www.pewresearch.org/fact-tank/2019/03/11/us-metro-areas-unauthorized-immigrants/.

248  Lehmkuhl, "Overwhelmed Texas Border Community."

249  Ronn Blitzer, "Schools Close, Switch to Remote Learning Due
to Heat as DOE Blames Climate Change," Fox News, September
8, 2022, https://www.foxnews.com/politics/schools-close-
switch-remote-learning-due-heat-doe-blames-climate-change.

250  "'Sobering' Early Glimpse at Pandemic's Effects on Young
Students: 9-Year-Olds' Reading and Math Scores Fell Sharply,"
CBS News, September 1, 2022, https://www.cbsnews.com/
news/pandemic-reading-math-scores-sharp-fall-federal-study/.

251  Richard Fry, "Some Gender Disparities Widened in the
U.S. Workforce During the Pandemic," Pew Research
Center, January 14, 2022, https://www.pewresearch.org/
fact-tank/2022/01/14/some-gender-disparities-widened-
in-the-u-s-workforce-during-the-pandemic/.

# ACKNOWLEDGMENTS

Eunice Schwartz, your memory lives on.

# ABOUT THE AUTHOR

Jacqueline Toboroff, Manhattan native, divorced mom of two, is a private citizen who ran for City Council as a Republican. She was appointed VP of the Manhattan GOP and helped organize Moms for Lee (Zeldin), former NY Republican gubernatorial candidate.

A published writer and featured guest speaker, Jacqueline is focused on NYC issues, finding solutions, and providing a platform for mothers who are fed up with having their parental rights challenged by the government. She serves as editor-in-chief at CD Media's online news publication the *Manhattan*. Her column "On the Sidewalks of New York" is a weekly feature at *Human Events*.

Made in the USA
Columbia, SC
02 September 2023

63ac7f5b-b70b-4bde-95e3-57580b525f63R01